The Internet

THE ROUGH GUIDE

There are more than 100 Rough Guide travel,
phrasebook, and music titles, covering
destinations from Amsterdam to Zimbabwe,
languages from Czech to Thai, and musics
from World to Opera and Jazz.

To find out more about Rough Guides, and to
check out the biggest and best travel database
online, get connected to the Internet
with this guide and find us on the Web at:

www.roughguides.com

Rough Guide to the Internet Credits

Text editors: Mark Ellingham, Orla Duane
Design and layout: Henry Iles
Production: Susanne Hillen
Proofread by Elaine Pollard

To Shelley

This fourth edition published Oct 1998 by Rough Guides Ltd
            62–70, Shorts Gardens, London WC2H 9AB
            375 Hudson Street, New York 10014
            Web site: http://www.roughguides.com
            Email: mail@roughguides.co.uk

Reprinted in December 1998.

Distributed by The Penguin Group
Penguin Books Ltd, 27 Wrights Lane, London W8 5TZ
Penguin Books USA Inc, 375 Hudson Street, New York 10014
Penguin Books Canada Ltd, 10 Alcorn Avenue, Toronto, Ontario MV4 1E4
Penguin Books Australia Ltd, PO Box 257, Ringwood, Victoria 3134
Penguin Books (NZ) Ltd, 182–190 Wairau Road, Auckland 10

Printed in the United States of America by R. R. Donnelly & Sons

© Angus J. Kennedy, 1998

512 pages; includes index

A catalogue record for this book is available from the British Library

ISBN 1-85828-343-4

The Internet

THE ROUGH GUIDE

by

Angus J. Kennedy

Acknowledgements

Writing any book takes a fair amount of patience, not just from the writer but also from those whose lives become involuntarily entwined in it. This book has been no exception. I'd like to thank my friends and family who've understood this and stuck by me through the madness that has coincided with researching and writing each edition.

I am especially indebted to those who contributed text. Garret Keogh brought me up to date with the inner machinations of the Online Services; David Pitchford shared his expertise in Web authoring; Gerry Browne and Jason Smith misspent their time well in Online Gaming; and Richard Baguley, of Internet Magazine, joined in the missing dots in ISPs. I would also like to thank the hundreds of you who sent me URLs, news clippings, and feedback on the third edition.

Finally, I'd like to express the greatest appreciation of my editor Mark Ellingham and all at the Rough Guides and Penguin, particularly Andy Hilliard, Henry Iles, Eleanor Hill, Orla Duane, Kate Hands, Susanne Hillen, Richard Trillo, Simon Carloss, Jean Marie Kelly, SoRelle Braun, and Nicole Lyons, for doing such a remarkable job of polishing up this book and putting it in more hands than I'd ever imagined.

Angus Kennedy
angus@easynet.co.uk

Contents

Help us update

Trying to keep up with the ever-changing Internet is a near impossible task. So don't be alarmed if you find a few addresses that don't work, or dubious recommendations. It was all correct at time of press. Honest. But it's sure to change. So, if something's not right, or you think we could have explained it better, please let me know via email at: angus@easynet.co.uk and I'll attend to it in the next edition.

In the meantime, keep an eye on:
http://www.roughguides.com/net/

Read Me

There's nothing worse than feeling left behind – when everyone is talking about something, but it just doesn't gel. The Internet's had this effect over the last few years. Everything you pick up. Internet this, cyber that. But, unless you've been connected, you're still in the dark. Getting to grips with the Net can be daunting, but it's a short (if steep) learning curve, and the basics don't take long to master. This small guide is crammed with nuggets of practical advice, troubleshooting tips, step-by-step tuition, and addresses of the places you'll need to go. We'll make you a Net guru in the shortest possible time. Guaranteed!

Internet books mostly fall into two categories: the brick-sized volumes that tell you far more than you want to know in unimportant areas and not enough on shortcuts; and the patronizing simplistic ones, that make it look easy in the bookstore with cute icons and catchy titles, but aren't much use once you start having problems. And, if they're written before mid-1998, they should be filed under ancient history. The truth is you don't need a fat book to get started on the Internet. It's too much work. And boring.

This Rough Guide gives it to you straight. In plain English. We think the Net is a pushover. If you can figure out how to use a word processor, you'll master the Net. Sure, you'll have teething troubles, but we show you how to solve them and where to go for help. Rather than compile everything there is to know about the Net, we give you the basics and show you how to use the Net itself to find out more. Since the Net and its associated technology changes almost daily, it's wiser to get your information from where it's always fresh.

What's more, we'll show you how to: get the best deal on Internet access, send messages across the world instantly for the price of a local call, find all the software you'll ever need free, become an expert in the most important Internet programs, and locate anything, anywhere, on the Net without having to learn any difficult commands. Or, if you're really impatient, you can wing it and go straight to our listings chapters to explore the weird, wild, and wonderful World Wide Web, or get those nagging questions off your mind in one of the special interest newsgroups. Who knows, you might even make a few friends along the way.

Well, what are you waiting for?

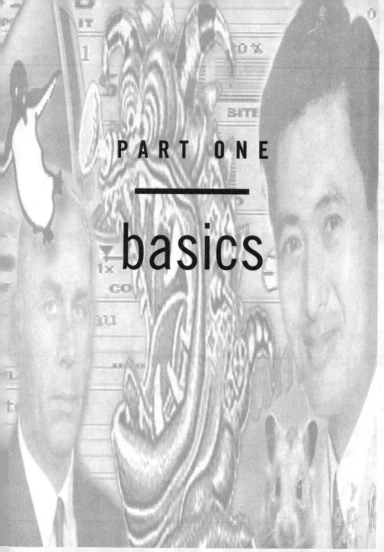

PART ONE

basics

Frequently Asked Questions

Before we get into the nitty gritty of what you can do on the Internet – and what it can do for you – here are some answers to a few Frequently Asked Questions (or FAQs, as acronym-loving Netizens call them).

Big-picture questions

Okay, what's this Internet good for?

The Internet, or the **Net** as it's more often called, is a real bag of tricks. Some say it's like having 100 million consultants on tap – free of charge. You can seek and usually find answers to every question you've ever had, send messages and documents across the world in a flash, shop in another continent, sample new music, visit art galleries, read books, play games, chat, catch the latest news in any language, meet people with similar interests, grab free software, bet on the stock market, or just fritter the hours away surfing across waves of visual bubble-gum.

The Internet is also an invaluable business tool for everyday correspondence, marketing products, providing support, inviting customer feedback, and publishing. In the last couple of years it has become as integral to business as the telephone and fax machine.

Sounds like fun, but what is it exactly?

It's getting tougher to define the Internet – it's changing that quickly. Once it was simple. You could just explain that the Internet was an **international network of computers** linked up to exchange information. The word Internet is a contraction of international and network.

The core of this international network consists of computers permanently joined through high-speed connections. To get on the Internet, you simply connect your computer to any of these networked computers via an Internet Service (or Access) Provider. Once you're **online** (connected) your computer can talk to any other computer on the Internet whether it's in your hometown or on the other side of the world.

That's plain enough, but if you want to be picky you have to consider it's not just the computers hooked up by fancy telephone lines that make up the Internet. It's what it's used for as well. Mostly, that's the transfer of **electronic mail** (**email**) and digital publishing on the **World Wide Web**. So when people say they found something on the Internet, they didn't find it randomly zipping around the wires hooking up the computers, they either retrieved it from where it was stored on a computer connected to this international network, or someone sent it to them by electronic mail.

But most importantly, the Internet is not really about computers. It's about people, communication, and sharing knowledge. It's about overcoming physical boundaries to allow like minds to meet. And that's why you want it.

So, is this the Information Superhighway?

Only buffoons refer to the Internet as the Information Superhighway. But, it is the closest thing we have to a prototype of Al Gore's vision as talked up by software magnate Bill Gates and pals. It has huge capabilities for cheap, global, and immediate communication; it may grow to dominate areas of **publishing, news, and education**; it is already providing an alternative **shopping mall**; and it will almost certainly make major inroads into **banking and customer support**.

Nonetheless, to get big-screen action like video on demand, we'll need a much faster network than today's Internet. Right now the Net's main arteries are already straining under the pressure of new users, and some fear it might get even worse before it gets better. Until the **Internet backbone** can withstand the added demands from **high-speed alternatives** such as ADSL, cable, and direct satellite feeds, the real digital "revolution" is still very much on hold.

Can I shop online?

It won't be long before you can buy almost anything you want via the Internet. There are already thousands of **online stores** – including success stories in book, CD, and computer stores – but Net shopping has yet to take off in a big way. It suffers from the usual reticence towards mail order and has been hindered by hype surrounding credit card fraud. Of course you can be conned on the Net, as much as anywhere else, but your card details are actually a lot more secure on the Internet than when you make a purchase face to face in a shop.

Can I make money out of the Internet?

Yes, no, maybe – perhaps it's better to ask yourself the question "Can I continue to make money without the Internet?" The last few years have seen a gold rush in the computer hardware, software, training, and publishing industries. Some, who got in early, made a killing getting businesses on the Web – the Net's "commercial zone." Today, it's settled down somewhat. Web page designers are commonplace, and can no longer charge extortionate rates unless they're tied in with a major agency. However, those with serious technical and programming skills are always in high demand.

If you're wondering whether to throw a Web site into your existing **marketing mix** to help boost sales, the answer's probably yes. But rather than use it to try to attract customers, it's better to think of the Net as a place to post in-depth product literature, provide customer support, and canvass feedback. Not too many companies are making money from **direct sales** – though that's improving, particularly for hard-to-get products, or deep-catalog items like CDs and books.

Another way to profit is by charging others to **advertise on your Web page**. To do so, you'll either need to run a very popular site or attract a certain type of customer, and you are usually paid according to the number of times visitors pursued links from your site to your sponsor's. Alternatively if your site generates heavy traffic and looks promising, someone may want to buy you outright.

Advertising on the World Wide Web is perfectly acceptable but emailing protocols are more delicate. **Never, ever, ever, send bulk email** other than to people you know or who've requested information. And never post an advertisement in Usenet or to a mailing list.

Junk email is called spam, and spammers are universally detested. Try it and you'll be flooded with hate mail, and potentially kicked offline. On the other hand, email is by far the most efficient direct response device you'll find. For instance, you could set up an **autoresponder** to send out product details upon receipt of a blank message. No dictating over the phone, no data entry from a coupon and not only that, it's instant and informal. Plus, you'll have their email address on record to follow up later. So next time you put your telephone number on an advertisement, put your email address up, too.

Is there a lot of really weird stuff on the Net?

Yes, lots. Just like in real life, except it's easier to find.

So who's in charge?

Well, technically no-one, though a number of powerful commercial players such as **CompuServe**, **America Online (AOL)**, **Microsoft**, **Cisco**, **MCI**, **Worldcom**, and **Netscape** have played major roles in putting the framework in place, and there are various bodies concerned with the Net's administration. Foremost among the latter are the **Internet Network Information Center** (InterNIC), which registers domain names, the **Internet Society** which, amongst other things, acts as a clearing house for technical standards, and the **World Wide Web Consortium**, which discusses the future of the Web's programming language.

No-one, however, actually "runs" the Internet. As the Internet is, in effect, a network of networks, most responsibilities are contained within each local network. For instance, if you have connection problems, you would call your connection supplier. If you object to material located on a server in Japan or Ireland, say, you'd have to complain to the administrator of that local server.

While it certainly promotes freedom of speech, **the Internet is not so anarchic** as some sections of the media would have you believe. If you break the laws of your country while using the Net, and you're caught, you're liable to prosecution. For example, suppose you publish a document in the US outlining the shortcomings of a military dictator in Slobovia. It might not worry the US authorities, but it could be curtains for any Slobovian caught downloading the document. The same applies to other contentious material such as pornography, terrorist handbooks, drug literature, and religious satire. **The Internet is not an entirely new planet.**

But isn't it run by the Pentagon and the CIA?

When the Internet was first conceived 30-odd years ago, as a network for the American Defense Department, its purpose was to act as a nuclear-attack-resistant method of exchanging scientific information and intelligence. But that was then. In the 1970s and 80s several other networks, such as the **National Science Foundation Network** (NSFNET), joined, linking the Internet to research agencies and universities. It was probably no coincidence that as the Cold War petered out, the Internet became more publicly accessible and the nature of the beast changed totally and irreversibly. These days, intelligence agencies have the same access to the Internet as everyone else, but whether they use it to monitor insurgence and crime is simply a matter for speculation.

So is the Net basically a geek hangout?

It's about as geek as you want it to be, which can vary between twin hip-slung multi-meters with a matching pocket protector, to not in the slightest. They say if you're bored with the Net, you're bored with life itself.

Okay, but what about deviants?

Today, just about anyone who's anyone has a Net account. Most politicians in North America and Europe have email accounts. Celebrities – pop stars, actors and travel authors especially – often look themselves up to see what's said about them and join discussions. Doctors, lawyers, journalists, and scientists use the Net to trade knowledge with their peers. Students use it for research and to hand in assignments. It's something different for everyone.

So sure, there may also be perverts, gangsters, and con artists, but probably no more than you mix with every day in "real life".

But isn't it yet another male-dominated bastion?

Well, there are reckoned to be close to twice as many men as women online, but for no very good reason. Some argue that women, more than men, are daunted by the technological hurdle and expense involved in getting connected, others that women have less of men's "hobbyist" and "listing" obsessions. Whatever. Recent surveys suggest, however, that the gap is starting to close. AOL, for example, now claims that 52% of its members are women.

In theory, the Net is as level as playing fields get – and its usage is likely to become little different from the phone, fax, and home video. After all, it's meant for communication and entertainment, and no-one can stop you, your views, your work, or your peers from getting online.

Will I make friends on the Internet?

It's easy to meet people with common interests by joining in **Usenet (newsgroup) or mailing list discussions**. And being able to discuss sensitive issues with strangers while retaining a comfortable degree of anonymity often makes for startlingly intimate communication.

Translating email pen pals into the real world of human contact, or even romance, is another thing. You won't be able to tell your new e-pal Alex's age, sex, appearance, or motives at first glance. And there's nothing stopping anyone from assuming the name of their pet, town, fantasy, or idol as an email user name or IRC nickname. Or from re-inventing themselves. So if you find yourself in private council with a "Prince", don't swoon too soon. After all, on the Internet no-one can tell if you're a dog.

More technical questions

What's electronic mail, again?

Electronic mail or **email** is a method of sending text files from one computer to another. You can send messages across the world in seconds using Internet email.

What's the difference between the Internet, the Web, AOL, CompuServe, and the Microsoft Network?

The **World Wide Web** (or Web) is a user-friendly point-and-click way of navigating data stored on the Internet. CompuServe, AOL, and the Microsoft Network are called **Online Services**. They plug in to the Internet, and thus form part of the Internet, but each also has exclusive services and content available only to their members and not the general Internet public. You'll find more about them in "Online Services" (see p.43), and more on the Web in "Surfing the World Wide Web" (see p.75).

What about a BBS?

Once upon a time **BBSs (Bulletin Board Services)** were like computer clubs, where you could dial in to post messages and trade files. However, these days the definition is far fuzzier. All Online Services, such as CompuServe and America Online (AOL), are technically BBSs. That is, they have a private network or file area which is set aside out of the public domain of the Internet. The big Online Services are not what most people refer to as BBSs, though. The term is usually taken to mean a small network which primarily acts as a place to download and trade files.

There are well over 100,000 private BBSs in the USA alone, most often devoted to particular or local interests, and sometimes access is free. They customarily have areas to play games, chat, use email, post messages, and sometimes get limited access to the Internet through their own private network connections.

And what about Intranets?

The mechanism that passes information between computers on the Internet can be used in exactly the same way in a **local network** such as in an office. When this is not publicly accessible, it's called an **Intranet**. Many companies use Intranets to distribute internal documents – in effect publishing Web pages for their own private use.

What are newsgroups and mailing lists and chat?

Usenet – the Net's prime discussion area – comprises over 25,000 **newsgroups**, each dedicated to a specific topic. So if you have a question, this is the place to raise it. Usenet messages are stored on the Internet for a matter of days or weeks, a bit like an online notice board.

Mailing lists perform a similar function, though the messages aren't kept on the Internet. The discussions are carried out by email. Each list has a central email address. Everything sent to that address goes to everyone on the list.

Chat, on the other hand, is instant, like a conversation. It's typically more of a social medium than an information tool. For more on Usenet, see p.128; Mailing lists, see p.123; and Chat, see p.180.

How can I get my own Web page?

Putting a page on the Web is a two-step process. First, you have to prepare it in **HTML**, the Web's mark-up language. A word processor, such as Word 97, can do a basic job of this by saving a document as HTML. To prepare something more elaborate, you need to use a dedicated HTML editing tool, or to learn HTML code – which isn't too hard for a computer language. Once you have an HTML document ready to go, you need to transfer it to your own special reserved **Web space**. For more on this, flip to page 200.

Can I rely on email?

In general Internet **email** is considerably more reliable than the postal service. If a message doesn't get through, it will generally bounce back to you telling you what went wrong. Occasionally, though, mail does go astray. During 1997, AOL and Microsoft Network – to name just the big players – had severe mail outages resulting in the delay, and in some cases loss, of email. And many corporate mail servers have had growing pains, too, experiencing holdups and the odd deletion. But on the whole you can confidently assume that email will arrive. If you don't get a reply within a few days, of course, you can always send your message again. At worst, it will act as a reminder. If you find your mail regularly takes more than a few minutes to arrive, you should seriously consider switching providers.

Who pays for the international calls?

The Internet is barely affected by political boundaries and distance. For example, suppose you're in Boston, and you want to buzz someone in Bangkok. Provided you both have Net access, it's as quick, easy, and cheap as sending a message across the street. You compose your message, connect to your local Internet Service Provider, upload your mail and then disconnect.

Your **mail server** examines the message's address to determine where it has to go, and then passes it on to its appropriate neighbor, which will do the same. This usually entails routing it toward the **backbone** – the chain of high-speed links that carry the bulk of the Net's long-haul traffic. Each subsequent link will ensure that the message heads towards Bangkok rather than Bogotá or Brisbane. The whole process should take no more than a few seconds.

Apart from your Internet access subscription, **you pay only for the local phone call**. Your data will scuttle through many different networks, each with its own methods of recouping the communication costs – but adding to your phone bill isn't one of them.

Then how does the pricing model work?

Once you're on the Net, most of what's there is free. But unless you have free access at work, school, or college, you'll need to pay for the privilege of being connected. That means paying an **Internet Service Provider** (ISP) to allow you to hook into its network. Depending on where you live, that could be a set price per month or year, or an hourly rate. Then on top of that, you'll have some sort of **telephone, ISDN, or cable charge**.

It's possible – indeed probable – that none of this money will ever go to the people who supply the content you'll be viewing. It simply goes toward maintaining the network. This imbalance is unlikely to continue, in the future it's likely that many publications (or sites) will charge a subscription for entry. As yet, that's still rare, other than for technical and financial publications, so enjoy it while it lasts.

What are hosts, servers, and clients?

In Net-speak, any computer that is open to external online access is known as a **server** or **host**. The software you use to perform online operations such as transfer files, read mail, surf the Web, or post articles to Usenet, is called a **client**.

A Web client is more commonly called a **Web browser** – a field dominated by **Netscape** and **Microsoft (Internet Explorer)**. A **Web server** is a machine where Web pages are stored and made available for outside access.

How do I read an email address?

Internet **email addresses** might look odd at first glance but they're really quite logical. They all take the form someone@somewhere As soon as you read that aloud, it should begin to make sense. For example, take the email address angus@roughguides.com The "@" sign says it's an email address. It's pronounced "at," so the address reads "Angus at Roughguides.com." From that alone you could deduce that the sender's name is "*Angus*" and he's somehow associated with "*Rough Guides*." It's not always that obvious but the format never changes.

The *somewhere* part is the **domain name** of the Internet **host** that handles *someone's* mail – often their Access Provider or workplace. Anyone who uses *someone's* provider or works with them could also share the same **domain name** in their email address, but they wouldn't be called *someone*. That's because the *someone* part identifies who, or what, they are at that host address. It's usually a name or nickname they choose themselves, or, with companies, a function like "help" or "info."

What's a domain name?

A **domain name** identifies and locates a host computer or service on the Internet. It often relates to the name of a business, organization or service and must be registered in much the same way as a company name. It breaks down further into the subdomain, domain type, and country code. For example, consider the email address: sophie@thehub.com.au In this case, the subdomain is thehub (an Internet Service Provider), its domain type com means it's a company or commercial site, and the country code au indicates it's in Australia.

Every country has its own distinct code, even if it's not always used. These include:

au	Australia
ca	Canada
de	Germany
fr	France
jp	Japan
nl	Netherlands
no	Norway
se	Sweden
uk	United Kingdom
tw	Taiwan

If an address doesn't specify a country code, it's more than likely, but not necessarily, in the USA. At present, domain types are usually one of the following, however the range will expand dramatically as recent changes to the domain registration system filter through:

ac	Academic (UK)
com	Company or commercial organization
co	Company or commercial organization (UK)
edu	Educational institution
gov	Government body
mil	Military site
net	Internet gateway or administrative host
org	Non-profit organization

What's an IP address?

Every computer on the Net has its unique numerical **IP (Internet Protocol) address**. A typical address looks like: 149.174.211.5 (that is, four numbers separated by periods). This is its official location on the Internet.

Your computer will be assigned an IP address when you log on. If it's **dynamically allocated**, the last few digits could vary each time you connect. That's usual with a PPP (Point to Point Protocol) dial-up connection. SLIP (Serial Line Internet Protocol) connections tend to use a fixed IP address. (There's more on this later).

Internet traffic control relies on these numbers. For example, a router might send all addresses beginning with 213 in one direction, and the rest in another. Eventually, through a process of elimination everything ends up in the right place.

Thankfully, you don't have to use these numbers. Why? Because, it's a recognized fact that humans are numerically dim. So we use domain names instead, by matching up the names and numbers in a table. After all, isn't it easier to remember "roughguides" than 204.62.130.112?

Not all IP addresses have attached domain names, but a domain name will not become active until it's matched to an IP address. The table is coordinated across a network of Domain Name Servers (DNS). Before you can send a message to someone@somewhere.com, your mail program has to ask your Domain Name Server to covert somewhere.com into an IP address. This process is called a **DNS lookup**.

What's bandwidth?

A higher (or fatter) **bandwidth connection** means the capacity to carry more data at once – just as a thicker pipe means you can pump more water. But unlike water, where pressure can increase, data is limited by electron speed. When a connection is at full capacity, it can't be pushed faster, so data goes into a queue – thus forming a bottleneck that slows things down. So even if you have a high bandwidth connection to the Internet, you could be impeded by insufficient bandwidth between you and your data source.

What if?

What if I'm harassed by another user?

It's possible to be harassed on the Internet by someone sending you unwelcome email, posting hostile replies to your comments in a newsgroup, pestering you in a Chat/Internet Phone channel or publishing something

on a Web page. The simplest thing to do is ignore them –
and if you've provoked the harassment, then you should
take it as a lesson. It's all too easy to **abuse or criticise
people by email** (especially work colleagues) in ways
you'd never imagine doing in person, or by regular
mail. And it's all too easy to send email – and worse,
with the mail copied to others adding to the humiliation.
Think before you click!

If you are having serious problems with someone you
don't know personally, then the best route is to forward
the messages or **pass their details to your Internet
Access Provider**. Even if your harasser has masked their
identity, they're probably still traceable. Your provider
should contact their provider, who'll most likely warn
them or kick them offline.

It's not easy to seriously harass someone via the Net
and get away with it. After all, it generates evidence in
writing. There have already been convictions for relatively mild threats posted to Usenet Newsgroups. Apart
from the nature of the harassment, whether you have a
case for action will depend on where you're both based.
For example, across US State lines it becomes an FBI
matter. Internationally, you might have no recourse
other than to appeal to their Access Provider. For more,
see: http://www.cyberangels.org

What if my children discover pornography or drugs?

If you're at all prudish, you'll get a nasty shock when
you hit the Web. You only need type the merest hint of
innuendo into a search engine to come face to face with
a porno advert. In fact, what once wasn't much more
than schoolboys trading Big & Busty scans has become
the Net's prime cashcow. Most perfectly normal kids will
search on a swearword the first chance they get. After

all, children are pretty childish. Consequently, if they're the slightest bit curious about sex, it won't be long before they end up at a porno merchant. That's the truth, if you can handle it.

What can you do about it? Well that depends on whether you'd rather shield kids from such things or prepare them for it. There is a large range of **censoring programs** available which attempt to filter out questionable material, either by letting only known sites through, banning certain sites, or withholding pages containing shady words. Internet Explorer, for example, comes with a **Content Advisor,** which can restrict access according to a rating system. Bear in mind that a smart kid – and no doubt that's what you're trying to raise – might be able to find a way to veto these filters. Whatever the case, if you're worried about your kids, the Net, and sex, then talk to them about it.

As for **drugs**, there's no way to get them from the Net. If anything, they're likely to find out the dangers of abusing them. So when they come across them in real life at least they'll be informed. Surely, that has to be a good thing.

Will being on the Internet put me at risk?

It's unlikely that someone is so interested in you that they could be bothered trying to worm their way into your PC to read or interfere with your files. So it's more a hypothetical question of whether it's possible for someone to break in. Security is tightening all the time, but yes, though highly unlikely, it's not entirely impossible. Nonetheless, the truth is **it's easier to break into your house** – and burglary is harder to trace.

Most professional Web sites issue you a "**cookie**" file to identify you when you visit. If that bothers you, and it shouldn't really, unless your Net interests are pretty unwholesome, then just switch off the option to accept them. For more on cookies, see p.75.

What about viruses?

You are far more likely to catch a virus from a corporate network or a friend's floppy disk than the Internet. Still, it pays to run a **virus check** regularly and keep your virus checker's signature file up to date.

It's almost unheard of to get a virus by **downloading programs** from a reputable site. Sure, there are regular scares that controls embedded into Web pages could exploit browser security flaws and harm your PC. But fixes generally appear days later. And these flaws are rarely exploited. The two risk areas are decoding unknown programs posted to **Usenet newsgroups**, and running programs sent to you as **email attachments**. Be particularly cautious of Microsoft Word and Excel documents, as they can carry malicious macros. For more on this, if you're running Microsoft Office, read http://www. microsoft.com/office/antivirus/

While it's possible for an attachment to contain a virus, **plain text email** is entirely harmless. Despite this, there's a glut of hoax letters circling the Net warning you not to open email with certain subject headings. These are in effect nothing more than chain letters. If you get such a message direct the sender to: http://kumite.com/myths/

Messages sent in HTML carry the same risks as **browsing the Web**. For example, it's possible to crash a computer by overloading its processing resources. All the same, it's not something you should worry about.

Getting online

What's full Internet access?

You can access the Internet – and send email – through several channels. But not all methods will let you do everything. The **World Wide Web**, **IRC**, **FTP**, and **Telnet** – key areas of the Net which we'll deal with later in this book – require **"full Internet access"**.

You can get full Internet access through an **Online Service** like CompuServe or America Online (AOL), or with what's called an **IP (Internet Protocol)** account from any **Internet Service** or **Access Provider** (**ISP** or **IAP**). You'll encounter a range of IP accounts, which may include **SLIP** (Serial Line Internet Protocol) and **PPP** (Point to Point Protocol) for standard modem dial-ups, **ISDN**, and **cable**. Regardless of what grade IP access you choose, you'll be able to do the same things, though perhaps at different speeds.

What do I need to get started?

You can get to the Net aboard an increasing number of devices from mobile phones to televisions, but the most popular and flexible route is via a home **PC**, hooked to an Internet Service Provider through a **modem**. So if you have a PC, a modem, and a telephone line, all you need next is an account with an Access Provider and possibly some extra software to get rolling. This is all covered in detail in the following chapters.

Where can I get an email address?

You should get at least one email address thrown in by your Internet Provider with your **access account**. Many providers supply five or more addresses – enough for the whole family. The only problem with these addresses is that they tie you to that provider. If you want to switch providers, you either have to negotiate a mail-only account or obtain an address that can move with you (see p.219). It's a hassle, either way, so choose your provider carefully.

If you already have an email address, say at work or college, but want a **more personal or funky sounding address**, you can ask an Access Provider for a POP3 mail only account, try a mail specialist such as Mail-Bank (http://www.mailbank.com), or sign up with a Webmail or redirection service (see p.117). That way you can choose an address and use it over any connection.

Will I need to learn any computer languages?

No. If you can work a word processor or spreadsheet, you'll have no difficulty tackling the Internet. You just have to get familiar with your Internet software, which in most cases isn't too hard. The biggest problem most people have is **setting up for the first time**, but it's becoming less of an issue as most Internet providers supply start-up kits that make it easy.

Once online, most people access the Internet through **graphical menu-based software**, with a similar feel to most Macintosh and Windows programs. And on the World Wide Web – the most popular part of the Net – **you hardly even need to type**: almost everything is accessible by a click on your mouse.

The one time you might need to use **UNIX commands** – the Internet's traditional computer "language" – would be when using Telnet to remotely log on to a UNIX computer. And that's something most of us can avoid.

Can I use the Internet if I can't use a computer?

As mentioned above, even if you can't type, you can still
use the World Wide Web – all you have to do is **point
your mouse and click**. That's about as far as you'll get
though. If you've never had any contact with computers,
consider the Internet your opportunity. Don't think of
computers as a daunting modern technology. They're
only a means to an end. The best way to learn how to
use a computer is to grab one and switch it on.

So, how do I get connected?

Good question, and worth a whole chapter. Read on.

Getting Connected

There are all kinds of ways to access the Internet. It's likely you're already in contact with a Net-connected terminal: maybe at your work, college, school, local library, or even your local coffee shop. But if you're not in that position already, you needn't wait. It's possible to get everything you need to be up and running within a few days. The good news is it's no longer expensive or complicated, and it's getting cheaper and easier by the day.

You don't need to be a computer expert

Perhaps you're not already hooked up because you find the whole computing world a bit off-putting. Well, this is the perfect opportunity to get over it. The rewards of being online far outweigh the effort involved in learning to use a computer.

Although there's enough information in this guide to get you started on the Internet, if you're entirely new to computers it might be a good idea if you asked someone computer literate to sit with you for the first couple of sessions. If you don't know anyone suitable, then drop into a **cybercafé** (see p.223) and ask an attendant to kickstart you onto the World Wide Web. That's their business, they won't laugh at you, so don't be scared to admit you're green. You should be able to figure out how to surf the Web within a matter of minutes. Finding your way around is another matter, but you're at an advantage – you have this guide.

In addition, if you strike problems remember that the **online community** – other folks on the Net – is out there for help, though be sure that you direct your queries to the right area. Just wait and see, before long you'll be sharing your newfound expertise with others.

What you'll need

Before you can get connected, you'll need three things: a **computer** with enough grunt to handle the software, an account with an **Internet Service Provider**, and a hardware device – usually the fastest **modem** you can afford – to connect your computer to the Internet. How you connect can make the difference between pleasure and frustration. You don't necessarily need state of the art computer gadgetry, but no matter what you have, you'll find a way to push it to the limit.

Computer firepower

It's possible to access the Net in some way with almost any machine you could call a computer, but if you can't run your Web browsing and mail software together without a lot of chugging noises coming from your hard drive, you're going to get frustrated.

To drive browsing software comfortably, you'll need at least a **486 SX25 IBM-compatible PC**, or a **Macintosh 68030** series, equipped with **8Mb RAM**. This won't be enough to run the latest Net software, but you should be able to get by at a pinch if you stick to old versions. For more flexibility, add more RAM.

You can also connect to the Net with Ataris, Amigas, PCTVs, Psion Organizers, Palmtops, and even the Nokia 9000 cellular phone, but you'll be severely restrained by the lack of software. Unless you just want to use these devices for email, you'll be far happier with something faster and more versatile.

If you're in the market for a new computer, your first decision will be to decide between **PC or Mac**.

Apple Mac computers are said to be more user-friendly, especially by their fiercely brand-loyal users. They also shine at image handling - one reason why they've become institutionalized within the graphic art, publishing and media industries. Hence, they're worth considering if you intend to work in these fields, as you'll find it much easier to share files and knowledge with peers. Apple has done it tough in the 90's, but things are looking brighter with new manage- ment and the birth of the impressive and affordable I-Mac. Just beware though, if you buy into Apple, you'll be locked into a proprietary system that's comparatively starved of software.

On the other hand, if you join the masses and head down the PC track, you'll get more bangs per buck, a far wider range of software and greater flexibility when it's time to upgrade and expand.

With PCs, brand names are less important than **after-sales service**. PC components often come from several different manufacturers. The crunch comes when some-thing goes wrong. Find out how long you'd be without your computer if it needs repair. Your corner shop might be able to do it on the spot, or help you set up your soft-ware. Name brands often offer a range of service agreements ranging from same day replacement to potentially leaving you stranded for weeks. Don't underestimate the worth of a guarantee. And consider seriously buying the exact same set-up as a friend, so you have someone to turn to for help.

Whatever you buy, bear in mind the Net is a full multimedia experience, so pack it with as much **memory** or RAM (32+ Mb) as you can afford, a decent **hard drive** (2+ Gig), a fast **CD-ROM or DVD drive** (for loading software and playing movies), and check out the advanced options in **sound and video**.

Note: If you're on a network at work or college, don't attempt to connect to the Net without your systems manager's supervision. Networked PCs and Macs can use the same software listed later in this book, but may connect to the Net differently.

Connecting your computer to the Net

A powerful computer won't make up for a slow link to the Internet. Get the fastest connection you can afford.

Unless you're hooked up through a network, you'll need a device to connect your computer to the telephone line or cable. There'll be a similar device at your Access Provider's end. This device will depend on the type of Internet account. The two main types are **Leased Line** and **dial-up**. Leased Lines are expensive and aimed at businesses that need to be permanently connected. Dial-up suits the casual user. Investigate the Net through a dial-up account before contemplating a Leased Line.

Modems – the plain vanilla option

 The cheapest, most popular, but slowest, way to connect is by installing a **modem** and dialing up through the standard telephone network. Modems come in three flavors: internal, external, and PCMCIA. Each has its advantages and disadvantages.

The cheapest option is usually an **internal modem** – unless you have a portable, for which internal modems are often comparatively pricey. An internal modem plugs into a slot inside your computer called a bus. Installation is not difficult but does require that you take the back off your computer and follow the instructions carefully (or get your computer store to do it). Because they're hidden inside your computer, internal modems don't take up desk space, clutter the back of your computer with extra cables, or require an external power source. They do, however, generate unwanted heat inside your computer, place an extra drain on your power supply, and lack the little lights to tell you if or how the call is going.

An **external modem** is easier to install. Depending on the make, it will simply plug straight in to your computer's serial, parallel, or SCSI port, making it easily interchangeable between machines (and simple to upgrade). External modems require a separate power source, maybe even a battery. And they usually give a visual indication of the call's progress through a bank of flashing lights (LEDs).

The credit-card-sized **PCMCIA modems** are a mixture of the two. They fit internally into the PC card slots common in most modern notebooks and remove easily to free the slot for something else. They don't require an external power source, but are expensive and sometimes fragile.

The need for speed

Whichever type of modem you choose, the major issue is speed. Data transfer speed is expressed in bits per second or **bps**. It can take up to ten bits to transfer a character. So a modem operating at 2400 bps (2.4 Kbps) would transfer at around 240 characters per second. That's about a page of text every eight seconds. At 28.8 Kbps, you could send the same page of text in two-thirds of a second.

A 14.4 Kbps (V.32) modem can browse the World Wide Web, but you'll be much happier with something faster. A faster modem might cost a little more, but it will reduce your online charges, and give you more for your money. At time of writing, the standard has reached **56K (V.90)**, which can theoretically download at up to 56 Kbps, and upload at up to 33.6 Kbps. Unfortunately, because of phone line dynamics, you may never get to connect at the full speed, but you should still be able to get well above 33.6 Kbps, the previous speed barrier. If you have an X2 or K56flex modem, upgrade to V.90, if possible. (See http://www.56k.com).

Finally, **make sure whatever you buy will work with your computer**. PCs need a high-speed serial card with a 16550 or 16650 UART chip to process any more than about 9.6 Kbps reliably. Most modern PCs have them as standard, but check anyway. It's not an expensive upgrade.

Faster ways to connect

What's good about modems is that they are the right-here right-now accepted worldwide standard and work over the regular telephone system without any excess charges. But they are slow and unstable compared to what's around the corner. If you're into seriously fast connections and enjoy new technology, then read on – and check the Web addresses given for further details. If you just want to get up on the Net, skip this section.

ISDN

ISDN is a vast improvement on modem technology, not just for speed, but for superior line handling and almost instantaneous connections – and it is already available.

It provides three channels (1x16 Kbps and 2x64 Kbps) which can be used and charged for in various ways. ISDN Internet accounts don't usually cost more but, depending on where you live, the line connection, rental, and calls can cost anywhere from slightly to outrageously more than standard telephone charges. That's up to your telco. Connecting through ISDN, rather than using a modem, you'll need a slightly more expensive device called a **Terminal Adapter**, plus appropriate software, and possibly an upgrade to your serial card. For details on how to install ISDN under Windows 95 see: http://www.microsoft.com/windows/getisdn/

Cable and xDSL

Fast though ISDN is, it looks dead in the water as other copper-wire technologies promise to bring far higher bandwidths into homes at a fraction of the cost.

A much superior option, if you can get it, is **cable access**. Cable offers mega-speed rates (up to 10 Mbps) without call charges, but suffers slightly from having to share the line with your neighbors. It's already available as a cable TV sideline in many cities in the US and Australia, and should become widespread within Europe and Asia soon. So, if you have cable in your street, ask if it's available.

Next on the horizon are the various strands of **xDSL**, such as ADSL, CDSL and RADSL. You'll most likely see CDSL first, in the form of a 1Mbps modem that can operate over normal telephone lines. Rockwell (http://www.rockwell.com) and Nortel (http://www.nortel.com) already have the hardware; it's just a matter of rolling it out. Nortel is testing delivery at similar speeds via the power lines. ADSL is much faster still, with download speeds up to 6Mbps, and uploads up to 640 Kbps, again via the normal telephone system. It has looked great in trials, but as yet there's not much commercial action. For more, see: http://www.adsl.com

Satellite

If you need zippy delivery and you need it now, your best choice might be via **satellite**. You receive through a small TV dish, and send through a standard dial-up or leased line account with an Access Provider. So you can in theory browse the Web at up to 10 Mbps, but send email or upload material at a standard modem rate.

DirecPC (http://www.direcpc.com) has two home user access accounts with rates of up to 200 Kbps and 400 Kpbs. Satellite access might even become the norm if the Boeing/Gates funded global broadband "Internet in the sky" project has its way. See: http://www.teledesic.com

Doubling up modems

It's possible to bind two or more modems together using multiple telephone lines in parallel. In theory, this should give you a bandwidth equal to the sum of the combined modems. It's simple to set up in Windows 95 (or later versions): just right-click on your provider's Dial-up Networking entry, choose Properties, and add another device under Multilink. If you don't see a Multi-link option, install the latest Dial-up Networking and Winsock upgrades from: http://www.microsoft.com/windows95/info/updates.htm The hardest part is finding a provider that supports it.

Okay – I have a computer and modem. So, how do I get an Internet connection?

To connect to the Internet, you'll need someone to allow you to connect into their computer, which in turn is connected to another computer, which in turn . . . that's how the Internet works. Unless you have a working relationship with whomever controls access to that computer, you'll have to pay for the privilege.

IAPs and ISPs

A company in the business of providing Internet access is known as an **Internet Access Provider (IAP)** or **Service Provider (ISP)**. This is a highly competitive business, with providers galore touting **free trial periods** and **software**, and (something you may well want to take advantage of) **free Web space** for your own homepages.

However all providers aren't equal. Some are excellent and established, providing licensed software and top class service to thousands of subscribers. Others, by contrast, may be financially shaky: bad news, since if they go broke you'll not only lose your connection but maybe your email address as well. Others, still, are just plain not very good, trying to squeeze too many folk online, resulting in frequent busy tones when you dial, and slow transfer rates once you're online.

It pays to ask around for personal recommendations, or check local **Internet or computer magazines** (who are forever doing comparative tests of speed, service, and so forth), before choosing your IAP/ISP. An added bonus to Internet and computer magazines is that they often carry cover-mounted disks with all the Net software you'll need to get started – and maybe introductory accounts with reputable providers.

To help with your quest, there's a **list of IAP/ISPs** at the end of this book (p.487), along with a **checklist of questions to ask them** – some of which will be important to you, others not, depending on cirumstances.

Online Services

An alternative to the dedicated IAPs and ISPs is to sub-scribe to one of the major **Online Services** – such as **CompuServe**, **America Online (AOL)**, or **Microsoft Net-work** – which offer full Internet access at increasingly commercial rates. Most of these commercial giants offer two separate services: access to the Internet proper and access to their own private network. On the Internet front, they can be appraised in the same way as any other ISP, and are reviewed in the following chapter.

How much will it cost?

Have you ever shopped for a mobile phone? Well, that was easy compared to trying to get the best deal on Internet access. As the gates to the Net are in the hands of small and large business, there's a puzzling array of providers and pricing structures.

The biggest issue is **time charges**. Where local calls are fixed or free, as in North America, Asia, and Australasia, providers began by either restricting the number of access hours included in the monthly charge or charging by the minute. The idea being to discourage line hogging. So in the **US** typical charges started at $20 per month for the first 40 hours access and then $2 per hour thereafter. However, due to fierce competition most US providers have switched to "all you can eat" accounts for a single monthly fee, usually about $20. In the **UK** and other countries where local calls are timed, lengthy connections mean hefty phone bills, and line hogging is not an issue. In the UK it's common just to pay a single monthly fee of £10–15 or an annual fee of £120–200. In **Australia**, where access rates vary as wildly as the quality of the networks, untimed accounts are rare and relatively expensive. A cheap deal works out around $20 for the first 50 hours each month. Sometimes **cable** can be just as cheap if you subtract the phone call charges. For instance, the US Internet cable provider, @Home (http://www.home.com), charges between $30-50 flat per month depending on the cable reseller. Be more wary of cable providers which have an excess rate per Mb downloaded, which can work out prohibitively expensive if you're cruising the Web and downloading software in excess of 30 Mb per hour.

In addition to these monthly charges many Access Providers charge a **once-off setup fee** (usually about the same as a month's access), which should include up-to-date **software for email and browsing the Web**. Other providers, especially the Online Services, might offer a **free trial period**, but if you check their pricing for an average year it mightn't work out cheaper overall.

Mind your phone bill: POPs

If you plan to connect through a telephone line, make sure you choose a provider with a **local dial-up number**. And, if you travel, you will want to have a range of access numbers, otherwise you might run up some serious phone bills.

These dial-up numbers are called **Points Of Presence (POPs)**. In the US, if you need to call your provider from interstate, it may offer a free 1-800 number with a flat fee of about 15¢ per minute including the call. If you have free local call access, then make sure your provider has a POP in your local zone. In the UK, unless you restrict your access to nights and weekends, your phone bill will usually outweigh your Internet access bill.

Most telcos offer a discount to your choice of frequently called **"Friends and Family"** numbers. Put your provider on this list as it's sure to become your most called number.

Online Services

AOL, CompuServe, Line One, Microsoft Network (MSN), and Prodigy provide Internet access to their subscribers but are commonly called Online Services rather than Internet Service Providers (ISPs). That's because they supply more than just Internet access. Each offers its members private, customized content, either on an exclusive network separate to the Internet or in a password-protected Web site. They can be more expensive than a regular ISP but might be worth considering as they are well organized, secure, regulated, easy to navigate, simple to install and tend to throw in a bit of free Web space for your own pages.

In addition, AOL and CompuServe, in particular, maintain discussion forums that rival Usenet, and offer a broad range of both local and international numbers (POPs) to dial in. If you want to pick up mail on your travels, this can be a big plus – see our section "On The Road" (p.217). All the Online Services supply free (and simple) connection kits, which makes the initial sign-up process more straightforward than usual. Unfortunately, they can also make your online experience cumbersome, as they tend not to be as efficient as the simple Internet browser/mail alternative.

Following are brief summaries of what's currently on offer from the major Online Services. Be warned, though, that they are all in a state of flux, shifting material from their private networks to the Web proper, and integrating software such as Internet Explorer. The traditional gap between Online Services and IAPs/ISPs continues to narrow as Online Services are forced to compete on price, Web access and Internet mail standards. Eventually, the only issue will be content.

Choosing an online service

Online Services can be a gentle introduction to the online world. They're simple to set up, easy to find your way around and packed with consistently high-quality content. The trouble is, many users find they spend most of their time on the Internet, so they don't want to pay extra for exclusive content, chat rooms, and forums they rarely use. You can only work out what's best for you by having a look around first.

So, try them out – the lot, if you have time. It won't cost you anything, because they're all mad on free trials. Between ten hours and a month is typical. Take a close look at the content, forums and chat rooms; check that localized content, such as news services, are available and that the content you pay for is useful; and if you enjoy one, then sign up. But if you're serious about using the Net you should try at least one dedicated ISP, too, so you can compare speed and service.

America Online (AOL)

With well over thirteen million account holders, **America Online (AOL)** is currently the world's largest Online Service. In fact, it could have several times that number of users, because each member is allowed five "screen names". That means five people – your friends and family, say – can each have a sub-account at no extra cost. They can then log in and do everything you can with a full account. With one exception. As account holder, you control how much they can access. So if you don't want your kids near binary newsgroups (mostly porn and pirate software), you can bar them, or ban decoding and downloading.

These **screen names** are actually email addresses. So if you choose the screen name Shelley, your email address would be Shelley@aol.com Unfortunately, with potentially forty million screen names, it's hard to get one quite that simple. Especially as once you've taken one, and changed it, it can't be reused by anyone else. Still, you might get Shelley159 if you move fast.

AOL has been aggressively pushing its software to the point where any computer magazine buyer in the US or UK should have several copies of its access program, and **signing up** couldn't be easier. You just pop in the disk, type in your personal details, click "yes" a few times, and within seconds you're asked to choose a screen name. And then you get a month's free access to not only all AOL's content but the full Internet as well.

Despite its name, AOL is not entirely American. UK members, for example, are greeted by Joanna Lumley's voice and UK news, travel, and entertainment guides. In addition to its range of **online encyclopedias, magazines, and databases**, AOL's greatest strength lies in its sense of community. AOLers do tend to mix online with other AOLers, aided by an Instant Messaging system which lets them know when their "buddies" are online. This eager AOLer personality shines through in AOL's **chat forums**, where lucky members get to grill popstar bigwigs like Oasis, Paul McCartney, and the Spice Girls.

Although it now ships **Internet Explorer** integrated into its software bundle, of all Online Services, AOL seems the most reticent to switch over to a Web/POP3 base. Consequently, you'll need the AOL program to access its mail and much of its exclusive content. However, you can still install other Net software and use it like a regular ISP.

For a free trial and local pricing call: ☎1300 654 633 (Australia); ☎800 827 6364 (North America); ☎0800 279 1234 (UK).

CompuServe

 CompuServe started Online Services in the late 1970s and now has POPs in over 142 countries, more than five million members (including almost two million in Japan!) and a content range second to none. It has support forums for just about everything supportable, company searches, online shopping, news, magazines, professional forums, chat, software registrations, program archives, flight reservations, and more services than you could look at in a lifetime. CompuServe is also a truly **international** access provider. No matter where you join, you can dial in to any of its international numbers to browse the Internet or pick up your email. It's simple to register and provides all necessary software, including Microsoft's **Internet Explorer**, for free.

Although CompuServe, like AOL, delivers its share of home info-tainment, such as online grocery shopping and entertainment guides, that's just floss on the cake. Since being taken over by AOL in early 1998, CompuServe has focused its efforts on becoming more of a

business, professional and technical service than an AOL-styled family funshack. Around the same time as the AOL takeover, its physical network was bought out by cable giant Worldcom, and is now run as a separate business. As yet, this has all been transparent to members but by early 1999 AOL and CompuServe intend to share the same software. The other approaching development will be the move of all CompuServe's content, including a mass of third-party content deals, to the Web. Once this happens, CompuServe should be almost entirely navigable with any Web browser – which means non dial-up members should soon be able to access it across the Net on some sort of pay per view basis.

One thing that's long bugged everyone about CompuServe has been its dreadful mail system. Thankfully, that's starting to change. Although new members still receive an email "number" (eg 12345.671@compuserve.com) they can instantly change it to a name (eg MilesAlmo@compuserve.com) and then redirect it to a POP3 address (eg MilesAlmo@csi.com). Although POP3 is available, it's not actively supported (ie they deny it exists) in some countries, for example the UK. Don't listen to them, just GO POPMAIL once online. And then never ever use its mail program again. Got it? Don't hold your breath – because nothing ever happens in a hurry at CompuServe – but it's rumored to be upgrading to IMAP, which is even better than POP3.

CompuServe's charges can be complex, with premiums for some services, and different payment structures for different countries. Internet-only access is offered in some areas at a discount.

For a free trial and local pricing call: ☎1300 555 520 (Australia); ☎800 524 3388 (North America); ☎0800 442 374 (NZ); ☎0990 000 200 (UK).

LineOne (UK Only)

LineOne, launched in 1997 by the combined forces of Rupert Murdoch and British Telecom, only offers dial-up access within the UK. However, members can access its content from anywhere via the Web. Apart from Internet access and POP3 email, its main selling proposition is its traditional British family-values content enhanced by the online debuts of *The Sun* and *News of the World* (Murdoch's *Times* and *Sunday Times* are available on LineOne, too, but already have established Web editions). So you can start your day with Uri Geller, Mystic Meg, Betty Shrine, a bit of footy gossip, a Page 3 stunner, and a randomly selected lotto number.

As with AOL, you can set up five **sub-accounts** and restrict their access, say, to strictly educational matter. And as well as the tabloid fluff, there's up-to-the-minute news and sport, Sky video feeds, HarperCollins reference titles, financial data and portfolio management, Kiss FM and Classic FM in Real Audio, online gaming and entertainment listings. A recent deal with United Media promises to bring other titles online such as the UK's *Daily Mail* and *Yorkshire Post*. It's all entirely Web-based, squats neatly inside **Internet Explorer**, doesn't meddle with your system, and hence isn't a bad introduction to the Net. After all, if it's not your style, you already have the Web software, so signing up with another ISP is as simple as switching your dial-up settings. Then again, maybe you'll become a *Sun* convert.

There are three LineOne **charging** options. Unlimited access costs £14.95 per month. Alternatively, you can opt for three free hours and pay £2.35 per subsequent hour. If you already have Internet access, or live outside the UK, a content-only subscription costs £4.95 per month. For details, call: ☎0345 777 464 (UK).

Microsoft Network

 **Microsoft's** original masterplan was to create an ubernetwork, powerful enough to topple the Internet. With $US1billion to blow on content, a link on every Windows 95 desktop, and Bill Gates belligerently tooting its horn, that seemed possible. However, four relaunches later, Microsoft Network (MSN) has finally refashioned itself as one of the Net's biggest, and perhaps even best, free Web sites, with just a small amount of password-protected exclusive content, perched over a rented network. Microsoft has, it seems, given up on the access game to concentrate on content – and, in particular, transactions, with its hugely successful travel agency, Expedia.

Thus when you dial into MSN, you'll actually dial into whichever ISP or media empire it's in cahoots with. This gives Microsoft the flexibility to pull out if need be, and switch providers, perhaps to cable, ADSL or low orbit satellite. Take Australia, for example, where it's called **NineMSN**. It has colluded with Telstra Big Pond for access and Kerry Packer's PBL media circus for content. This has brought ACP titles (like Dolly and HQ) and Channel 9 shows (like Wide World of Sport and Business Sunday) together under one online roof. As you'd expect, by teaming a country's main telco with its largest media force, Microsoft has created a Web site that's close to a household name.

This very focused development hasn't been repeated in all territories, as yet, and there are those who suggest that Microsoft doesn't have a clue where it's headed. But then if the Net has taught Bill Gates a lesson, it is perhaps the value of flexible thinking – and U-turns. After all, Microsoft began by dismissing the Net as an area of no commercial interest.

Technically, MSN is, as you'd expect, a professional package. It gives you everything you'd expect from a regular ISP including full Internet access, POP3 email, Usenet, free software and good support. The only question is whether you want to pay a premium price.

To **register with MSN**, you can simply click on the icon in Windows 95/98, and follow the instructions. Or to save your phone bill, call and get the latest software updates on disk.

For details call: ☎1300 300 679 (NineMSN Australia); ☎800 386 5550 (North America); ☎0345 002 000 (UK), and ask how much they'd like to charge you today. Or visit: http://www.msn.com or http://ninemsn.com.au (Australia).

Prodigy

Prodigy was the first Online Service to add full Internet access. That used to be its drawcard. These days it's more like an ISP with the bonus of a reasonable wad of prime proprietary content, like Study Web and Investor's Business Daily, plus an aggregation of material plucked from the Web into a form that might make more sense to a newcomer. To date it's been primarily focused in North America, but it has recently made inroads into East Africa, Latin America, and Asia, including China. If you want an ISP, with a little of the added comfort and community of an Online Service, but without the associated annoyances like non-POP3 mail and clunky software, Prodigy might do the trick.

For a free trial in North America, call: ☎800 776 3449.

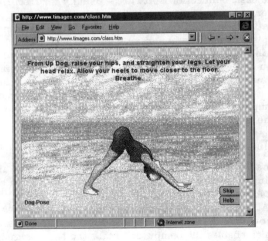

Connection
Software

It's standard practice for Access Providers to supply
the basic connection software – usually for free. However, because the Internet is constantly evolving, no
matter how good the starter kit, you'll soon want to
replace or add components. It's not crucial to start out
with what's state of the art, because once you're online,
you can download the latest versions of everything -
again, usually for free. Or you can get it in disc form
as a cover-mount from one of the many Internet and
computer magazine titles: just browse the racks to see
who is offering the month's best package.

The connection essentials

What you stand to get from a provider could be anything from the bare minimum needed to dial in and
establish an IP connection to a full Internet toolkit.

At the heart of every package is the TCP/IP software,
known as the stack or in Windows as the Winsock,
which enables the computer to talk the Net's language.
It needs to know your IP address and your provider's
DNS server addresses (see pp.24), information that you
will have to enter, either by running an installation program or manually. It must be set up properly otherwise
none of your Internet programs will work.

Once the TCP/IP stack is correctly configured for your provider, you can pick and choose whatever components as you see fit.

Windows 95/98/NT, OS/2, or Mac?

If you're running **Windows 95/98/NT**, IBM's **OS/2**, or Macintosh **System 7.5 or later**, you already have all the TCP/IP software you need to get started.

In Windows 95/98, right-click on the desktop Network Neighborhood icon and check you've installed the Client for Microsoft Networks, TCP/IP protocol and Dial-up Adapter. If not, click "Add" and install each in turn. Microsoft is the manufacturer in all cases. Then choose Client for Microsoft Networks as your Primary Network Logon. Do not enable File or Printer sharing unless you want to let outsiders from the Net into your computer.

Your provider will either supply you with an installation program or give you written instructions on how to set up the finer details. Failing that, have someone walk you through it over the phone. Once that's done the rest is easy.

Earlier systems

If you are running an **earlier version of Windows**, or a **pre-System 7.0 Mac**, you'll need to either upgrade your operating system or obtain a TCP/IP program.

Of the several **TCP/IP programs** for **Windows 3.x**, the most popular is **Trumpet Winsock**. It's freely available on the Internet and used as the core of many ISPs' Windows 3.x bundles. It's not actually free, though. If you want to use it after a trial period, you are requested to pay the author. Its dial-up scripting takes a while to figure out, but once you have it going it's rock solid and works with everything. A better choice, if offered, is the version of **Internet Explorer 3.03 for Windows 3.x** that includes its own Winsock. Setting it up is as simple as following the prompts. It is available for free on the Net, if you can get someone to download it for you, at:

http://www.microsoft.com/ie/win31/

Macintosh users need look no further than **MacTCP**, or its successor **Open Transport**, which can be obtained separately from most Access Providers or from your Apple dealer as part of the **Apple Internet Connection Kit**. Open Transport is superior, but will not run on 6800 or 68020 systems.

Getting it to dial

Unless you're connecting via a Local Area Network (LAN) you'll also need a **dialer** to automate the dial-up and log-in procedure. You can generally configure this in the same process as TCP/IP. This means if you're setting up through a step-by-step wizard, you'll usually enter your TCP/IP configuration, user details, password, provider's telephone number, and then attach a dial-up script (if used), all in one go. Depending on the set-up program you might also be able to configure your mail and news programs in the same process. After it's all configured, you should only need to click on "connect", or something similar, to instruct your modem to dial. You shouldn't need to enter your dial-up (or mail, if it was included) password again.

Windows dialing

Dialing is the part of **Windows 95** that's gone through the biggest evolution on its path to **Windows 98** via its controversial Web browser program, **Internet Explorer**. If you have the first release of Windows 95, you might need to install a dialing component, as this was originally a Plus pack extra called the "Dial-up Scripting Tool." (There have been so many incarnations since it's hard to keep track). But if you've been supplied with Internet Explorer 4.0 or later, either as part of Windows 98 or otherwise, you'll be able to set it all up in a jiffy through the **Internet Connection Wizard**. If not, your access provider will be able to supply you with enough to get you connected.

Once online, drop into http://www.microsoft.com/windows95/info/updates.htm and update your system to Dial-up Networking 1.2 and Winsock 2.0.

Mac dialing

Macs need a separate program to enable dialing. The most popular choices are: **FreePPP**, from http://www.rockstar.com; **ConfigPPP/MacPPP**, part of the Apple Internet Connection Kit; and **OT-PPP** for Open Transport, also from Apple. If you don't already have one of these, your provider should be able to oblige.

Once you're online visit http://www.info.apple.com for system upgrades and support. Articles 18238 and 24138 in the Tech Info Library explain how to obtain and configure Open Transport.

Dialing different providers

Once your connection software is set up you should be able to forget about it, unless you have to **dial a different provider**.

It's simple to set up **Windows 95/98/NT** to handle multiple providers, or switch to a new one. Just start a new account under Dial-up Networking and then set the TCP/IP under Properties, or do it all in one go with the Internet Connection Wizard. The same goes for Mac users with **FreePPP**, **MacPPP**, and **OT-PPP**. Just look for the option "New" to start a new account. There's no need in any case to install new software, you just have to change the TCP/IP and dial-up settings. That should only take a few minutes.

However, if you've installed a **Windows 3.x** ISP bundle, under any version of Windows, you might encounter conflicts. When you install Windows 3.x TCP/IP software, it deposits its own version of a file named winsock.dll into your system path. If you install two TCP/IP packages from different vendors you could have two such files in different directories, but both in your system path, or one could overwrite the other. Make sure this doesn't happen. If you need to install a new package, uninstall the old one first. Don't install an ISP kit under **Windows 95** that isn't specifically designed for it. In fact, there's absolutely no reason to use any TCP/IP dialer combination other than what Microsoft supplies.

Did you get all that TCP/IP stuff?

If you didn't understand a bar of the last few pages on
getting connected, don't worry! Internet connection and
TCP/IP configuration is your Internet Access Provider's
specialty. It's in their interest to get you up and running, so if things go haywire, or you're confused, do
things the easy way – give them a call. After all, if you
can't get connected, they're not going to get paid.

Setting the settings . . .

There are so many ways to get onto the Internet,
it's impossible to draw up a set of generic step-
by-step instructions. That's why we suggest you
follow whatever directions you're given on your
first sign-up. However, if you have to enter the
settings yourself, these are the main ones you'll
strike:

TCP/IP settings
IP address: Your location on the Internet. It's
likely your ISP's server will allocate this afresh
each time you log in. If so, you won't be given a
numerical address, you'll be told to choose
"server assigned" or "dynamically allocated."
Two DNS server addresses: The servers that
convert friendly domain names into numerical
Internet addresses. These will be numerical, in
the form 123.345.123.12
Domain or Search Domain: This will look
something like: provider.net It's not used in
Windows 95/98.

Dialer settings
User name: Your account name with the ISP.

Dial-up password: Your secret access code.
Dial-up access number: The number your modem dials to access the ISP.

Mail settings
Full email address: The address where you'll receive your mail. Will be in the form someone@somewhere where the somewhere part is a domain name.
Mail login: The name you choose as the someone part of your email address.
Mail password: The secret code you use to pick up your mail.
Outgoing mail server (SMTP): The server that will handle all mail you send. It will be a domain name.
Incoming mail server (POP/IMAP): Where your mail is stored. It will also be a domain name.

Other settings
News server address (NNTP): Most providers maintain their own Usenet services. This domain address goes into your newsreader preferences. (See p.128)
Proxy settings: Some providers use a gateway between you and the Internet to manage traffic. These settings go into your Web browser. (See p.96)
IRC server: Not all providers support chat locally, but they should be able to recommend

a server to start you off. Enter this into your chat software preferences. (See p.180)

FTP server: Where to transfer files to and from your ISP's local storage space. This isn't something you configure, you type it into your file transfer program. (See p.146)

If you'd need further instructions on **tinkering with your TCP/IP settings** once you're online, a good place to start would be your provider's homepage on the Web. Most ISPs maintain a set of pictorial instructions of what to fill in where for various operating systems. The best thing about these instructions is that they'll be tailored for your situation. If yours isn't so helpful, you could try another provider such as:

http://www.dial.pipex.com/support/connect/
http://www.mr.net/technical/dialup/
http://www.ozemail.com.au/internet/support/

Right – is that it, or do I still need more software?

The **TCP/IP** and **dialer** (Dial-up Networking) combination is enough to get you connected to the Net. But you'll need more software to actually use it. Your access provider should supply some start-up software on a disk, or alternatively instruct you to download it off a local server using a Terminal program such as Hyper-Terminal. If your provider doesn't provide software, they're maybe not a great choice, though, as noted previously, you can get a range of current software from Internet or computer magazine cover CDs.

The one thing you'll definitely need is a **Web browser**. In fact, the latest Web browsers are so complete you might not feel the need to get any other software program. You certainly won't need a **mail** program as the ones that come bundled with browsers are as good as they come – and free. Most people these days also use their browsers (or the programs which come with them) to download other software (see p.146) and read newsgroups (see p.128).

In any case, once you have a browser you can surf around for new or specific programs at will, enabling you to chat, play games and whatever else you desire. Don't worry, they're not hard to find with the whole Internet at your disposal – and they needn't cost a penny. For more on how to choose the right browser, and what it can do for you, read on.

The Web Browser

A Web browser is the most important piece of Internet software you'll ever install. It will serve as the window through which you look at the Net and act as a springboard to almost everything you do online. A year or so back, the browser was basically a tool for viewing sites on the World Wide Web but today's generation of programs – essentially a choice between Microsoft's Internet Explorer and Netscape – come integrated with a whole assortment of Internet accessories that handle such tasks as email, news, Internet telephony, chat, homepage editing and multimedia playing. That makes your choice of browser pretty crucial.

Choosing a browser

You may not get to choose your own browser - at least initially - as your Access Provider should supply one as part of its start-up kit. This is likely to be **Internet Explorer**, as most providers and Online Services adopted it during the period when it was free and Netscape wasn't. Now that Netscape is also free, you might even be given both. And if you're using Microsoft Windows 98, you will find Internet Explorer seamlessly bundled into the operating system – the contraversial move that resulted in anti-trust action in the US courts (for more on which, see our History of the Net, p.443)

Not that **Netscape** is exactly hard to obtain – you can download it from the Net (see p.67), or load it onto your system from one of the myriad free disks mounted on computer or Internet magazines. If you're serious about the Net, you should try both programs and see which you prefer. In fact, if you can afford the disk space, you might like to keep both browsers on your system. This isn't such a bad idea as some sites work better with one or the other. And, of course, like everything on the Net, browsers are in a constant state of evolution, so a new release from either party could turn things around overnight.

Unraveling the numbers

 Both Microsoft Internet Explorer and Netscape Communicator have a **range of versions** available, catering to Windows 95/98, Windows NT, Windows 3.1, Power Mac, Mac 68k, Unix, and in Netscape's case, OS/2.

You can tell which is the **latest release of the program** by its number. For example, in Netscape Communicator, version 4.03 is newer than 4.02. The first number is the **series**: these are both "4.0x" series browsers (as you'd expect, the "4.0x" series, came after the "3.0x" series). The second number, after the decimal point, tells you if it is the **original release** (.0) or an **interim upgrade** (0.1, 0.2, etc) within the series. Such upgrades generally fix problems and add on a few minor features. In doing so, the previous release in that series becomes obsolete, and in the case of betas (test programs), expires.

A **new series release** – which at present happens at least once a year – heralds major changes and new features, and usually adds extra system demands. Thus, if your computer resources are low, you may find an earlier series more suitable (see opposite).

System requirements

Browsers take up a lot of **disk space**, especially the full installation of Internet Explorer 4.0x. Internet Explorer also hogs your system resources even after you shut it down. This means you might find your computer unreasonably slow after a long Web session and have to reboot. Hopefully, Microsoft will fix this, but don't bet on it.

PC requirements

PC users will need at least a 486 DX66 PC, with **16 Mb of RAM** to get either **Internet Explorer or Netscape** to run comfortably under Windows 95/98/3.x, and 24-32 Mb to run other programs at the same time. Windows NT versions demand at least 24 Mb of RAM: depending on which optional components you install, Netscape 4.0x requires between 18-30 Mb of hard disk space, and Internet Explorer, between 40-73 Mb.

Mac requirements

For the Mac, Internet Explorer 4.0x has three versions: Power PC, 68K, and Fat Binary, which all require MacOS 7.1 or later, and **12 Mb of RAM**. Netscape 4.0x supports Power PC and 68K, requiring MacOS 7.5 or later with 12 Mb of RAM. All work best with **Virtual Memory switched on**.

Humble machines

The best choice for older machines running Windows 3.1 is **Internet Explorer 3.03**. It can get by (just about) on 4Mb of RAM and as little as 7 Mb of disk space for a browser-only installation, plus it also includes all the TCP/IP dialing software that Windows 3.1 omits. The Mac equivalent also requires somewhat less RAM and disk space than its successor. If that's still too heavy, **Netscape 2.0x** is better than no browser at all.

Alternatively, if you don't mind paying for it (after a free trial period), investigate the much less well known but distinctly impressive **Opera** program. This packs a browser, mail program and newsreader into only a couple of Mb – and it's even slightly quicker than 4.0x series browsers. You can download it from the Net at: http://www.operasoftware.com

There is also a browser called **Voyager** designed specifically for **Amigas**. It is available on the Web at: http://www.vapor.com/voyager/

Explorer v. Netscape: what's on offer?

Okay, let's assume your computer is up to running the latest versions of Netscape Communicator and Internet Explorer. What's on offer?

Microsoft Internet Explorer 4.0x (IE4.0x)

Internet Explorer 4.0x comes close to assembling a best of the Net in its **package of tools** – more so than Netscape. If you are running Windows, it also has the plus of familiarity. Its look is exactly that of Windows 98 and Microsoft's policy (logical as well as commercial) is to integrate the Web browsing experience into Windows.

Thus, once you install the Desktop Update, Windows Explorer and Internet Explorer share the same interface – whether you're surfing the Web or ferreting through your hard drive. Installation, too, is a breeze, guided by the built-in **Internet Connection Wizard**, which can also

Content Advisor

Ratings | General | Advanced |

To specify which sites users are allowed to see, select a category, then adjust the slider.

Category: RSAC
- Language
- Nudity
- Sex
- Violence

Description

The Recreational Software Advisory Council rating service for the Internet. Based on the work of Dr. Donald F. Roberts of Stanford University, who has studied the effects of media for nearly 20 years.

To view the Internet page for this rating service, click More Info...

OK   Cancel   Apply

refer you to a local Access Provider, if you haven't already signed up to one.

IE4.0x's notable features include **Content Advisor**, which provides a way to bar kids from unsavory Web sites, and **Subscriptions**, which can download whole or partial sites at prescribed intervals for you to **read offline**.

Optional extras include: **Outlook Express**, an outstanding Internet email and news program, particularly for those with multiple accounts; **Netmeeting**, an Internet telephony, video conferencing and collaboration tool; **Microsoft Chat**, a cute comic-based chat client; **Front Page Express**, a basic homepage editor; **Netshow**, a video broadcast player; Media Player (**Active Movie**); a movie-clip player; plus most of the Web's essential multimedia accessories such as **Shockwave Flash and Director**, **Real Player** and **VDOlive**.

The other notable feature – which is an abomination – is **Active Desktop**, which feeds channel junk from the Net onto your desktop. This was being touted as the future of the Net a few months back but it's far from it in this incarnation, at least. Thankfully, it has been dumped in Internet Explorer 5.0x.

Internet Explorer also has a **Macintosh version** which shares the same appearance, but is written entirely afresh for MacOS. Its developments tend to lag behind the Windows equivalent and bundled extras are somewhat more limited.

Netscape's Communicator 4.0x browser is available in two flavors, **Standard** and **Pro**. Standard is free and aimed mainly at home users; Pro is a commercial version, designed mainly for business. Both are based around the same browser called Navigator, which is also available as a standalone (in case you'd rather use another mail program).

Standard contains the **Navigator** browser; **Messenger**, a fully-featured HTML email program; **Collabra**, a newsreader plus Intranet discussion tool; **Conference**, an Internet telephony and collaboration client; **Composer**, a basic homepage editor; **Netcaster**, a push (see pp.90–91) client which can receive Web "broadcasts" and download sites of your choice; and **AOL Instant Messenger**, a skeletal chat tool which alerts you when your buddies are online. Navigator is also available separately.

Pro adds: **Calendar**, a basic scheduling program; **Host on demand**, for sharing IBM host systems applications and data across networks including the Internet; and **AutoAdmin**, for managing browser settings across an office installation. As such, it reflects Netscape's targeting of the corporate Intranet market.

Okay – so which one, then?

It **sounds like a fudge** but if you've been provided with either Explorer or Netscape, there's no great need to change. Both have their strengths, neither is perfect, and ultimately it comes down to a matter of personal preference. Right now, I'd say IE4.0x is the winner on points through its better help documentation, its inclusion of TCP/IP and dialer support, and a richer bundle.

But then again, you mightn't end up using anything more than its browser and mail program, in which case you'll find it bulky.

If you have enough disk space, there's no harm in **installing both browsers**, as some Web pages work better with one program than the other. If you want Netscape to be your default (main) browser, you should install it last.

How to get the latest versions

If you already have a browser, you can download the latest Netscape release from: http://www.netscape.com and Internet Explorer from: http://www.microsoft.com/ie/

To update Netscape, go online and **choose Software Updates** from the Help menu. In Internet Explorer, choose **Product Updates** from the Help menu. In both cases, the server will automatically interrogate your system to determine which components you need to bring yourself up to date. Then it's just a matter of picking what you want.

Before you start, bear in mind that the entire kits weigh in between 12 to 30 Mb. This means **the download could take anywhere up to a few hours** – depending on which options you pick, how busy the sites are, and at what speed you connect. Count on about 6 Mb per hour with a 28.8 Kbps modem. So, if you're paying by the minute to be connected, you might find it cheaper and more convenient to buy a computer magazine with the browsers (and more) on a CD cover disk. Plus you'll have a backup copy handy if you need to re-install.

Want more information?

For the latest news on what's happening in browsers, reviews, comparisons, tips, and downloads for a wider range of brands and platforms, see Browsers.com at: http://www.browsers.com and Browser Watch at: http://www .browserwatch.com

More Net software . . .

Once you've installed your browser, you can surf the Web looking for other software. We have selected a few of the best programs from each category in the **Software Roundup** (p.425). But that's only a smidgen of what you'll find in some of the software guides recommended in our Web directory (see p.250).

Connecting for the First Time

If you've configured your TCP/IP, dialing, and mail software to your provider's specification, you should be ready to hit the Net. Hopefully, you also have a Web browser installed, as the ideal exercise for your very first connection would be to get straight onto the World Wide Web.

Connect that modem . . .

Once you're set up, and browser-ready, **connect your modem** (or terminal device) to the phone line, and **instruct your dialer to call**. If your modem speaker volume is turned up (look under your modem Properties), it will make all kinds of mating noises while connecting, like a fax machine.

These sounds will cease once the connection's negotiated. At this point your provider's server will need to identify you as a customer, so if you haven't already entered your **user name and password**, you'll have to now. Once that's done, **click the box that says "Save Password,"** otherwise you'll have to enter it every time you log in. Make sure you keep this password private – anyone could use it to rack up your bill or, perhaps worse, read your mail (although you should be issued with a separate password to retrieve mail).

Now **start your Web browser** and try accessing a few of the addresses from our Web Guide (p.237). You'll find instructions on how to browse the Web in the next chapter. If you can access the Web, it's close to plain sailing from now on. If not, you'll need to find out what's wrong. Read on . . .

Troubleshooting

To access all the **connection settings** in **Windows 95/98** (modem, scripting, TCP/IP, phone, and dialer), open Dial-Up Networking (under My Computer), right-click on the connection, and choose **Properties**. To change the log-in settings, simply left-click as if dialing.

If you are using a **Mac with Free PPP** (or equivalent), you can access the settings by opening the **Free PPP** window and clicking on "General," "Accounts," or "Locations." You may also need to adjust the settings in your **TCP/IP file**, which you access through the Control Panel under the Apple symbol (top left-hand corner of the screen).

If you didn't get through

If you **didn't succeed in connecting to your provider**, there's probably something wrong with your dialer or modem configuration. The most common errors are:

* No modem detected: Is your modem installed, plugged into the right port, and switched on? To install or diagnose a modem in Windows 95/98, click on the Modem applet in the Control Panel.

* Dial tone not detected: Is your phone line plugged in? Try disabling Dial Tone Detect or

Wait for Dial Tone under the modem settings. The initialization string for this is X1.

* No answer: Do you have the right phone number? You can verify your modem's working by dialing a friend's phone number. If the phone rings you know your dialer and modem are talking to each other properly.

* Busy/engaged: Access providers' lines can be occupied at peak hours like the end of the working day. Keep trying until you get in: even though you dial a single number, there are several modems at the other end. If it happens often, complain, or get a new provider with a **lower user to modem ratio**.

You got through but were refused entry

If you **succeeded in connecting** but were **refused entry**, check your username, password and script (if used). If it **failed to negotiate network protocols**, verify your TCP/IP settings. You might need your provider's help on this one. Keep the settings on screen and phone them.

You're online but not on the Web

If you've **managed to stay connected, but can't access any Web sites**, either your DNS settings are incorrect, you've failed to establish an IP connection, or there's a temporary outage. Log off, verify your TCP/IP settings, and try again. DNS servers go down occasionally, so (unless yours are server-assigned) make sure you specify more than one.

For details on how to troubleshoot Web access see: Finding It (pp. 176–179).

Your connection keeps going down

If everything works fine but **your connection often drops out,** you'll need to check each link in the chain between you and your provider. Unfortunately, there are a lot of links, so it's down to a matter of elimination.

Does it only happen after an extended period of inactivity? Then it could be an automatic defense mechanism in your dialer or at your provider's end.

Do you have telephone Call Waiting? If it's enabled, and you're called while online, those little beeps will knock out your connection.

Pick up your phone. Does it sound clear? Crackling sounds indicate a poor connection somewhere. Modems like a nice clean line.

Do you share a line? Picking up an extension will drop your connection.

Do you have the latest modem driver and firmware revision? Check your modem manufacturer's homepage.

As a **last resort** try a different Access Provider, phone line, and modem.

Okay, it works – but it's very slow

When the **Net gets overloaded**, transfer rates slow down:
it can happen to the whole Internet backbone at peak
usage times, particularly with TransAtlantic routes. If
transfers are slow from everywhere, however, it usually
means the problem lies closer to home. It could be that
your **provider or office network** has too many users
competing online, or too much traffic accessing its Web
area from outside. In this case your provider or office
needs to increase its bandwidth to the Net.

Access Providers tend go through cycles of difficult
traffic periods. If they have the resources and the fore-
sight to cope with demand,
you won't notice. But as it's
such a low margin business,
they're more likely to stretch
things. Always call your
provider when you have com-
plaints with its service and if
you're not treated with
respect, no matter how triv-
ial your inquiry, take your
money elsewhere. There's a
prevailing arrogance within
the computer industry. Don't
tolerate it. You're the customer; they're not doing you
a favor.

Finding the bottleneck

If you'd really like to know
what's slowing things down,
you can arm yourself with
some network diagnostic tools

from the Net. The staples are: **Ping**, which works like a radar to measure how long it takes a data packet to reach a server and return; and **TraceRoute**, which pings each router along the path to see which one's causing the hold-up.

Windows users have plenty of choices for obtaining these programs. NetScan Tools (http://www.nwpsw.com) has Ping, TraceRoute and loads more. NetMedic (http://www.vitalsigns.com) can tell you exactly where it's breaking down, whether your provider is falling short, monitor trends, and send off a complaint report. Neo-Trace (http://www.neoworx.com) adds another level to TraceRoute by identifying who owns the routers, and then maps it all out in Hollywood style.

Mac users can enlist WhatRoute (http://crash.ihug. co.nz/~bryanc/) for tracing routers, and CyberGauge (http://www.neon.com) to monitor bandwidth.

The single best piece of advice

If you know someone who's a bit of an Internet guru, coax them over to help you hook up for the first time. Throw in enough pizza, beer, and compliments about their technical prowess, and you'll have an auxiliary support unit for life.

Surfing the
World Wide Web

When you see www.come.and.get.me or suchlike on an advert or business card, or as further reading for a news article or academic report, you're being invited to visit an address on the World Wide Web (the Web), the biggest development in communications since TV. Once you're online, you can find any such address with ease as the Web is the genuinely user-friendly face of the Internet.

In fact, it's not too hard to find anything on the Web, once you get started. Because the Web is such an easy, inexpensive and flexible platform for expression, it has sparked off more publishing, both professional and DIY, than at any time in history. Consequently, its content spans an exhaustive range of topics across an expanding variety of media formats.

Although the Web is undeniably simple to use, you'll still need a little help to get off the ground. As preparation, we've dedicated this chapter to explaining **how to set up your Web browser** and point it in the right direction, another chapter on **how to find things** once you're there (see 160), and most of Part Two of this book (see p.235) to reviews of **interesting and useful sites**.

What to expect

The Web is the Internet's glossy, glamorous, point-and-click front door: a media-rich assault of shopping, music, magazines, art, books, museums, games, job agencies, movie previews, self-promotion, and much, much more. It has information on more than a million companies and is accessed by more than a hundred million users in every corner of the globe from Antarctica to Iceland. It will bring the world to the keyboard of your computer. It's better than the best encyclopedia, and for the most part, it's free. There's no doubt, if you're not on the World Wide Web, you're missing out.

Hypertext and links

Web pages are written in **HTML (HyperText Markup Language)**, which means **links** to other documents can be embedded within the text. This creates a sort of third dimension. If you've used Windows Help or Macintosh Hypercard, you'll be familiar with the concept.

Depending on how you've configured your browser, **text which contains links** to other documents (or another part of the same document) is usually highlighted in another color and/or underlined. In addition, when you pass over a link (which can be an image as well as text) your **mouse cursor** will change from an arrow to a pointing hand and the target address will appear in a bar at the bottom of your browser.

To pursue the link, simply **click on the highlighted text or image**. When the new document appears, it will be entirely independent of the one where you found the link. The previous document is now history. And as the new document needs no connection with it, there might not be a reciprocal link. However, there is an easier way to return, as we'll explain soon.

Home pages

On the World Wide Web, **home page** has two meanings. One refers to the page that appears when you start your browser and acts as your home base for exploring the Web. Whenever you get lost or want to return to somewhere familiar, you can just click on the "Home" button on your browser menu and back you go. The other usage refers to the front door to a set of documents that represents someone or something on the Web. This set of interconnected documents is called a **Web site**.

For instance, Rough Guides' "official" home page – found at: http://www.roughguides.com – acts as the publishing company's site index. You can access every page in the Rough Guides site by following links from the home page. Play your cards right and you'll end up at this book's home page.

If a site hasn't been endorsed by whomever it represents it's called an **"unofficial"** home page. This is typical of fan sites for rock bands, many of whom have dozens (in some cases hundreds) of fan sites.

How to read a Web address

Web addresses are formally known as **URLs** (Uniform Resource Locators). Every Web page has a unique URL which can be broken into three parts. Reading from left to right they are: the **protocol**, (such as http:// ftp:// news: or gopher://); the **host name** (everything before the first single forward slash); and the **file path** (everything after and including the first single forward slash). Consider the address: http://www.star.com.hk/~Chow/Yun/fat.html The http://www. tells us it's a HyperText file located on the World Wide Web, the domain star.com.hk tells us it's in Hong Kong, and the file path indicates that the file fat.html is located in the directory /~Chow/Yun/

If a URL doesn't have a file path, it's called a **root URL**. Anyone who's serious about their presence on the Web has their own root URL. Typically, a company will choose an address that relates to its business name or activity. It's also common, but certainly not a rule, for such addresses to start with http://www. For example, you can find: Apple computers at http://www.apple.com; the BBC at http://www.bbc.co.uk; and some cheap airfares at http://www.bargainflights.com

What to do with Web [http] addresses

To visit a Web site, you must first submit its address to your browser. This can be done by clicking on a link or by keying in the address. The box to enter URLs runs horizontally above the browser panel. In Netscape, when it's blank, it says "**Go to**" beside it, and when it retrieves a URL the wording changes to "**Location**" or "**Netsite**" (for sites housed on Netscape servers). In Internet Explorer it says "**Address**." You can bring up an alternative box by choosing Open or Open Page under the File menu. Key the address you're looking for into either box, hit your enter (or return) key, and wait.

Your browser will examine the address and work out what to do next. If it's recognized as a legitimate Web address it will contact your DNS server to convert the host name into an IP address. You'll see this process happening in the lower right corner of your screen. Once it's converted, the browser will contact the Web site's server and request the page.

It rarely takes more than a minute or two to locate and load Web pages, and if you've a fast connection, it can be a matter of seconds. If all works well, your browser will retrieve the page and display it on your screen. If you receive an error message, try again. If that fails, follow the instructions in "Finding the right Web address" (see p.176).

Take care with capitals

Note that URL path names are **case sensitive**. So key them carefully, taking note of capitals as well as their sometimes bizarre punctuation. Host names are almost always written in lower case, but are actually case insensitive. Don't bother keying in the http:// part as your browser will automatically add it on if you omit it.

Other addresses (non http]

You can also access **FTP** (see p.146), **Gopher** (see opposite), **Telnet**, and **Usenet** (see p.128) sites from the helm of your Web browser.

To **use FTP**, you just add ftp:// to the file's location. So, to retrieve duck.txt located in the directory /yellow/fluffy from the anonymous FTP site ftp.quack.com you should enter: ftp://ftp.quack.com/yellow/fluffy/duck.txt (In fact, with recent browsers you can omit the ftp:// part as they know that any domain starting with ftp. is an FTP site.)

Gopher and **Telnet** work in exactly the same way. So does **Usenet**, except that it omits the // part. Thus, to access the newsgroup alt.ducks key: news: alt.ducks

Addresses starting with file:/// are located on your own hard drive. You can browse your own computer by entering a drive letter followed by a colon (eg, c:).

Gopher

Before the Web's explosion, **Gopher** was the smartest way to archive data on the Internet. As the name suggests, Gopher is used to "go for" information. Although it stores data in an entirely different architecture, it looks and acts similar to the Web. In many ways, the Web is its natural successor as what was once stored in Gopher is now on the Web – and for most purposes you need not read on. However, certain old battlers like government bodies and universities still use it to archive stuff, so we feel grudgingly obliged to mention it.

Gopherspace is a separate entity from the Web, although when you link out of the Web and into a Gopher site you may not recognize the difference. Its clickable directory listings work just like hyperlinks, however these Gopher burrows are dead-ended. You can surf from page to page following links all day on the Web, but with Gopher, once you find your text file, you have to tunnel back out again.

To get to a Gopher from the Web, key in gopher:// before the address in your Web browser. For example, to access the "Mother of all Gophers" at Minnesota University, key: gopher://gopher.tc.umn.edu It has all you need to know about Gophers, including how to search by subject or geographic region.

For more on searching Gophers, see "Finding It" (see p.172).

The main browser navigation buttons

All the main **navigation buttons** are located on the toolbar above the main browser panel. Displaying them is optional, but they're hard to live without.

The most useful are probably the back and forward buttons. To **go back to a page** you previously visited, just click the "Back" button until you find it. To **return to where you were**, keep pressing "Forward." And to go back to your start-up page hit **"Home."**

You can go back and forward through pages pretty much instantly once you've visited them during a session, as your computer stores the document in its memory. How much material you can click through in this fashion, however, depends on the amount of storage space that's been allocated to **cache** or **temporary Internet files** in your settings. We explain cache later under "Browsing Offline " (see p.89).

Two other important buttons are stop and reload. To **cancel a page request**, because it's taking too long to load a site, or you've made a mistake, just hit the **"Stop"** button. Occasionally you might have to hit "Stop" before "Back" will work. Alternatively, if a page doesn't load properly, you can hit **"Refresh"** or **"Reload"** to load it again. You'd also do this if a page changes regularly, and you want to load a new version rather than one that's stored in your session "cache."

Use your mouse

The next most important navigation controls are in your **mouse button** (the right button on PCs). Just hold it down and try them all out. The menu will change depending upon what you click. For instance, if you click on a link, you'll have the option of opening the target page in a new window or saving it to disk. The latter is sometimes handy if you want to save time loading a large page or image. The saving process goes into the background while you continue in the foreground.

URL shortcuts

Not only do you not have to key http:// but you can sometimes get away with **just putting in a company's name** if its URL starts with www. <u>and</u> ends in .com So to reach Yahoo in Netscape or Internet Explorer, simply key in yahoo and hit enter. Internet Explorer will also autoscan the other common root domains (.edu and .org, with and without www.) and then give you the option of looking it up in a search engine (see p.161).

Current versions of Netscape and Internet Explorer will also attempt to **guess which URL you're entering** by looking at your History file (see p.87). So for Yahoo, you might only need to type in www.y and key return/enter, and they'll guess the rest. Clever, huh?

How to find a page later

Whenever you find a page that's worth another visit, you should file its location. In Netscape that's called

adding it to your "**Bookmarks.**" Internet Explorer calls it adding to "**Favorites.**"

Both of these file addresses into folders for later retrieval, but they approach the task from very different angles. That's most apparent if you want to send the addresses to someone else. **Netscape** stores them in an **HTML file** – that's actually a Web page in itself. That means you can put it on the Web, specify it as your home page, or send it to a friend as a single file. **Internet Explorer** stores each address as an individual "**Internet Shortcut**" in the same way it makes shortcuts to programs in Windows 95/98. You can mail individual links, or folders, to a friend but only if they're using the same setup.

To **arrange your Favorites** into logical folders, choose Organize Favorites from the Favorites menu. You can do the same in Netscape by opening Edit Bookmarks in the Bookmarks menu.

When you add an address to your Favorites in IE4.0x, it will ask if you'd like to **subscribe to the page**. If you agree it will check the page at whatever intervals you specify to see if it's changed. At the same time, it can also download the page, and others linked to it, so that you can browse the site offline later (see "Browsing Offline" – p.89). Netscape can't do that, but you can run through your Bookmarks and see which sites have changed by choosing Update Bookmarks from under Edit Bookmarks.

You can also **save an address as a shortcut or alias** on your desktop. In Netscape, just drag the icon on the Toolbar to the left of where it says "Location" or "Netsite" and plonk it down wherever you like. In Internet Explorer drag and drop the page icon to the left of the address or choose "Send Shortcut to Desktop" from under the File menu.

Downloading files

Almost, if not all, your **file downloads** and **software upgrades** can be initiated by a link from a Web page. When you click on that link both Netscape and Internet Explorer will start an **FTP operation** in the background, and let you carry on surfing.

Depending on your settings, once the file is found, you'll be asked where you'd like to save it. If it can log in but can't find the file, or you'd like to browse the FTP site, copy the address using the mouse menu, paste it to the URL window, and delete the file name from the address. Then you can log into the FTP server and browse it like a Web site.

For more on file transfer, see p.146.

Saving an image, movie or sound file

Web pages often display reduced images. In Web art galleries especially, such images often have links to another with higher resolution. To **save an image**, select it and then choose "Save as" or "Save image as" from the File, or mouse button, menu. Windows 95 browsers can also save images as desktop wallpaper. To save a movie or sound clip, click on the link to it and choose "Save Target as", or "Save Link as", from the mouse menu.

Copying and pasting

To **copy text from Web pages**, highlight the section, choose "Copy" from the Edit menu (or use the usual shortcut keys), then switch to your word processor, text editor, or mail program and choose "Paste."

Uncovering the source

The smartest way to **learn Web design** is to peek at the raw HTML coding on pages you like. Choose "Source" from the View or mouse button menu. (For more on Web page design, see p.200).

Changing the settings

You can reconfigure Internet Explorer by either choosing "Internet Options" under the View Menu, "Internet " in the Windows 95/98 Control Panel, or by right-clicking the desktop Internet icon and selecting Properties. In Netscape, the option is under "Preferences" in the Edit menu. Following are a few things you might change.

Choose your own home page

Browsers come preconfigured with a **default page** – their own, or that of whoever supplied it to you. It will come up every time you start your browser, or when you hit "Home." This is one of the things you can change in Options (Preferences). You can specify any page you like, even one located on your own hard drive such as your Bookmark file. It's generally more convenient to start with a blank page. That way you don't have to wait for anything to load before you start a Web session.

How to tell where you've been

An **"unvisited" link** is like a signpost to a new page. You click on the link to go there. After you've been, nothing changes on the page, but your browser records your visit by storing the URL in a **history file**. It's then called a **"visited" link**.

You can customize links by displaying them as **underlined** and/or in a **special color**. The default is usually underlined blue for unvisited links and either black, purple or red for visited links. See how this works for yourself. Look at any page. Links you haven't followed should appear blue and underlined. Now click one and load the page. Next, click "Back" and return to the previous page. The link should have changed color.

What's more, visited links will appear in the new color wherever they crop up, even on a completely different page that you are visiting for the first time. This can be useful if you're viewing directories and lists, as you can instantly see which sites you have previously visited.

Visited links eventually expire and revert to their old color. You can set the **expiration** period under Internet Options (Preferences). It's wise to keep the expiry short (no more than 20 days). A big History file can dramatically slow things down, especially if you surf a lot. After a month or so, click on Clear History in your settings and see if it speeds things up. If it does, reduce your expiry period.

History files

During a session browsing the Web, you can **return to recently visited sites** through the drop down menus found by either holding down the back and forward buttons or clicking on the adjacent down arrows. And you can return to the sites you visit most by scrolling through the drop down menu where you enter URLs.

These, however, are but a pale imitation of the **History file**. You'll find the main History file under the Communicator or Window menu in Netscape, or on a toolbar button or under the File menu in Internet Explorer. Think of it as a collection of signposts. You can use it to return to a visited page, rather than clicking the "Forward" and "Back" buttons. We'll discuss another use for the History file ahead in "Browsing Offline"

Sending email from a Web page

You'll often come across an invitation to **email someone from a Web page**. It mightn't look like an email address – it might be just a name that contains a link. Whatever, it will be obvious from the context that if you want to contact that person you should click on the link. If you pass your mouse over this link it will read something like: mailto: someone@somewhere.com. And then when you click on it, a new message will pop up addressed to someone@somewhere.com Just type your message and send it. Any replies will arrive through the normal email channels.

If it doesn't work, your **browser/mail combination** isn't set up properly. Before you can send email, you have to complete your email details. Generally this is automated in your setup process. If not, you'll have to open your browser and email settings and enter it yourself. You can use any mail program with Internet Explorer. Just choose it from the list under Programs in Internet Options. Netscape forces you to use Messenger. For instructions on setting up mail, see p.104.

Joining a newsgroup from the Web

A Web page might **refer you to a newsgroup** for more information. When you click on the link Netscape or Internet Explorer will open a newsreader in a separate window. You can continue surfing the Web in your browser while you wait for the newsgroup subjects to arrive.

Again you'll need to have your **newsreader set up** to get the link to work. With Internet Explorer, if you're using any Usenet program other than Outlook Express or Internet Mail & News, you'll have to specify it in Internet Explorer under Programs.

For more on newsgroups, see p.128.

Browsing Offline

If time online is costing you money, consider spending it **gathering pages** rather than reading. Allow each page you want to read to load fully and it will cache for

reading offline later. Then you can run back through your session, after you hang up, by choosing **"Go Offline"** or **"Work Offline"** under the File menu in Netscape Navigator and Internet Explorer, versions 4.0x or later.

Once in this mode, you can **call up sites** either by typing in their addresses or following links as if you were online, or by clicking on sites in your History file. This works by retrieving files stored temporarily in a folder called **"cache"** in Netscape and **"Temporary Internet Files"** in Internet Explorer. Their primary purpose is to speed up browsing. When you return to a page, your browser will check the cache first rather than download its components again from the Net.

These pages won't sit on your hard drive forever – they're governed by your **Cache or Temporary Internet Files settings** and they'll also be overwritten next time you visit that same address. However, if you want to **archive a page**, you can choose "Save as" from the File menu. The only problem is it won't save the images as well. You'll need to save all those separately.

You'll find your Cache (Temporary Internet Files) settings in your Preferences (Options). While you're there, it's best to select the **option to check for newer versions** just once per session. Then if you suspect the document's changed during a session revisit, just hit "Refresh/Reload". Unless you plan to read offline, it's wise to delete these files regularly as, like the History file, if it gets too big, it can slow things right down.

Push, Channels, and Subscriptions

Push was the hype technology of 1997. It was supposed to become the next big thing. Now the same commentators are saying it's dead. Perhaps that's a bit harsh but

Internet Explorer's **Active Desktop** and Netscape's **Net-caster** are both actively worth avoiding. The Web is traditionally a "pull" kind of thing: you click on a link to make something happen. Push is more like email or a TV broadcast. It's something sent to you.

To **get something pushed to you** (or at you) you specify all sorts of rules, like how and when you want stuff delivered, and what to include or exclude. Your push software then periodically retrieves (or a third party sends) you items relating to your request. These could vary from world and sports news to stock prices or new CD releases. They can be (kind of) useful, though most people find them the Web equivalent of junk mail and a strain on system resources. Even Microsoft has given Push the thumbs down by dropping it outright in the beta of IE5.0x. Nevertheless, if you're terminally curious, click the Channel button on IE4.0x or open Netcaster from under the Communicator menu in Netscape 4.0x. Start out by subscribing to just one channel and see how long you can stand it.

Subscriptions

If you'd like to **read an online newspaper offline** – for example on the train to work – you can set up Internet Explorer to go online while you sleep and download as much of the site as you want. (This is also handy if your access or phone charges are less late at night and you'd like to browse a large site during working hours). Just save the site to "Favorites", choose "download the page for offline viewing," and then click on Customize to set how many pages to download and when to grab them. To edit or delete your deliveries, choose "Manage Subscriptions" from the Favorites menu.

You can do something similar under Netscape Netcaster by creating a new channel.

Making the most of your session

Since things never happen instantly on the Net, make sure you're always doing at least three things at once. You might as well download news, mail, and the latest software releases while you browse several sites at once.

Opening multiple sites is simple. While you wait for one page to load, you just open a **"New Window"** or **"New Browser,"** and look at something else while you wait. For instance, when reading an electronic magazine, scan for interesting stories, and then quickly fire them all open in separate windows. Just click each link in turn and select "Open in a New Window" from your mouse menu. Then you can read it all instantly, perhaps even offline.

Bear in mind, however, that each process is competing for **computer resources** and bandwidth, so the more you attempt, the higher the likelihood that each will take longer – and that your machine will crash.

Turn off your multimedia

The drawback of the Web's graphic richness is the time it takes to download images and sounds. To speed things up, you have the option of **not showing images and** in IE4.0x's case, other multimedia. You'll find this in the advanced section of your browser settings.

It's well worth declining images if you're only interested in text. The catch is some pages contain nothing but images with links behind them. If you strike such a page, select the broken image, and choose "Show Image" from your mouse menu on Explorer, or "Show Images" from Netscape's View menu, or change your settings and refresh the page.

Plug-ins and ActiveX

Although your browser can recognize a mind-boggling array of multimedia and other file formats, every so often you'll come across something it can't deal with. Generally, there'll be an icon nearby suggesting you grab a **"plug-in"** or an **"ActiveX control."** If not, you'll see a broken image which when clicked on will tell you what you need and where to get it.

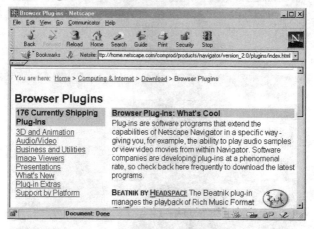

A **plug-in** is an auxiliary program that works alongside your browser. You download this program, install it, and your browser will call on it when need be. **ActiveX controls** work similarly, although their scope is far greater. When you arrive at a site that relies on an ActiveX control, it checks to see if you already have it, and if not, installs it automatically after you approve the publisher's certificate. As a rule, don't accept certificates unless you're satisfied the publisher is reputable.

Currently, ActiveX only works under Windows 95/98/NT versions of Explorer, or Windows 95/98/NT versions of Netscape when aided by the NCompass ScriptActive plug-in (http://www.ncompasslabs.com). Both Netscape and Microsoft plan to eventually introduce ActiveX as a standard across all platforms.

To **see what plug-ins are already installed** in Netscape, choose "About Plug-ins" from the Help menu. Then follow the link to see what else you can try. Remember, plug-ins consume hard disk and memory, and you can do without most of them, so choose carefully.

RealPlayer and ShockWave

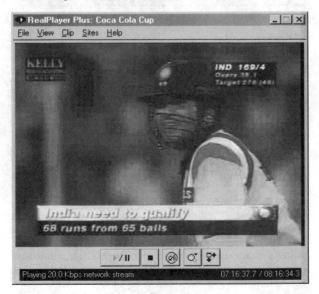

There are two plug-in/ActiveX controls you'll definitely need: the **RealPlayer** (which includes **RealAudio** and **RealVideo**) for Internet music and video broadcasts; and **Shockwave Director** and **Flash** for multimedia effects. Once you have RealAudio you can sample CDs before you buy at online music stores, listen to live Internet concerts or if you're lucky, archives of your favorite radio shows. ShockWave is commonly used on elaborate sites, like movie promotions.

Whether you've already been given them, for example with IE4.0x, you should still stop in and grab the latest versions at: http://www.real.com and
http://www.macromedia.com/shockwave/

Java

When **Java** – Sun Microsystems' vision of a platform independent programming language – arrived, it was instantly pounced upon by the Web community. What once was a static environment quickly sprang to life with all sorts of "animated" applications thanks to its simple HTML adjunct, **Java Script**. The main difference between Java and JavaScript is that Java involves downloading and running a small program (called an Applet) whereas JavaScript is interpreted by your browser.

Java and JavaScript applications can be cool items but they are the worst and most consistent culprits for crashing your browser. Script that works fine with Netscape can cause Internet Explorer to crash, and vice versa. It's even more pronounced if you're running an old version. If it's causing you too many problems, open your settings and disable Java.

To find out more about Java and its latest applications, see Gamelan at: http://www.gamelan.com

Proxy settings

Many Access Providers have a server that caches copies of popular Web sites. If you specify this machine's address as your **proxy server,** it might make browsing faster. Ask your provider for its IP address and enter it in your settings under Connection in Internet Explorer or Advanced in Netscape.

Cookies

A **cookie** is a small file, placed on your computer by a Web server, as a sort of ID card. Then, next time you drop by, it will know you. Actually, it doesn't quite know it's "you," it only recognizes your individual browser. If you were to visit on another machine or with a different browser on the same machine, it would see you as a different visitor. Or conversely, if someone else were to use your browser, it couldn't tell the difference.

Most Web sites routinely **log your visit**. They can tell a few harmless things like what browser you're using, which pages you've requested and the last site you've seen. This is recorded against your IP address. However, because many dial-up users are issued a different IP address each time they log on, this information isn't useful for building individual profiles. If analysts can log this data against a cookie ID instead, they have a better chance of recognizing repeat visitors. Amongst other things, this makes their lives easier when it comes to looking for sponsorship, which means the site has a better chance of staying afloat.

On the next level, if you **voluntarily submit further details**, they can store it in a database against your cookie, and use it to do things like tailor the site to your preferences, or save you entering the same data every time you check in. This won't be stored on your computer, so other sites can't access it. And most importantly, they won't know anything personal about you – not even your email address – unless you tell them. So unless you have a good reason for hiding your visit to that site, go ahead - accept the cookie.

Censoring Web material from kids

If you want to do so, it's possible to **bar access to certain sites** which might be on the wrong side of educational. Internet Explorer is most advanced on this front, as it employs the **PICS** (Platform for Internet Content Selection) system. You can set ratings for language, nudity, sex and violence under the Content settings in Options. AOL also gives you similar control.

There are several third party programs such as **Surf-Watch**, **ImageCensor**, **Cybersitter** and **NetNanny** which can impose all sorts of restrictions. None, however, are foolproof. See: http://www.peacefire.org

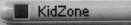 If you're really concerned about what your children are viewing on the Web, you might do better spending a few hours each week surfing the Web with them. After all, having access denied to a site does add glamor.

Help

If you need step-by-step help using or configuring your browser, refer to your **Help menu**. Microsoft provides excellent help, including all manner of troubleshooting wizards. Netscape's is adequate for basic instructions, but you'll need to go online to view it.

If you strike serious **problems with Internet Explorer**, you can search Microsoft's Knowledge Base at: http://support.microsoft.com or try an appropriate newsgroup from: http://support.microsoft.com/support/news/

For **Netscape problems** see: http://help.netscape.com/nuggies/ and http://www.ufaq.org

Email

If you need one good reason to justify hooking up to the Internet, email should suffice. Once you gather enough email contacts and get used to communicating this way, don't be surprised if it becomes your preferred way to get in touch. You'll be able to write more and respond faster – and that means you'll probably become more productive. Probably: but be warned that email is as time consuming as it is addictive. At first you might rediscover the joy of old fashioned letter writing, but because it's so easy to copy (cc) a message to everyone in your address book it may invite more mail than you can handle. On the plus side, though, it distinctly reduces phone time at work.

Why email will change your life

Email is such an improvement on the postal system it will revolutionize the way and the amount you communicate. You can send a message to anyone with an email address anywhere in the world, instantaneously. In fact, it's so quick that it's possible they could receive your message sooner than you could print it.

All you need to do is **key an address**, or choose it from your **email address book**, write a brief note, and **click "send"**. No letterheads, layout, printing, envelopes, stamps, or visiting the post office. And once you're online your mailer can automatically check for post at whatever interval you like. You don't have to wait for the postie to arrive. Email is delivered 24 hrs, 7 days a week.

Email is also better than faxing. It's always **a local call to anywhere, at any time**. No busy signals, paper jams, or failed attempts. Plus you receive the actual text and not a photocopy, or an actual image file and not a scan. So that means you can send **high resolution color** and **lengthy documents**. Each edition of this book has been submitted and edited by email.

Email also **beats the phone** at times. You can send a message to a part of the world that's asleep and have a reply when you get up the next morning. No need to synchronize phone calls, be put on hold, speak to voice-mail, or tell some busybody who's calling. With email, you take the red carpet route straight through to the top. And you don't have to make small talk, unless that's the purpose of the message.

Replacing the post and fax is not email's only strength. You can also **attach any computer file to a message**. That means you can forward things like advertising layout, scanned images, spreadsheets, assignments, tracks from your latest CD, or even programs. And your accompanying message need only be as brief as a Post-it note or compliments slip.

What's more, with email **everything you send and receive can be filed** in a relatively small amount of disk space. No filing cabinets, no taped phone calls, and no yellowing fax paper. All in writing, and instantly searchable for later reference. You just need to back up occasionally in case someone steals your computer.

Challenging the establishment

Email is steadily overcoming formal business writing. Since email messages are (for the most part) simply text files, there's no need to worry about fonts, letterheads, logos, typesetting, justification, signatures, print resolution, or fancy paper. It distills correspondence down to its essence – words.

But email has gone farther than that – it has encouraged **brevity**. This could be the result of online costs, busy users, or just the practical mindset of the people who first embraced the technology (back in the days when you needed to know UNIX code). Whatever the reason, it's good discipline and it means you'll be able to deal with several times more people than ever before.

Conversely, email is also putting personal correspondence back into letters rather than phone calls. Almost all new users remark on this – and the fact that email often seems to spark off a **surprising intimacy**.

What you'll need

To get started, you'll need a connection to the Net, an **email program (mailer)** – included in Web browsers – and an **email address**. You don't need a full Internet connection to use email: you just need access to a gateway that leads on to the Net.

You will automatically get an **email address** when you sign up with an Access Provider or an Online Service. If you access through work or someone else's account, you could shop around your local providers for a mailbox only account or try one of the free email address services on the Net (see p.117 for details).

You should get an **email program** with your Internet access account, but if it's not up to scratch, it's easy to scrap it for another.

Choosing an email program

As your **email program** will become the workhorse of your Net toolkit, you should choose it as carefully as your browser. Still, that need only be one decision, because Netscape 4.0x's **Messenger** and Internet Explorer 4.0x's **Outlook Express** are the two best mailers around. They're reliable, user-friendly, cutting edge, and free. Like their respective browsers, it's tough to say which is better. Both are first-class products which improve with each release, but neither is perfect.

If it comes down to nitpicking, **Outlook Express** is better equipped to handle multiple mail accounts, is smarter at organizing mail into folders and has a few unique features such as background stationery and spell checking. **Messenger,** concentrates more on getting the basics perfect than trying to be clever. That means there's never a hitch carrying out simple everyday tasks like replying to a message, or forwarding it to someone else. Outlook Express isn't quite as well polished in this regard as we'll explain later.

It's probably not worth your effort trying to mix and match the browser suites as neither Outlook Express nor Messenger can be installed without their respective browsers.

Other Mail Programs

Microsoft has put out some real email stinkers over the years such as Exchange (built into Windows 95) and Outlook 97 (part of Office 97). Exchange should be avoided at any cost, but Outlook 97 can be improved by installing the free Outlook 98 patch upgrade at: http://www.microsoft.com/outlook/

Outlook 98 is also touted as the next step up from Outlook Express. Although it adds contact, calendar, and task-management tools along with some neat features like mapping and return receipt, you can safely get by without them. And unless you're using it for internal office mail, ensure you choose the "Internet mail only" installation - it loads faster.

Internet Mail & News, which accompanies IE3.0x, however, is simple, elegant and ample to the task if you're strapped for disk space.

If you'd prefer a custom-built email program, **Eudora** remains the choice option. It maintains two versions: Light, which is free, and Pro, which is free for thirty days and then you have to pay. If you're presently using Light, check through the features at: http://www.eudora.com and decide if it's worth the upgrade.

Where to get an email program

For addresses of where to **download email programs and add-ons**, see our "Software Roundup" (p.425). If you're using any type of Microsoft mail, including Outlook 97/98, grab all the latest Internet upgrade patches from the appropriate sections under: http://www.microsoft.com/products/

Setting up for email

Before you can use your email, you'll need to fill in a few **configuration details** for whoever supplied your email account (usually your provider). This process is often automated by a wizard or by your Access Provider's software, but it's worth taking some time to understand your email profile so you can enter it on other machines. (For more on email addresses, see p.22).

To **start a new account in Outlook Express**, open "Accounts" under the Tools menu, choose Add Mail and follow the prompts. To change the settings select the account and choose properties.

In **Netscape 4.0x**, close the browser, open "Profile Manager," click on

"New" and follow the prompts. To change your details later, open "Mail & Groups" under Navigator's Preferences.

The settings

Let's say you're Garret Keogh and your email address is garret@lard.com Open your settings in any mail program and here's what you'll strike:

Name: Garret Keogh
   (Who or what will appear as the sender of your mail.)
Email Address: garret@lard.com
   (Where mail you send will look like it came from.)
Return Address: garret@lard.com
   (Where replies to your mail will go. Most users opt for their regular email address but you could divert it to a work account, for example.)
Outgoing Mail (SMTP): mail.lard.com
   (The server to handle your outgoing mail – usually your own provider. If you're on someone else's machine, and don't know what to put, try smtp.site1.csi.com or mail.geocities.com as a temporary measure.)
Incoming Mail (POP3): mail.lard.com
   (Where your mail is stored. This should be the same as the last part of your email address, though often with pop. or mail. added at the start.)
Account Name: garret.
   (The first part of your email address.)
Password: ******
   (Careful, don't let anyone see you enter this one.)

Note that the above only applies to **POP3 based mail systems** which at present doesn't include AOL. For more on POP3, including how to upgrade your CompuServe address, see p.217.

Sending and receiving email

You needn't be connected to the Net to **compose an email message**. You just have to open a new message, address it either by entering an address manually or by selecting a name from your **address book**, add a **subject**, write the note, and then click **send**. But before you can actually deliver it you need to **go online**. Sending is usually tied in with receiving (read on for more detail on both operations). Normally you do both at the same time, although it's possible if necessary to separate the two.

Outlook Express and Messenger store **unsent mail** in a folder either called the **Outbox** or **Unsent Messages**. Once it's dispatched, it moves into the **Sent** folder. Other programs may do it differently. For instance, Eudora marks unsent mail with a Q which changes to an S after it's sent. Incoming mail arrives in the **Inbox** or wherever your filters dump it.

When mail arrives you'll hear a sound, get a message and/or see a little envelope in your system tray. That depends on what you configure in your settings. You can change the new mail sound in Windows 95/98 under Sounds in the Control Panel. Unlike Eudora Light, Outlook Express and Messenger both let you **read mail as it arrives**, as well as preview messages in a separate panel. You can tell which messages are new as they'll be bold and the little envelopes next to them will be closed.

Addressing email

Open up a new mail message window, and you'll see a line starting with "To:" That's where you type in your **recipient's address**. Internet email addresses should be along the lines of someone@somewhere where someone is the sender's account name and somewhere identifies the server where they collect their mail.

If you submit a wrongly constructed or a non-existent address, your message should bounce back to you with an **error message** saying what went wrong. This tends to happen within a matter of minutes. Sometimes, however, mail bounces back after a few days. This usually indicates a physical problem in delivering the mail rather than an addressing error. When it occurs, just send it again. If it's your end that's caused the problem, you might have a whole batch of mail to resend.

Sending mail to CompuServe and AOL

To make life a little harder, some addresses – namely **CompuServe** and **AOL** – don't follow the standard someone@somewhere format.

CompuServe members have been able to change their addresses from numbers to names for some time but many members remain unaware of this and stick to the old system. If someone has given you a CompuServe address that looks something like 12345,671 you'll can convert it to an Internet email address by replacing the comma with a dot and adding @compuserve.com at the end. Thus to send mail to CompuServe member 12345,671 you need to address it to 12345.671@ compuserve.com

To send mail to an **AOL nickname** simply tack @aol.com on the end. So to contact Kickme at AOL, address it to kickme@aol.com

Of course, with both AOL and CompuServe, you can reply to mail sent to you simply by keying "Reply" – more on which below.

The address book

Despite first appearances, Internet email addresses aren't so hard to recall. CompuServe numbers apart, their name-based components are stacks easier to remember than telephone numbers and street addresses. However, there's no real need to memorize them, nor do you have to type in the whole address every time. Not when you have an **address book**.

Start your address book by putting yourself in. Open it in Outlook Express from under the Tools menu or by clicking on the book icon. In Messenger it's under the Communicator menu. Choose "New Card" or "New Contact" and fill in the blanks. To **import addresses from messages** simply right click (or click in Macs) on the sender's name and choose "Add to Address Book" from your mouse menu.

You can **send a message to someone in your Address Book** in several ways, from within the Address Book or the New Message window. Start off by entering every email address you know, and click on all the options until you know it inside out. With most email programs you can either **click** or **double click** on addresses in your address book to create new mail, or with Netscape **drag and drop addresses** into the "To:" or "CC" fields of a new message.

You can also **assign nicknames** which will act as shortcuts – and even if you don't the programs are smart enough to help you out. For example, you might only have to enter a few letters of a name, an address or a nickname and it will search the address book for the closest matches.

It's worthwhile experimenting to see which way you prefer. Understanding your address book's capabilities will save you loads of time and tedium in the long run. But the simplest way to address a message is by replying to one previous. Here's how.

Replying to mail

Yet another great thing about email is how you can quote received mail. To **reply to a message**, simply select it and choose "reply". This will automatically copy the original message and address it back to the sender.

Depending how you set this up in your settings (check your help file or experiment), this new message will commonly appear with quote tags (>) prior to each line. You can **include parts or all of the original message**, including the subject – or delete the lot. So when someone asks you a question or raises a point, you can include that section and answer it directly underneath or above. This saves them having to refer back to the message they sent. It also saves keying their address.

Don't fall into the habit of including the entire contents of the original letter in your reply. It wastes time for the receiver and its logical outcome (letters comprising the whole history of your correspondence) hardly bear thinking about.

Note also that the **"reply all"** option addresses your message not only to the sender but also to all recipients of the original. That's not something you'll always want to do.

Unfortunately, replying is the one area that Outlook Express has serious **flaws**. If you leave your mail sending format set in the default (plain text, Mime, encode using "none"), your replies will look messy with intermittent orphan lines. You can work around it by selecting encode using "quote printable," however not all mailers, for example Exchange, like this format. If someone complains your mail comes through with symbols like "=20" at the end of each line, that's what's causing it.

Forwarding email

You can also **forward** or (with Eudora only) **redirect a message** to somebody else. Forwarded messages may be quoted and edited like replies. Redirecting means sending it without the > tags. All programs handle this differently. If you choose quote tags in Outlook Express you have to temporarily change this option to omit them (this will be fixed in IE5.0x). In Messenger, all the variations are on the mouse menu (three cheers!).

Carbon copies (cc) and blind carbon copies (bcc)

If you want to send two or more people the same message, you have two options.

When you don't mind if recipients know who else is receiving it, one address will have to go in the "To:" field, and the other addresses can also go in this field or in the **"CC"** (**carbon copy**) field.

If you put recipients into the "**BCC**" (**blind carbon copy**) field their names and addresses are masked from all others. However everyone, including those in "BCC", can see who's in the "To" and "CC". To send a bulk mailer without disclosing the list, put yourself in the "To:" field and everyone else in "BCC."

The subject

Let your email recipients know what your message is about. Put something meaningful in the "**Subject:**" heading. It's not so important when they first receive it – they'll probably open it even if it's blank. However, if you send someone your résumé and you title it "Hi," two months down the track when they're looking for talent, they'll have a hard time weeding you out of the pile.

Filling in the subject is optional when replying. If you don't enter anything, most mailers will retain the original subject and insert "**Re:**" before the original subject title to indicate it's a reply.

Signatures

All mailers let you add your personal touch at the end of your composition in the form of a **signature file**. This appears automatically on the bottom of your email, like headed notepaper. It's common practice to put your address, phone number, title, and perhaps round off with a witticism. There's nothing to stop you adding a monstrous picture, frame, or your initials in ASCII art. Except you have more taste than that.

```
   ////\\       //|\\       //\|\\       ///||\
  /`0-0'`      ` @ @\      //o o//        a a
    ]            >         ) | (          _)
    -            ~            ~            ~
  John          Paul       George       Ringo
```

Attaching non-text files to your email

Suppose you want to send something other than just a text message – such as a **word processor document, spreadsheet, or an image** – via email. It's quite feasible, and no longer requires technical expertise. To send a file, look in your mail menu for something along the lines of "Send Attachments" or "Attach File." Either that or try dragging and dropping the file into the new message window. It will normally work without a second thought from you.

How it does it is like this. Internet mail messages are transmitted in plain ASCII text and must be no larger than 64 Kb. That means to send anything larger than 64 Kb and anything other than text it has to be processed first. This includes all binary files such as images, spreadsheets, word-processor documents, and programs. Thankfully, these days, your mailer can handle this for you. It converts the binary coding into 7-bit ASCII and chops the message into units less than 64 kb. Then when the message arrives, it's automatically decoded, then lobbed into a designated download directory or can be accessed from an icon in the message.

Well, it's almost that simple. A residual problem, while people are using a variety of mailers, is that both parties' mailers need to support a common encoding standard, otherwise it will appear in gibberish. The most used methods are **MIME** and **Uuencode**. It doesn't really matter which you use as long as it works every time, so try a practice run first.

If you have problems getting a file to someone, refer to your Help file on how to specify an encoding method, as it varies between packages. MIME is gaining acceptance across all platforms (it's all that Netscape's older mailers recognize), so if you have the option, set it as the default. Eudora for Macs includes Binhex, Apple Single and Apple Double. Always choose Apple Double.

If your mailer doesn't automatically decode attachments, ditch it for one that does. It's not worth the bother. Old office systems like early Microsoft Mail are notoriously fussy. If you're not allowed to use an email program that handles attachments with grace, consider a new job.

How to send a CD track

If you'd like to share a tune from your new CD try encoding it with **RealEncoder** (http://www.real.com) and attaching it to a message. All your friend will need is the RealPlayer from the same address.

HTML mail and sending Web pages

Not long ago, email was a strictly plain text affair. The odd mailer such as Microsoft Exchange allowed formatting, but it didn't really make an impact until Netscape introduced **HTML mail** as a new standard. Today, if your mailer lacks HTML support you'll feel a bit backward.

HTML mail blurs the distinction between email and the World Wide Web, bringing Web pages right into your mailer. This means Web publishers, particularly magazines and news broadcasters, can send you regular bulletins formatted as Web pages complete with links to further information. It also means you can send Web pages by email. Either drag and drop them into a message or choose Send Page from under the File menu. Just make sure your recipient also has an HTML compliant mailer, otherwise they'll get all the formatting as a useless and time-wasting attachment.

Additionally, although the concept of fancying up your email by adding color, logos, and signatures might seem appealing, it's unlikely to increase your productivity and actually detracts from one of email's strongest features – simplicity. So don't spend too much time worrying about the appearance of your email. Just get the words right.

For a quick lesson in Internet Explorer 4.0's HTML mail see Outlook Expressions: http://www.barkers.org/ie/oe/ and the newsgroup: microsoft.public.inetexplorer.ie4.outlookexpress.stationery

Managing email

If your provider or phone company charges you by the minute to stay connected, it's best to **compose and read your mail offline** (ie when you are not connected by phone). That way, while connected you're actually busy transferring data, and getting your money's worth. Most mailers give you the option to send your messages immediately or place them in a queue, as well as to collect mail at regular intervals or on request.

Unless you're connected for long periods, you should select **choose not to send mail immediately** and **check manually**, otherwise your software will try to send and collect when you're offline. It's best to go online, collect your mail, upload your unsent mail, reply to anything urgent, log off, deal with the rest, and send your new bag of letters next time you go online.

Netscape Messenger detects whether you're online and should sort it out automatically. Well, it should, but you might have to choose "Go Offline" to get it to work. Then "Get Mail" to send it. Try it and see.

Filing

Just like you keep your work desk tidy, and deal with paper as it arrives, you should also keep your email neat. Most mailers can organize your correspondence into **mailboxes** or **folders** of some sort and offer you the option (worth taking) of automatically filing sent mail into a "Sent Mail" folder.

It's good discipline to use several folders for filing and to transfer your sent mail into monthly or bi-monthly folders, otherwise you'll be creating unwieldy (and possilbly hard to open) folders containing thousands of messages. Similarly, when you have dealt with mail, either send it to trash (and empty this folder regularly) or put it into a topic folder.

Sorting

To **sort your messages** by date, sender, size or subject, simply click on the bar at the top of each column. Click again to sort it in a different way.

Filtering

Most mailers can **filter** incoming mail into designated mailboxes, either as it arrives or on selection. It looks for a common phrase in the incoming header, such as the address or subject, and transfers it to somewhere other than the default inbox. This is indispensable if you subscribe to a lot of mailing lists (see the following chapter) or get a ton of junk office email.

Eudora Pro has a manual option which is useful in that you can leave messages in the Inbox until they've been handled, then transfer them into archives for later reference.

Etiquette and tracking replies

It's common courtesy – or netiquette – to **reply to email promptly**, even if just to verify you got it. After all, it only need be a couple of lines. Leave email in your Inbox until it's dealt with so you can instantly see what's current. Do the same with your Sent box. Just leave the mail that's awaiting reply.

As email is quick, and people tend to deal with it immediately, if you don't get a reply within a few days you'll know what to follow up. Once you've received your reply, you can either archive or delete your original outgoing message.

Sending your first email

The best way to get started is to **send yourself some email**. That way you'll get to both send and receive something. If you're dialing in, start this exercise offline with your mailer in offline mode.

1. To set up Messenger, open Preferences, then Offline, and choose "Offline Work Mode."

In Outlook Express, open Options, then Send and choose not to "send mail immediately." Then open Accounts from under the Tools menu, select your account, choose Properties, then Connection and check "Connect using Internet Explorer." Open Connection from Internet Explorer's Options, and set it up to connect to your ISP. If you need to dial through a different ISP later, change it in here.

2. Presuming you've completed your server details, the first step is to put yourself into the Address Book. Next, open up a new message, choose yourself from the Address Book, give the message a subject, enter something in the body and click "send" in the "New Message" window. If you're in offline mode, that will place your message in a queue to be sent once you go online. Otherwise, it will call up your dialer and try to send it immediately.

3. Now attempt to retrieve/send your mail. If you're offline, that should bring up your dialer. If not, and you

can't see how to make it happen automatically, call up your dialer manually, log in, and try again. Most mailers pop up a progress window to tell you what's going on.

Once you've sent yourself the message keep checking every 30 seconds until you receive it. It shouldn't take more than a few minutes. Now repeat this exercise until you're confident to face the rest of the wired world.

GET YOUR FREE EMAIL ADDRESS HERE

You connect to the Internet connection at work – but you don't want your business address for personal mail? No problem. You can score an extra email address and it needn't cost you a thing. You just have to suffer a little advertising.

There are three main options: **POP3 mail**, **Webmail**, and **mail redirection**. The best free deal going is Geocities (http://www.geocities.com). It provides a full POP3 address that works with any mailer, plus a free homepage in a sort of Web theme village. It might strike you as a bit corny, but it's exceptionally well organized.

Pick of the Webmail is probably Hot Mail: just log into http://www.hotmail.com and give a few details and you'll have a mail account in seconds. It's not like normal mail. It's all stored on and sent via the Web. That makes it handy for collecting and sending on the road, especially as you can use the same page to pick up your POP3 mail, but a bit inconvenient for everyday use. As you can give any details you like, it's perfect for anonymous mail – though abusers can still be traced by their IP address.

Other **Webmail** deals include: Rocket Mail (http://www.rocketmail.com); Magicia (http://www.magicia.com), which also provides free Web space; and NetAddress (http://www.netaddress.com) which provides **both Web and POP3** mail addresses ending in @usa.net

If you already have an email address and simply want a funkier address, you can get one ending in anything from @struth.com to @flippingheck.com through a **redirection service**. What's sent to this address gets redirected to wherever you choose. You're then free to switch providers while retaining a fixed address.

See: iName (http://www.iname.com), StarMail: (http://www.starmail.com) and NetForward (http://www.netforward.com).

Staying anonymous

Occasionally when sending mail or posting to a newsgroup, you might prefer to **conceal your identity** – for example, to save embarrassment in health discussions. There are three main ways to send mail anonymously. As mentioned in the box above, **Webmail** is one.

The second is less ethical. You can **change your configuration** so that it looks like it's coming from somebody else, either real or fictitious. However, if anyone tries to reply, their mail will attempt to go to that alias, not you. But, be warned, it's possible to trace the header details back to your server, if someone's really eager – and your national law enforcement agency might be if you're up to no good.

The third way is to register with a server dedicated to **redirecting anonymous mail**. These generally act as go-betweens. When someone receives such mail, it's plainly masked, as it comes from an obviously coded email address. When they reply, the anonymous server handles the redirection. That's as good as it gets, but if you break the law in the process, they can still find you by demanding your details from the server's administrator. For more information see: http://www.stack.nl/~galactus/remailers/

Privacy

Although there's been a lot of fuss about hacking and Net security, in reality email is way more secure than your phone or post. In fact, most new generation email programs (including Messenger and Outlook Express) have some kind of **encryption** built in. But it's not hackers who are most likely to read your mail – it's whoever has access to your incoming mailserver. If it happens to be at work, then you should assume your boss can read your mail. So that's another good reason not to use your work mail for correspondence that could get you in hot water.

If you're really serious about privacy, you may want to investigate **PGP (Pretty Good Privacy)**, a powerful method of encryption which generates a set of public and private "keys" from a passphrase. You distribute the public key and keep the private key secure. When someone wants to send you a private message, they scramble it using your public key. You then use the private key, or your secret passphrase, to decode it. For more on this, see: http://www.pgp.net/pgpnet/pgp-faq/

Digital Signing and Encryption

Internet Explorer 4.0x, Netscape Communicator 4.0x, and their associated mailers already support emerging

encryption and **digital signing** standards but it's yet to be seen how they'll be received.

Digital signing proves your identity via a third party certificate. Here's how to get yours. First up, fetch a personal certificate from Verisign: http://www.verisign.com You can't go wrong there if you follow the instructions. Once it's installed, open your mail security settings and see that the certificate is activated. You may choose to digitally sign all your messages by default, or individually. Then send a secure message to all your regular email partners, telling them to install your certificate. Those with secure mailers can add your certificate against your entry in their address books. From then on, they'll be able to verify that mail that says it's from you is indeed from you.

Encryption works similarly, though you'll also need your email partners' certificates to encrypt messages to them. Also, as each certificate only works on one installation, you'll need a different one for work and home. This makes it a bit cumbersome if you're collecting mail on the road. It also means anyone with access to your machine could pretend they're you.

Yes, it's all a bit flaky at this stage. So spend a few minutes in your help file figuring out the finer details, try it with your friends, and decide amongst yourselves whether it's worth the bother.

Finding an email address – and being found

If you'd like your long lost childhood sweetheart to track you down by email, you'd better list yourself in a few online email directories. See "Email Search" (p.248) in our Web Guide.

For advice on how to find someone else's email address, see our chapter on "Finding It" (p.171).

START YOUR SESSION ON THE NET WITH EMAIL

If you're running a dial-up account, the first thing you'll want to do once you go online is check your mail and send your queued email. So it makes sense to use collecting your mail as your springboard on to the Net. You may need to investigate your mailer's connection settings to work this out but it should be straightforward, particularly under Windows 95/98. Most of the time, it's the default setting.

If not, you might have to specify to connect to the Net as required or to tell it that you're connecting via a modem. Anyway just try it first and see what happens. Make sure everything's connected and select the option to retrieve mail. If that doesn't start up your dialer, you'll need to fiddle. As ever, refer to your help file for instructions.

The Net by email

If your Internet access is restricted to email only, you can still get to a fair bit of the Net via automatically responding **mail servers** (see the chapter on Mailing Lists, following). It's hardly on a par with full Internet access, but you're not shut out altogether. For example, if you can't use FTP, you could try using an FTP mail server to supervise the transfer. It's even possible to retrieve Web page text. To find out how, mail: mailbase@mailbase.ac.uk with this line only in the message body: send lis-iis e-access-inet.txt

Help

If you're frustrated by Microsoft's
Internet Mail & News or **Outlook Express** try
Ed Miller's IMN tips:
http://home.sprynet.com/sprynet/edm/ and
http://www.okinfoweb.com/moe/
or resort to the newsgroups:
microsoft.public.inetexplorer.ie4.outlookexpress or
microsoft.public.internet.mail

For **Eudora**, try: http://www.eudora.com
and the newsgroups:
comp.mail.eudora.ms-windows or
comp.mail.eudora.mac

For **Netscape**, try:
http://help.netscape.com/nuggies/
and the newsgroups:
comp.infosystems.www.browsers.ms-windows or
comp.infosystems.www.browsers.mac

Mailing Lists

If you want email by the bucketload, join a mailing list. This will involve giving your email address to someone and receiving whatever they send until you tell them to stop. There are thousands of lists and they fall into two categories: closed (one way) or open. Closed lists are set up by some sort of authority or publisher to keep you informed of news or changes. That could be anything from hourly Antarctic weather updates to product release announcements. They're one way only: you don't contribute. What comes through an open list is sent by its members – and yes, that could be you.

The purpose of most lists is to broadcast news or encourage discussion about a specific topic – anything from alien abductions to Japanese jazz. In some cases, the list itself forms a group, like a social club, so don't be surprised if discussion drifts way off topic or into personal and indulgent rants. You'll see. But you'll also find lists are an easy way to keep up with news and to meet a few peers, maybe in person, too. The only drawback is you have to browse a load of mail.

Climbing aboard

Joining is never hard. In most cases, you **subscribe** by sending a single email message. Or maybe by filling out a form on a Web page. It depends on who's running the list. Once you're on an open list, you'll receive all the messages sent to the list's address, just as everyone else on the list will receive whatever you send. Your first message will either welcome you to the list, or ask you to reply to confirm your email address (to stop prank subscriptions). Keep the welcome message as it should also tell you how to **unsubscribe**.

Mailing list basics

Each mailing list has two addresses: the **mailing address** used to contact its members; and the **administrative address** used to send commands to the server or maintainer of the list. Don't get them mixed up or everyone else on the list will think you're a twit.

Most lists are **unmoderated**, meaning they relay messages immediately. Messages on **moderated** lists get screened first. Moderation can be used for censorship but most often it's a welcome bonus, improving the quality of discussion and keeping it on topic by pruning irrelevant and repetitive messages. It all depends on the moderator, who is rarely paid for the service. Certain other lists are moderated because they carry messages from one source, such as the US Travel Warnings. Such lists often have a parallel open list for discussion.

If you'd rather receive your mail in large batches than have it trickle through, request a **digest** where available. These are normally sent daily or weekly, depending on the traffic.

These days most lists are maintained by a "robot," but some are still manual. For those, the administrative address is the same as the list's address with -request appended. For example, the administrative address of the list dragster-bikes@sissybar.net would be dragster-bikes-request@sissybar.net To subscribe or unsubscribe to such a list, send a one-line message (see below) to the administrator.

Listserv

LISTSERV, the most popular automated list system, uses listserv as the administrative address. So to join the list muck@rake.com you'd send a subscription message to: listserv@rake.com

Requests are interpreted by a program which usually reads only the message body. Messages may contain several requests as long as they're on separate lines, but you shouldn't include a signature/address at the end as it will confuse the program. Since all LISTSERV systems are hooked together, you can send your request to any LISTSERV host and your request will be redirected. If you're not sure which host to use, send your request to: listserv@listserve.net

How to use LISTSERV

To join a LISTSERV list, send the following message:
    SUB listname your name

To take yourself off, send:
    SIGNOFF listname

To find all options, send:
    HELP

To find out all the lists on a LISTSERV system, send:
    LIST

To find lists throughout all LISTSERV systems, send:
    LIST GLOBAL (It's over 500 Kb, so brace yourself!)

To hear of new lists as soon as they appear, send:
    SUB new-list to listserv@listserv.nodak.edu.

Note: many LISTSERV lists are mirrored in Usenet newsgroups under the bit.listserv hierarchy.

MajorDomo

MajorDomo is another list manager similar to
LISTSERV. It uses the address majordomo@host

How to use MAJORDOMO

To join a MajorDomo list, send:
  subscribe listname address

To get off, send:
  unsubscribe listname address

In both cases adding your email address is optional but
useful if you want to subscribe someone else.

To find out which lists you're on at any MajorDomo
host, send:
  which

As MajorDomo hosts are independent, you can't request
an overall list – you have to request it from each host
individually. To receive a list of all hosts, send:
  list

In-box Direct

You'll find the most organized collection of high quality
closed (or one-way) lists rounded up by Netscape and
loosely known as **In-box Direct**. These range from fashion probes like Elle Direct to techie bulletins like PC Week.
But they all have one thing in common: they're all sent
as Web pages, less the images. This means you need a
mail program – like those built into Netscape or Internet
Explorer – that reads HTML mail.

You don't actually need to use Netscape Mail for this
but the whole process may work more smoothly if you
sign up using a Netscape browser. The initial signup is
real pain; you have to go off and fetch a digital certifi-

cate and fill out too many details. Nonetheless, it's worth it. To sign up, look for a link from Netscape's home page at: http://home.netscape.com and follow the instructions. It takes weeks to get on some lists but persevere, it does eventually work. Or bypass this and go directly to each home site and sign up there. In the same way, keep your eye out for interesting lists as you browse the Web. Almost all the best sites have them. For more on **finding a list to join**, see our chapter on "Finding It" (p.175).

Starting your own list

If you'd like to **create your own list** check out Coollist (http://www.coollist.com). It's free, and simple to manage from the Web. Then if you want to get serious, ask your access provider or a list specialist from:
http://www.cs.ubc.ca/spider/edmonds/usenet/ml-providers.txt
For help **tuning Listserv** see The List Owners Survival Guide at: http://www.lsoft.com/manuals/owner/owner.html

Privacy

You should consider anything sent to a mailing list to be **in the public domain**. That means discussions could end up archived on the World Wide Web. This isn't usually the case, and may not even be legal, but it's safer not to test it. So take care not say anything you wouldn't like to see next to your name on the front page of your local paper.

Vacation alert!

If you're going on vacation or away from your mail for a while, consider unsubscribing to lists for a while. Otherwise you might face a serious mail jam when you return.

Usenet Newsgroups

The Internet is a great place to catch up on the latest
bulletins, health warnings, celebrity gossip, sports
results, TV listings, film reviews, and all that stuff commonly called "news." You can even have it delivered by
email, like a virtual newspaper run. But, don't be confused – that's not what's called "news" on the Internet.
In Net-speak, if you're "downloading news," you're
retrieving messages posted to Usenet discussion groups.
And these can make the regular news look positively
out of touch.

Usenet is where the Net community meets to kick
around just about every subject imaginable. It consists
of over 25,000 **newsgroups**; each dedicated to a single
theme. So whether you're interested in baseball, be-bop,
Buddhism, or brewing beer, there's sure to be a newsgroup deliberating over the issues closest to your heart.
And with an Internet population of over 100 million,
you should have access to the world's experts (and
loonies) in every field. Want to know the recipe for Lard
Surprise, whether it's safe to go to Kashmir, Unreal's
secrets, or where to sell that unexploded land mine in
your garden? Fine, just find the right newsgroup, post
your query, and wait for the results. It's the Net as

virtual community in action: fun, heartwarming, contentious, unpredictable, and ultimately useful – and, after email, arguably the Internet's most valuable resource.

We've listed a selection of popular and interesting newsgroups in our "Guide to Newsgroups" (see p.398). This chapter covers the basics of how to jump in and join their discussions.

Tapping into Usenet

Usenet can be accessed in several ways. If you have **full Internet access** you can read and post messages – or **articles** as they're sometimes called – online, switching between newsgroups as you please. It's possible to read any message, in any group, as long as it remains on your news provider's system.

If you only have a **BBS (Bulletin Board) or a "shell" account**, you'll have to subscribe to groups and then wait for messages to arrive. A third route is **via satellite**. A few companies provide read-only access through a decoder that sits between the dish and your computer. They transmit the entire Usenet database overnight. You can subscribe to what you want and scan through it over breakfast. But, as it's a one-way feed, you still have to post conventionally.

Even a full Internet connection does not guarantee **access to all groups**. Sometimes newsgroups are cut, due to logistics or because of a policy to exclude certain types. That decision lies with whomever supplies your **newsfeed**. Although most newsgroups cater to above-board hobbies, there's a share of pornographic, incendiary, provocative, and plain moronic material. So it's not surprising that many government, educational, corporate, and conservative bodies want to filter them.

How Usenet works

A Usenet newsgroup is a bit like a **public notice board**. When you **send (post) a message** to a newsgroup, everyone who reads that group will see it. And if someone replies, they will see that reply as well.

Usenet articles are like email messages but are transmitted in a separate system called NNTP (Network News Transport Protocol). Your Usenet provider (usually your ISP) maintains an independent **database of Usenet messages**, which it updates in periodic exchanges with its neighboring news servers. It receives and dispatches messages anything from once a day to instantly. Due to this pass-the-ball procedure, messages will appear immediately on your screen as you post them, but propagate around the world at the mercy of whoever's in between. Exactly how much **newsfeed** you get, and what you see, depends on your provider's neighbors and how often they update their messages. Most of the time, these days, it's almost as fast as email.

No provider, however, can keep messages forever, as it needs the space for new ones, so it **expires postings** after a certain holding period. It's usual to delete messages after about four days and even sooner for large groups and **binaries** (messages containing encoded programs, images, or formatted text). Each provider has a different policy.

In addition, some newsgroups are "**moderated**" – which means that postings are screened before they appear. Officially moderated groups are screened by whoever started the group or an appointee, but it's possible, though uncommon, that messages could be censored anywhere between you and the person who posted.

How to read newsgroup names

Newsgroups are divided into specific topics using a simple **naming system**. You can usually tell what a group's about by looking at its name. The first part is the broad category, or **hierarchy**, it falls under. Here are just some of the top-level and most popular (asterisked) hierarchies:

Hierarchy	Content
alt.	Alternative, anarchic, and freewheeling discussion*
aus.	Of interest to Australians
ba.	San Francisco Bay Area topics
bionet.	Biological topics
bit.	Topics from Bitnet LISTSERV mailing lists*
biz.	Accepted place for commercial postings
clari.	ClariNet subscription news service
comp.	Computing discussion*
ddn.	The Defense Data Network
de.	German groups
k12.	Education from kindergarten through grade 12
microsoft.	Microsoft product support
misc.	Miscellaneous discussions that don't fit anywhere else*
news.	Discussions on Usenet itself*
rec.	Hobbies and recreational activities*
sci.	All strands of science*
soc.	Social, cultural, and religious groups*
talk.	Discussion of controversial issues*
uk.	British topics

Newsgroups

News servers:

news.msn.com

news.compu...

Display newsgroups which contain:

ham

News groups

- alt.music.chameleons
- alt.music.hammond-organ
- alt.music.hamsters
- alt.music.shamen
- alt.pets.hamsters
- alt.religion.drew-hamilton
- alt.religion.shamanism
- alt.southampton.goth.commandoes
- alt.star-chamber
- alt.star-chamber.louise.woodward
- alt.tv.friends.northamerica
- de.comm.ham

All | Subscribed | New

Subscribe
Unsubscribe
Reset List

Go to | OK | Cancel

Note that **newsgroup names** contain dots, like domain
names, but they're interpreted differently. Each part of
the name distinguishes its focus, rather than its location. The top of the hierarchy is at the far left. As you
move right, you go down the tree and it becomes more
specific. For instance rec.sport.cricket.info is devoted to information about the compelling recreational sport that is
cricket. Also, though several groups may discuss similar
subjects, each will have its own angle. Thus while
alt.games.gravy might have light and anarchic postings,
biz.market.gravy would get down to business.

To find which newsgroups discuss your interests,
think laterally and use your newsreader's filtering capabilities to **search its newsgroup list** for key words. Or
easier still, search **DejaNews** (http://www.dejanews.com), the
biggest newsgroup directory on the Web.

Getting access to more groups

Your **newsfeed** might not carry every hierarchy, nor
every group within that hierarchy. Many local-interest

categories, for example, will only be available within their own localities. Your newsfeed provider selects the groups it wants to maintain and that's all you get to see.

This is not entirely a bad thing as it takes less bandwidth to keep the Usenet file up to date and thus reduces the general level of Net traffic. And **most providers are flexible**. If, say, your provider has arbitrarily decided to exclude all foreign-language and minor regional groups, and you're interested in Icelandic botany and Indian plumbing, you might be able to get the **groups added to the feed** simply by asking. However, sometimes omissions are due to **censorship**. Many providers remove groups on moral grounds, or to avoid controversy. The usual ones to get the chop are the alt.binaries.pictures. erotica (pornography), alt.sex and alt.warez (software hacking and piracy) hierarchies. No great loss.

If you can't get the groups you want from your provider or your account doesn't come with a newsfeed (eg at work), you needn't resort to another ISP. You could sign up for a **news-only account** with SuperNews (http://www.supernews.com) or try a publicly accessible news server with a better selection. See: http://www.jammed.com/ ~newzbot/.

Or, if you're really desperate it's possible to read and post your news for free **via the Web** at SuperNews or DejaNews.

Frequently Asked Questions (FAQs)

Every newsgroup has at least one **FAQ (Frequently Asked Questions)** document. This will describe the newsgroup's charter, give guidelines for posting, and compile common answers to questions.

Many newsgroups carry FAQs on various topics. They should always be your first source of information. FAQs are periodically posted, and usually updated every few weeks. To view a huge selection on the Web, see **FAQ Finder**: http://ps.superb.net/FAQ/ or http://www.lib.ox.ac.uk/internet/news/

Choosing a newsreader

Newsreaders – the programs you use for viewing and posting to newsgroups – are the most counterintuitive and inconsistent of all Internet appliances. You can be proficient with one yet bewildered when faced with another. That particularly goes for the set of various mutations bundled throughout the history of Microsoft's and Netscape's Web browsers.

If you are running **Netscape Communicator 4.0x (Collabra)** or **Internet Explorer 4.0x (Outlook Express)** you shouldn't need to look for another newsreader unless you have high demands. (Earlier versions, Netscape Navigator 3.0x and Internet Mail & News are satisfactory though not cutting edge.) However if you want more power and value from your session, you might consider a dedicated client. For PCs, try **Agent** from Forté. It has two versions: Free Agent which is free, and Agent, the registered full-featured Swiss army knife edition. **NewsWatcher** is probably the pick the of the Mac crop.

As ever, for download addresses, see our "Software Roundup" (see p.425).

Getting started

Before you can get your news you'll need to tweak a few knobs on your **newsreader**. It's hard to give definitive instructions because the features differ so markedly between programs. However, here's what to look for.

Configuring the newsreader

To start with, you'll need to specify your **news server**, your **identity**, and your **email address**. It should be part of your initial set-up routine. If not, to add a new Usenet service in Outlook Express, open Accounts from under the Tools menu, select Add News and follow the prompts. In Netscape Collabra, open Preference from under the Edit menu, and enter your news server under Groups Server.

Most newsreaders then offer a whole bunch of options for how long you want to keep messages after you've read them, how much to retrieve, and so forth. Leave those in the default settings and go back when you understand the questions and know your demands. Right now, it's not so important.

Building your group list

Before you can jump in, you'll need to **compile a list of newsgroups** available on your server. Your newsreader should do this automatically when you first connect to your news server– but be warned, it could take several minutes to arrive.

As the newsgroups arrive on your list, they either appear in a window titled "New Groups" or go straight into the main list (commonly called "All Groups"). To **compile your newsgroup list** in Outlook Express, go online and click on your news server entry at the bottom of your mail folder list. In Collabra (Netscape Message Center), choose "Go Online" and then "Subscribe to Discussion Groups" (both under the File menu).

Reading messages

The newsgroups list only contains the group names, not the actual messages. You have to **retrieve the messages** in a separate two-part process. But first you might need to **subscribe** to the group. This simply means putting a newsgroup into a special folder so that it's away from the main list. You might be able to give it priorities, like automatically updating headers or retrieving all message bodies upon connection, or it might just make it easier to locate.

To **subscribe to a group in Outlook Express**, click on the news server entry and choose "Newsgroups" from the Tools or mouse menu. When the list appears, select a group, click "Subscribe," and then "Goto" to commence downloading the message **headers**. The **headers** contain the message subject, posting date, and contributor's name. They can be threaded (bundled together) by subject, or sorted by date or contributor. Once all the headers have arrived, clicking on a message will download its body. You can then read it in the preview panel. If you wish to read the group at a later date, just select it from under the news server folder and wait for the new headers to arrive. To **remove a Newsgroup**, choose "Unsubscribe" from your mouse menu.

The process is almost identical in **Collabra**. Choose "Subscribe to Discussion Groups," open the folders until you find your group, click on "Subscribe," then close the window. To start downloading headers, select the group, then choose "Open Discussion Group" from the File or mouse menu. Selecting a message will download its body and display it in the preview pane.

Other newsreaders, and probably later versions of these, will use a different combination of menu choices to go through the same motions. So to get this right, you'll need to either read the "Help File" or randomly click everything the first time. Yes, really: it's the best way. As long as you understand the process, it will all come together, whatever the terms and instructions.

Reading Offline

Reading articles one at a time online is convenient, but not if it's costing you to stay connected or you're tying up your only telephone line. If that's the case consider **downloading the article bodies along with the headers** to read offline at your leisure.

This is simple in Outlook Express. Before you go online, choose "Work Offline" from under the File menu, select the group, then open its "Properties" from under the File or mouse menu, and make your selection under the "Download" tab. Click on the group when you're next online, to retrieve whatever you've set. Once you're offline, switch to "Work Offline" mode and browse through the articles as if you're online.

Collabra makes a bit of a meal of the same operation, but it's still possible. One way is to select the group while online, choose "Discussion Group Properties" from under the Edit or mouse menu, then mark your preferences under the "Download" tab. You can either choose to "Download Now" or retrieve them as you

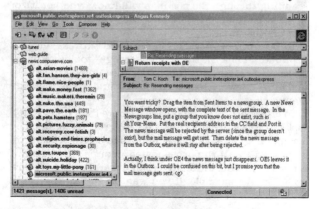

switch between Offline and Online mode. Just follow the prompts.

Contributing to a discussion

When a newsgroup message raises a new topic, it's called **starting a thread**. Replies to that initial message add to this thread. You can configure your Usenet reader to **sort threads** together to follow the progress of a discussion. But if you follow a group regularly you might find it more convenient to sort by date, to see what's new.

Posting

Posting is like sending email – and equally simple. You can start a new thread, follow up an existing one, and/or respond privately by email.

When you post, most programs automatically insert the newsgroup you're reading in the "Newsgroups:" line. When starting a thread, enter a **subject** that outlines the point of your message. That way people scanning through the postings will know whether it's of interest to them. The subject line will also be used to identify the thread.

To post a new message in Outlook Express, enter a group and click on the "New Message" toolbar icon or select "New Message" from under the Compose menu. In Collabra, "New Message" is located under the Message menu.

To **crosspost** (post a message to more than one group), just add those groups after the first group, separated by a comma, and then a space. Replies to crosspostings are displayed in all the crossposted groups. If you want replies to go to a different group, insert it after "Follow up – To:" For example, if you want to stir up trouble in alt.shenanigans and rec.humor and have the responses go to alt.flame, the header would look like this:

Newsgroups: alt.shenanigans, rec.humor

Follow-up – To: alt.flame

Replying

Replying (or responding) is even easier than posting. You can send your contribution to the relevant newsgroup(s) and/or email the poster directly.

It's not a bad idea to **reply as well as post**, because the original poster will get it instantly. It's also more personal and will save them having to scan through the group for replies. It's quite acceptable to continue communicating outside Usenet as long as it serves a purpose. Before long you'll have a circle of new virtual friends.

Like email, you also have the option of **including part or all the original message**. This can be quite a tricky choice. If you cut too much, the context could be lost when the original post is deleted. If everyone includes everything, it creates a lot of text to scan. Just try to leave the main points intact.

You'll find all the various reply options beside or below your "New Message" menu entries in all newsreaders.

Sending a test post

As soon as anyone gets Usenet access, they're always itching to see if it works. With that in mind, there are a few **newsgroups dedicated to experimenting**. Post whatever you like to alt.test, gnu.gnusenet.test or misc.test You'll get several automatic (and maybe even humanly) generated replies appearing in your mailbox within a few days, just to let you know you're in good hands.

Canceling a message

If you've had second thoughts about something you've posted select it in the newsgroup and choose "**Cancel Message**" from under the Compose menu in Outlook Express or the Edit menu in Collabra. Unfortunately it won't be instantly removed from every server worldwide so someone still might see it.

Kill files

If you don't like a certain person on Usenet, you can "kill" their mail. If your newsreader has a "**kill file**," just add their email address to that, or use your **Filters**. Then you'll never have to download messages they've posted again. You can also trash uninteresting threads in the same way, by setting a delete filter on the subject. But don't make it too broad or you might filter out interesting stuff as well.

Image and sound files – and decoding

As with email, Usenet can carry more than just text. Consequently there are entire groups dedicated to the posting of **binary files** such as images, sounds, patches, and even full working programs. Such groups usually have .binaries in their address.

Again like email, binary files must be processed, most commonly in UUencoding, before they can be posted or read. You can use a separate program to handle the **encoding/decoding**, but it's far more convenient to leave it up to your newsreader. As postings are restricted to 64 Kb, the file could need to be chopped into several messages. Each part will have the same subject heading followed by its number.

Depending on your newsreader, to **retrieve a binary file** you might need to highlight all the parts and decode them in one go. Agent/Free Agent recognizes a set, just by clicking on one part. Netscape's Collabra and Microsoft's Outlook Express both decode automatically within the window. To decode a multi-part attachment in Outlook Express, select the components and choose "Combine and Decode" from the Tools menu. Collabra, as yet, can't cope with parts. With some newsreaders, you might need to retrieve the message body and decode in two stages. Best to read your help file to get it straight.

To **post a binary**, just attach it as in email and your newsreader will look after the rest.

Warning: make sure you virus check any program you download from Usenet.

Starting your own newsgroup

With more than 25,000 newsgroups already existent, you'll need fairly specialized tastes to get the urge to start your own group – plus a fair bit of technical knowhow and a monk's patience. It's one of the more convoluted and arcane procedures on the Net.

First off, before you can create a new group – in anywhere but the alt. hierarchy – you need to drum up support. It's a good idea to start a **mailing list** first. To get numbers, discuss the proposal in the newsgroups related to your topic and then announce your list. Once you have a case, and support, you have to put it before the pedantic news.groups for a savaging. Then through a long process that culminates in an election where the number of "yes" votes must be at least 100 more than, and twice the number of "no" votes.

Starting alt. **newsgroups** is much easier. You just have to post a special control message. The hard part is getting people to frequent the group.

For more see the Web sites:
"So you want to create an alt. newsgroup"
   http://www.cis.ohio-state.edu/~barr/alt-creation-guide.html
and "How to write a good new group message"
   http://www.cs.ubc.ca/spider/edmonds/usenet/good-newgroup.html

Newsgroup netiquette

Apart from your provider's contract, the Net is largely devoid of formal rules. Instead, there are certain established, or developing, codes of conduct known as **Netiquette** (Net-etiquette). These apply mainly to Usenet.

If you breach Usenet netiquette, you could be ignored, lectured by a self-appointed Net-cop, or flamed. A **flame** is personalized abuse. You don't have to breach netiquette to get flamed – just expressing a contrary or naive opinion might do the trick. When it degenerates into name calling, it's called a **flame war**. There's not much you can do to avoid compulsive troublemakers, but if you follow these tips, you should be welcome to stand your ground.

Post to the right group

It's important to **get the feel of a newsgroup** before you post to it. If it's a big group you might get a fair idea of what's going on within one session, but more likely you'll need several. Download all the **relevant FAQs** first, to make sure your message isn't old hat. Some newsgroupies are not too tolerant of repeats.

Next, make an effort to **post in the most relevant group**. If you were to ask for advice on fertilizing roses in rec.gardening you might find yourself politely directed to rec.gardening.roses but if you want to tell everyone in talk.serious.socialism about your favorite Chow Yun Fat film, don't expect such a warm response.

Keep your cool

Never post in anger. You'll regret it later, especially when everything you send is archived at DejaNews. And beware of **Trolls**. These are baits left to start arguments or make you look stupid. If someone asks something ludicrous or obvious, says something offensive or inappropriate, or attacks you personally, don't respond. Let it pass. Tread carefully with sarcasm, too, as not everyone will get it, especially those nationalities with no sense of irony. (This is meant to be a joke, but how can you be sure?)

Less obviously, **never post in UPPER CASE** (CAPS) unless you're "**shouting**" (emphasizing a point in a big way). It makes you look rude and ignorant. And keep your **signature file** short and subtle. Some people believe massive three-page dinosaurs and skyscrapers sculpted from ASCII characters tacked to every Usenet posting gives them cred. That's unlikely.

In similar fashion, express yourself in plain English (or the language of the group). Don't use **acronyms** or **abbreviations** (unless they reduce jargon rather than create it). And avoid over-using **smileys and other emoticons** (see "Net Language" – p.464). Some might find them cute, but to others they're the online equivalent of fuzzy dice hanging from a car's rear view mirror.

In addition, don't post **email you've received from someone else** without their consent.

Get in there

These warnings aside – and they're pretty obvious – don't hold back. If you can forward a discussion in any way, contribute. That's what it's all about. **Post positively** and invite discussion rather than making abrasive remarks. For example, posting "All programmers are social retards" is sure to get you flamed. But: "Do programmers lead healthy social lives?" will get the same point across and invite debate, yet allow you to sidestep the line of fire.

Overall it's a matter of courtesy and knowing when to contribute. In Usenet, no-one knows anything about you until you post. They'll get to know you through your words, and how well you construct your arguments. So if you want to make a good impression, think before you post, and don't be a loudmouth.

If you're a real stickler for rules you should read: http://www.idot.aol.com/netiquette/ Or if all this seems a tad twee, you might appreciate 101 ways to be obnoxious on Usenet at: http://www.elsop.com/wrc/humor/usenet.htm

Or check Emily Postnews at: http://www.jammed.com/~newzbot/emily-postnews.html

Posting commercial messages

Having such a massive captive audience pre-qualified by interests is beyond the dreams of many marketeers. Consequently you will frequently come across flagrant **product advertisements and endorsements** crossposted to inappropriate newsgroups.

The process, called **spamming**, is a guaranteed way to incur the wrath of a high percentage of Usenetsters. It usually incites mass mailbombing (loads of unsolicited email) and heavy flaming, not to mention bad publicity. As a rule no-one who uses this technique to advertise is reputable, as with those who send mass emails.

If you'd like to make **commercial announcements**, you could try the groups in the .biz hierarchy, after all that's what they're for. The only problem is no-one reads them because they're so chocked full of network marketing schemes. In other groups, you'll need to tread more subtly with any mentions of your new book, CD or whatever; otherwise you might come in for a hard time. You can still do it, but only in the right groups and in the right context.

Ironically, nobody minds what you put in your **signature**, so if you put in your Web address it might attract a few visitors.

Searching Usenet

See our chapter on "Finding It" (p.170).

Downloading Software

If you're after a Web browser upgrade, the latest Quake patch, or some obscure CD mastering software, the Internet is the very first place you should look. Just about every program that's released nowadays finds its way on to the Net, and most of the time you can download a full working copy. If not, at the very least, you should be able to order it on disk by email direct from the publisher.

You mightn't be able to download a working copy of a big **commercial package** like Microsoft Office, Quark or AutoCad: that's not surprising as apart from being expensive some of these programs are so large they might take you a day to download. But you should be able to download all its **interim upgrades**, **patches** to fix problems, **extensions** and occasionally, a **trial (beta) version**.

What you certainly will be able to find is all the **Internet software** you'll ever need. And the good news is you can download the pick of the crop, for free. So don't be afraid to turf out components that you've acquired in a starter kit. As Internet software must comply with TCP/IP specifications, units should be seamlessly replaceable, and the only (minor) drawback in add-ons is that you might have to launch them by clicking on their icons and not from the menu in your all-in-one package. That's no big deal.

Incidentally, a bundle that won't let you mix and match components isn't worth keeping. That goes, in particular, for running **Windows 3.xx connection software** under Windows 95. Don't: instead, replace it with **Dial-up Networking** so you can run 32-bit software.

What you'll need

```
File Download                                    _ □ X

Opening:
SNEAKY.ZIP from mason.gmu.edu
■■■■■■■■■■■■■■■■■■■■■■■■■■■■■■■■
Estimated time left:  2 min 39 sec (736 KB copied)
Download to:         Temporary Folder
Transfer rate:       2.85 KB/Sec                 Cancel
```

Before you can download anything, you'll need an **FTP (File Transfer Protocol) program**. You can use a stand-alone dedicated program such as **WS-FTP**, **CuteFTP**, or **Fetch** (see our software roundup starting on p.425), but most of the time it's more convenient to do it all from your **Web browser**. Both **Netscape** and **Microsoft's Internet Explorer** browsers are continually improving for FTP, though dedicated programs are still worth checking out for serious use. They have more features, and if you're uploading or accessing password protected sites, you might find one necessary.

We've dedicated a whole chapter to a roundup of **Net software** (see p.425) which includes all the download addresses. You may want to refer to it in conjunction with this section.

Free software programs from the Net

While the Internet might be a veritable clearinghouse of freely available software, it's not all genuinely free. There are three types of programs you're allowed to use, at least for a while, without paying. They are called **freeware**, **shareware**, and **beta programs**.

Freeware

Freeware is provided by its author(s) without any expectation of payment. It could be a complete program, a demonstration sample with crippled features, a patch to enhance another program, or an interim upgrade. In some cases, a donation, or even an email postcard, is appreciated.

Shareware

Shareware usually has certain conditions attached, which you accept when you install or run the program. Commonly, these may include the condition that you must pay to continue to use it after an initial free trial period, or that you pay if you intend to use it commercially. Sometimes a shareware program, while adequate, is a short form of a more solid or better-featured registered version. You might upgrade to this if you like the shareware, usually by paying a registration fee, in return for which the author or software distributor will mail you a code to unlock the program or its upgrade.

Beta programs

Betas (and Platform Previews) are distributed as part of the testing process in commercial software development. You shouldn't pay for them as they're not finished products. But they're often good enough for the task, and usually right at the cutting edge of technology. Take Netscape's betas, for example. They've been the most popular programs to ever hit the Net.

With all betas, expect to encounter **bugs and quirks** now and again and don't be too upset by having to restart the program (or your computer) occasionally – it's all part of the development process. But do report recurring faults to the developers; after all that's why they let you have it free. If you notice a pattern, email the distributors and ask for a fix. If it's just too buggy, get an alternative.

How to download a file

The most popular way to transfer files across the Internet is by FTP. **Retrieving files by FTP** is straightforward if you have an FTP client with a graphical interface or a Web browser. Dedicated FTP clients are much alike – any of them will do to get started. And if you don't like one, you can use it to download another.

Unless you've been granted special permission to log into an FTP server to transfer files, you'll have to use one that permits "**anonymous FTP**." Such sites follow a standard log-in. Once you're in, you can look through the contents of a limited number of directories and transfer files to, and sometimes from, your computer.

Many **Net servers** have areas set aside for anonymous FTP. Some even carry massive specialist **file archives**. And most **software houses** provide updates, patches, and interim releases on their own anonymous FTP sites. No single server will have everything you need, but you'll soon find favorites for each type of file. Your **Access Provider** should have an FTP area, too, where you can transfer files for updating Web pages, download access software, and exchange files with colleagues.

FTP domain addresses

FTP domains are often prefixed by ftp. but that's not a rule. When you're supplied a file location it could be in the form ftp.fish.com/pub/dir/jane.zip That tells you that the file jane.zip is located in the directory pub/dir on the ftp.fish.com server.

Downloading from the Web

Netscape Navigator and **Microsoft Internet Explorer** are superb download clients for both **FTP** and **HTTP** transfers. You can kick off multiple transfers and then surf the Web while you wait for downloads to finish.

That's pretty convenient because most of your file leads will come from Web pages. And not just from specialist software guides either (see the software guides in our Web Guide, p.250). For instance, if you were to read a review of a computer game you can bet your back door it will contain a link to download a demo.

To retrieve it, all you need do is **click on the link and follow the prompts**. You might have to supply a bit of information, but it should all be self-explanatory. Once the transfer is initiated (you might have to wait a little longer than it takes to load a Web page), a window will pop up asking you whether you'd like to **open or save the file**. Choose "save" and key in where you'd like to put it on your computer. Once that's done a new window will appear estimating how long it will take to finish and logging the progress.

As with any FTP transfer, if the file has moved, you'll either be defaulted back to a higher directory or face an error message. If the file isn't where it should be, or you want to **enter an unlinked location**, just enter it as a Web address but instead of keying http: use ftp: as the first part of the address.

So, to look for a file at: ftp.chook.com in the path: /pub you enter: ftp://ftp.chook.com/pub Once connected, just click on what you want in the usual fashion.

If you're serious about your downloads, **Go!Zilla for Windows 95/98/NT** (http://www.gozilla.com) is a must have. You can assign it to take over whenever it detects a file download of a certain type such as .exe or .zip, or drag and drop links directly into the main window. It can search FTP space looking for alternative locations and tell you which one is quickest. And if you break the transfer it can take over where it left off (as long as the server supports **"resume downloads"**).

Resume downloads

As FTP downloads can take some time – hours, even, if it's a big program and your link is slow – it is essential to ensure your FTP program supports "**resume downloads.**" Then if you drop out, you can go back and pick up where you left off. That's a real lifesaver if you're 90% through downloading a 16 Mb browser upgrade. The latest versions of Netscape and Internet Explorer are both supposed to resume broken downloads.

Browsing an FTP site

If you'd rather use a dedicated FTP client, it's not much harder. FTP programs use different terminologies, so it won't hurt to read its help or "read me" file. It should tell you what to key in where. Basically, though, the procedure is fairly routine and goes like this:

To retrieve ftp.fish.com/pub/dir/jane.zip enter the server's address ftp.fish.com as **host name**, anonymous as **user name**, and your Internet email address (in the form user@host) as a **password**.

Next, enter the **directory** you wish to start looking in, in this case, /pub/dir Make sure the path and file details are entered in the correct (upper/lower) case. If you enter Dir instead of dir on a UNIX host, it will return an error because UNIX is case sensitive. If you have the file's full location, try entering that as the initial directory. However, don't be surprised if a file isn't where it's supposed to be – system managers are forever shuffling directories. And it's not necessary to get the location exactly right: once you're in, you can always browse around until you find it.

Having entered the details above, you're ready to **log in**. If it's busy, you may not be admitted the first time. Don't let that discourage you. If you can't get in within ten attempts, try again later, perhaps outside the local peak hours. If you're accessing a foreign site, try when that continent is asleep. You're likely to get a better transfer rate.

Once you're accepted, you'll see a listing of the initial **directory's contents**. Look for a contents file called readme, index, or the like. Read it if you're unsure of the

C:\Download\			▼ Browse	/pub/demos/pc/			▼
Filename	File Size	Date/Time		Filename	File Size	Date/Time	Description
🔼 Parent directory				📄 BaneDemo.exe	1278868	18-06-98 6:12:0...	
📄 viic97_100.zip	1134470	06-07-98 8:42:2...		📄 tsdem120.zip	2945022	18-06-98 9:53:0...	
📄 ie5setup.exe	463720	21-06-98 9:20:0...		📄 dsi103.exe	1300715	18-06-98 10:27:...	
📄 SMSoccer.zip.1	255136	15-06-98 3:30:0...		📄 earth2.zip	4936651	18-06-98 3:06:0...	
				📄 ...2 115 zip	2020120	18.06.98 10:12:1	

Filename		File Size	Date/Time	Destination	
⬅ 📄 /pub/demos/pc/scity102.zip		2861018	12-06-98 ...	C:\Download\	

contents, and read, too, any accompanying **text files** before downloading a program. You can usually do that by either clicking on them or selecting "view" or "read" from the menu.

Most FTP programs work in a similar way to Windows' file manager or the Macintosh folder system. That means when you click, something happens. Look at the top of the directory contents. **Clicking on ".."** will send you up a directory level. Directories should stand out from files by having a different color, typeface, folder icon, or at least not having extensions. **Clicking on a directory** will open it, clicking on a file or dragging and dropping it should start the download.

Make sure you select **"binary transfer"** before downloading any files other than plain text. If you're unsure of the file type, always choose binary. It will transfer text files as well. Although it may be slightly slower, text files aren't usually that large, so it's not really an issue. But if you download a graphic, sound, or program as "text" it will be useless. Everyone makes that mistake at least once.

Your FTP client should give you a **transfer progress report** to tell you how long it's going to take. You can either sit back and watch the bits zip into your hard drive or relegate it to the background while you do something else, like explore the Web. Unfortunately, if the **transfer fails or is canceled**, or your line drops out, you won't be able to pick up where you left off unless both your FTP program and the server both support "resume transfers." So bear this in mind when choosing an FTP client.

Uploading files

FTP isn't just for scoring files, you can **upload** as well. It might be more practical to submit stories, documents, graphics, and applications this way, rather than burden the email system with bulky attachments. For example, suppose you want to submit artwork to a magazine. You could FTP the scans to an area set aside for downloads (often a directory called "incoming"), and then notify your editor by email. The editor could then instruct staff to upload them for approval. If they're okay they could then be processed and moved to an outgoing directory for print house access.

In some cases an area is set aside where files can be uploaded and downloaded to the same directory. Useful maybe if you want to transfer files to a colleague who's having problems with handling mailed attachments (it happens!). It's frustrating waiting for several megabytes of mail attachments to download and decode before you can read your mail. Especially if it has to be re-sent.

FTP by email

Several services offer **FTP by email**. They can take up to a few days, but may save access charges over slow networks – it's usually quicker to download your mail from a local server than to transfer files from a distant busy server. If you're in more of a hurry to get offline than get the file, give it a shot. To find out how, mail: mailbase@mailbase.ac.uk with this line only in the message body: send lis-iis e-access-inet.txt

File types and compression

There are two reasons why archived binary files are **compressed**. One is to decrease their storage demands, the other to reduce transfer times. After you download a compressed file, you must decompress it to get it to work. Before you can decompress it you need the right program to do the job.

In general, it's easy to tell which technique has been used by looking at the file name or where it's located. Unless the site is specifically targeted at one platform, you're usually offered a **directory choice** between DOS, PC/Windows, Mac, and UNIX. Once you've taken that choice everything contained in that directory and its subdirectories will be for that platform only. If not, you can usually tell by the file extensions.

File extensions and decompress programs

The following table shows common **file extensions** and the **programs needed to decompress** or view them.

Extension	Filetype	Program to decompress or view
.arc	PC Compressed archive	PKARC, ARC, ArcMac
.arj	PC Compressed archive	UNARJ
.bin	MacBinary	MacBinary, usually automatic in Macs
.bmp	Bitmap	Graphics viewer, MS Paintbrush
.cpt	Mac Compact Pro archive	Compact Pro, Stuffit Expander
.doc	MS Word document	Word processor such as MS Word or Wordpad
.exe	PC executable	Self executing from DOS or Windows
.gif	Graphic Interchange Format	Graphics viewer
.gz	UNIX Compressed archive	GNU Zip
.hqx	Mac BinHex	BinHex, Stuffit Expander
.jpg	Compressed graphic	Graphics viewer
.lha, .lzh	Compressed archive	LHA
.mpg	Compressed video	Video viewer
.pict	Mac picture	Graphics viewer
.pit	Mac PackIt	PackIt
.ps	PostScript	PostScript printer or GhostScript
.sea	Mac Self-extracting archive	Click on icon to extract
.sit	Mac Stuffit compressed archive	Stuffit Expander
.tif	Tagged image format	Graphic viewer
.txt	Plain ASCII text	MS Notepad, text editor, word processor
.uu, .uue	UNIX UU-encoded	UUDECODE, Stuffit Expander
.z	UNIX Gnu GZip archive	GZip
.Z	UNIX compressed archive	UNCOMPRESS
.zip	PC PKZip compressed archive	PKZip, WinZip, Stuffit Expander
.zoo	Compressed archive	ZOO

PC archives

PC archives mostly end in .exe, .zip, .lzh, or .arj. The .exe files are usually **self-extracting archives**, which means they contain a program to decompress themselves. All you have to do is execute them. Just transfer them to a temporary directory and double-click on them in File Manager or Explorer. Or run them from DOS by changing into the temporary directory and typing what comes before the .exe. If you're on a PC, get the latest copy of **WinZip**, and the latest **Stuffit Expander** for Windows and place it on your desktop. The great thing about this combination is that it will handle just about everything, including files compressed on Macs. And it's easily configurable to automatically extract archived files just by double-clicking them in File Manager or Explorer, or by dropping them onto the Stuffit or WinZip icons.

Mac files

Compressed **Macintosh files** usually end .cpt, .sit, .sea, or .hqx. The .sea files **self-extract** by clicking on them, the rest by dropping on, or opening with, **Stuffit Expander**.

If you're **expanding a Mac file for PC use**, set the options under Cross Platform to "convert text files to Windows format when the file is known to contain text" and "never save files in MacBinary Format."

Audio and video files

All recent Web browsers add support above your standard multimedia software to cope with the most common **audio and video** formats. Anything else is likely to need a browser plug-in or specialist program. This includes compressed **multimedia files** like Fractal Image Format, Lightning Strike, and MP3.

Most of the time there'll be a link to download the player on the Web site where you found the file. See our **Software Roundup** (p.425) for details of how to obtain the above programs.

How to set up your directory structure

Before you start installing every Internet program you can find, sort out your **directory structure**. Otherwise, you'll make a jungle of your hard drive.

Hard drives are organized into tree-like structures. In DOS and Windows 3.x, each level is called a **Directory**. In Windows 95/98 and Macs it's called a **Folder**. Both mean the same thing, they're just represented by different icons. For simplicity's sake we'll call them directories. The top level of a drive is called the Root Directory. It's for system start-up files only, so don't lob anything in there. No matter what system you're running, you should create the following first-level directories:

Programs

Install all **programs** into their own separate subdirectories under a first-level directory called **Program Files**, **Apps**, or similar. It's wise to have a second level separating the types of programs such as Net, Graphics, Office, and such. Thus, you'd install Netscape and Eudora into their own subdirectories under Net; Word and Excel under Office; ACDSee and PaintShop under Graphics, and so forth.

Download

Configure your **Net clients** (programs) to download to a common Download directory and create a shortcut (alias) on your desktop to open it. Think of it as an in-tray and clear it accordingly.

Temporary

Once you've downloaded an application, extract it to an empty **Temporary directory** and then install it under the

Programs hierarchy. Once done, delete the contents of the Temporary directory. If you have space, keep the original installation file in case you need to reinstall it. Put it in your Archive directory.

Archive

Rather than clog up your Download folder, dedicate an **Archive directory** with enough **subdirectories** to make it easy to find things again. As you download new versions of programs, delete the old one.

You could open your archive to your peers through a Windows 95 Dial-Up, or FTP server. It should be the first place to delete files to make space.

Data

Put irreplaceable files, such as those you create, into a **Data directory** tree and regularly back it up onto another medium such as a floppy disk, Zip drive, or even an FTP site. Use WinZip or Stuffit to compress it all into manageable chunks.

Sending a file to a friend

If you use **ICQ** (chat – see p.188) to stay in touch online, rather than attach files by email, try sending them directly using its File option. It's more efficient.

Where to find an FTP client

See our "Software Roundup" chapter (p.425).

Finding Files

See the following chapter, "Finding It" (p.174).

Finding It

Once you've selected an Access Provider, installed your software, and the whole thing's purring along, you'll be faced with one further dilemma. How on earth do you find anything on the Net? Well relax, it's easier than it looks, once you've learned a few tricks. How you find something depends on what it is, how new it is, where it's likely to be stored, and who's likely to know about it. In this chapter, we show you the first places to look, and as you gain experience the rest will fall into place. We also show you how to fix addresses that won't work. Assuming you have Web access, the only program you'll definitely need for all this is a Web browser.

What's out there

Anything you can **link to through the Web**, you can find using a Web search tool. Plus you can find anything that's been **archived** into an online Web database, such as email addresses, phone numbers, program locations, newsgroup articles, and news clippings. Of course, first it has to be put online, and granted public access. Just because you can access US government servers doesn't mean you'll find a file on DEA Operative Presley's whereabouts.

First we'll examine the range of **search tools**. You'll find all the addresses detailed in the "Search Tools and Directories" section of our Web guide (see p.241).

The main search tools

There are three basic types of Web search tools: **search engines**, **search agents**, and **hand-built directories**. All have their specific uses.

Search engines

Search engines – the best of which are **AltaVista**, **Hot-Bot**, and **Northern Light** – run a program called a trawler, crawler, spider, robot, wanderer, worm, or some such name, that scouts around the Web and comes back with its findings. These pickings, such as each page's location, title, and an amount of text that varies between crawlers, are then stored in an online database.

You can search for something specific by **submitting keywords**, or search terms, to these databases through a simple Web page form. The results, which usually come back within seconds, are clickable like hot links on any other Web page.

Search agents

Search agents, or **searchbots**, gather information live from other sites. For example: metasearch agents such as Copernic, Dogpile, and MetaCrawler, can query multiple search engines and directories simultaneously; bargain finder agents, like **Virtual Outlet,** can look for the best deal across several online shops; and Web agents, like NetAttaché, can scan specific sites for pages which have changed or contain instances of an expression. Many are accessible through a Web interface, but the better ones are generally standalone clients.

Hand-built directories

The **hand-built directories**, such as **Yahoo**, **Magellan**, **What's New**, and **Cool Tools**, usually sort sites into categories and sometimes include reviews or comments. Sites are sorted by subject, date, platform, or even their level of "coolness." In the pages following, we call these **directories** or **guides** when they cover a broad range of subjects (like Yahoo), **specialist sites** when they are more focused in one area (like Cool Tools), or **lists** when they mainly rank sites (like Cool Site of the Day).

Directories

Finally, there are a few hybrids that might fit into a combination of these categories. If in doubt we'll call them **directories**.

Read me

As with just about everything on the Net, the easiest way to learn is to dive straight in to the search engines and explore how they work. But before you do, it's worth pausing to read the instructions first. Every search engine or directory has a page of "**Read Me**" tips on how to use them to their full potential. A few minutes study will make your searching more effective.

Search engines

Generally the quickest way to find specific reference to something on the Web is to use a **search engine**. These look like normal Web pages, with a form to enter the search terms of what you're looking for. It in turn feeds these terms into a database and returns a list of results or "**hits**".

Depending on the engine, the results should include enough information to judge whether the found pages will be useful. However, each engine can return only its crawler's most recent findings, which may be just a small proportion of what's actually there – and potentially, months old.

The various engines source, store, and retrieve their data differently. Always start with the best. Look for the biggest, freshest database and the ability to fine tune your search with extra commands and return the most relevant hits first. Currently, **HotBot**, **AltaVista,** and **Northern Light** appear to have the biggest databases. Of these three, AltaVista seems the biggest, fastest and freshest, but **HotBot is our pick,** as it's by far the easiest to tune, and can return **ten times as many hits per page**. Northern Light has an impressive database and a unique system of filing returns under subject folder but it's hard to tune.

Infoseek has a smaller database but gives quick accurate returns if you're just after a single URL. **Excite** and **Lycos** might prove useful if all else fails, but only if you use their advanced search forms. Otherwise, you'll have to wade through a lot of poor-quality results.

The **Search Engine Watch** (http://www.searchenginewatch .com) will tell you exactly how different engines rank plus whether they index the entire text, and not just extracts, of Web pages.

Getting the most out of a search engine

Call up a search engine and study its instructions or user tips. It's essential to know how to **state what should be included or excluded** (or more precisely, preferably included/must be included/must be excluded), and how to search for a phrase. HotBot is the simplest: you just choose the category from a pull-down menu.

For example, if you're looking for something about the band, Oasis, rather than somewhere to water your camel, you might decide to **include** "Oasis" and **exclude** "desert".

Since there's only one term to include, it automatically **must** be included. Now if you'd prefer something on Oasis, but don't want to exclude other Britpop acts, you could state that "Britpop" **must be included**, "Oasis" should **preferably be included**, and that "desert" **must be excluded**. In both AltaVista and InfoSeek you'd enter: +britpop oasis –desert The + **sign** says that it must be included, the – **sign** that it must be excluded. In HotBot, you'll need to click on the button "More Search Options" and open the "modify" option twice to get two boxes with pull-down menus. Then it's straightforward.

Now let's say you're specifically looking for something about the band Stereolab, preferably a review of their album *Mars Audiac Quintet*. The album name is an unusual phrase, and unlikely to result in false hits, so it would be a good term to specifically include. However, specifically including it would exclude any pages about Stereolab that don't mention that particular album. Thus it would be wiser to state that it should, rather than must, appear. And you'll need to instruct the engine to treat the **three words as one phrase**, or you'll get hits on Mars, Audiac, and Quintet – and lots of links to NASA and chocolate bars. So to refine it further, you could state that "Stereolab" **must appear**, the phrase "Mars Audiac Quintet" **should appear**, and "review" **should appear**. That way it's most likely that a page with all the terms will appear near the top of the results and the next most relevant under that.

Each engine has its intricacies in **grouping adjacent keywords into a phrase**, but if you enclose the words with quotes like this: "mars audiac quintet" it will work with Excite, InfoSeek, AltaVista, Northern Light and HotBot. And if you want to search on multiple phrases in HotBot, either use this method and search for "any of the words" or click on "More Search Options".

For more complex searches, refer to the individual engine's help file. Observe how they interpret capitals, dashes between words, brackets, and the Boolean operators such as AND, OR, NEAR, and NOT.

But, there's at least one product that can do all this for you, without you ever having to look at a search engine. Read on.

Search Agents

If you're a serious researcher, once you've tried **Copernic** you'll never want to use an individual search engine again. It's a standalone program that can query several search engines, directories, Usenet archives and email

databases, at once. And then it filters out the duplicates, displays the results on a single page in your browser and even automatically retrieves them for offline browsing. If you're running Windows 95/98/NT, don't pause for thought, download it now from: http://www.copernic.com

Unfortunately, the Web equivalents aren't as useful. Sure, they can query multiple search resources, but even the best, **Metacrawler** (http://www.metacrawler. com), will only return up to 30 hits from each site. The whole point of searching multiple engines is to get more hits, so you'd be better off starting with HotBot.

Shopping agents are likely to be the next big Web search growth area. There aren't many of these on the Web yet, other than **Virtual Outlet** (http://www.virtualoutlet.com) and **CompareNet** (http://www.comparenet.com) which can compare prices and stocks across selected online stores. Give them a try, but don't expect too much.

There are, in addition, **standalone searchbots** such as **WebFerret**, **WebSnake**, **NetAttaché**, and **WebCompass**, which like Corpernic, can query multiple engines and some can scan individual sites. However, they're a bit specialized and questionably useful, so we won't discuss them here. If you want to find out more, see the Software Roundup (p.425).

Note also that search engines are not the final word of what's on the Web. Just because they can't find something, doesn't mean it isn't there. It just means their trawlers haven't visited that site yet. Which means you'll have to turn to another, maybe fresher source. For instance:

Directories and lists

To browse a **range of sites within a subject category**, turn to one of the **directories**. These all seem to offer something unique. Indeed, they're so diverse that lumping them together is somewhat ambitious. What they do all have in common is that humans, rather than automatons, collate them, often add a comment, and catalog them in some kind of logical fashion.

You usually have the choice of browsing directories by **subject group** and sometimes by other criteria like **entry date or rating**. Or sometimes you search the directory itself through a form, rather like a search engine. Unlike search engines, directories don't keep the contents of Web pages but instead record titles, categories, and sometimes comments or reviews. So adjust your searching strategy accordingly. Start with broad terms and work down until you hit the reviews.

Good all-purpose directories include: **Yahoo**, **Magellan**, **Lycos 5%**, **The Internet Directory**, **Excite's Channels**, the **InfoSeek Guide**, the **Argus Clearinghouse**, and our own **Rough Guide** (we post online the Web sites and reviews in Section Two of this book). All these directories are useful for finding specialist sites, which in turn can point you to the obscure cauldrons of your obsessions.

Specialist sites

Whatever your interest, you can bet your favorite finger it will have several dedicated Web pages. And there's probably a page somewhere that keeps track of them all. Such **mini-directories** are a boon for finding new and esoteric pages – ones that the major directories overlook.

In addition, these specialist directories sometimes run **mailing lists** to keep you posted with news. If you have similar interests, you can email the Webmaster and introduce yourself. That's how the Web community works. You'll find hundreds of specialist sites all through our Web Guide, including the most popular in the **Internet Search Tools** category.

Lists

If you're not looking for anything in particular, just something new, entertaining, or innovative, maybe you'll find it in a **list**. In fact, it can be worth checking into a few lists like **Cool Site of the Day**, **Geek Site of the Day**, **Stroud's What's New**, **Gamelan**, and the **Internet Chart Show** regularly to keep up to date. And to see what's popular, try **100 Hot Websites**. Again, addresses for all these are featured in our Web Guide section.

Finding Stuff

If you start your search with the search engines and guides they'll invariably lead you to other sites, which in turn point you closer toward what you're after. As you get more familiar with the run of the Net, you'll gravitate toward specialist sites and directories that index more than just Web pages, contain their own unique content, and shine in specific areas. What's best depends largely on what you're looking for. When you find a useful site, **store it in your bookmarks, hotlist, or favorites**, so you can return. Here are a few examples, using a mixture of techniques to:

Find new and interesting sites

Search engines aren't good at finding the very latest sites. Nor do they give subjective advice, so you won't know what a site's like until you visit. Directories like **Lycos Top 5%** and **Magellan** are better because they review. But to find brand-new sites, try: **What's New**, **Internet Chart show**, and sites that showcase the latest technology, like **Macromedia ShockZone**.

Also scan **newspaper technology sections** and **magazines** like Wired, Internet World, Internet, .Net, and PC Magazine. And as mentioned before, **lists** like Cool Site of the Day,

Web100, and Geek Site of the Day are all great value for finding the cream.

Find out what others think on Usenet

You want to, but you don't know how. You want one, but you don't know which one. You have one, but you can't get it to work. You want more than just a second opinion. You want a forum on the subject. That's **Usenet** (see p.128).

There's no better place to find opinions and personal experiences than Usenet, but it's a lot of text to scan. Although it's sorted into subject bundles, if you had to find every instance of discussion about something, it could take you days. And if it was tossed around more than a couple of weeks ago, the thread might have expired.

With **DejaNews** (http://www.dejanews.com), however, not only can you scan close to all Usenet now, but a fair chunk of its history as well. That includes over 20,000 newsgroups going back, in many cases, to March 1995.

You can pursue entire threads and profile each contributor, just by clicking on the results. Which means you can follow a whole discussion, as well as check out who's who and how well they're respected. And on top of that, you can identify which groups are mostly likely to discuss something and then join the group. You'll get to the bottom of even the most obscure subject.

Like all search engines, DejaNews is pretty self-explanatory, but do yourself a favor and start out by reading: http://www.dejanews.com/jumpin.shtml

Find someone's email address

The best **email directories** are **Four11**, **Bigfoot**, and **WhoWhere**. These get most of their data from Usenet postings and visitors, so they're not in any way comprehensive, but they're pretty vast databases – and, of course, growing by the day. You can access them from their Web pages or directly from Outlook Express (Find People) and Messenger (Search Directory), both under the Edit menu.

If these fail, try searching on your quarry's full name in HotBot (choose look for the person) or DejaNews. Alternatively, if you know where someone works, search their company's Web pages – or (an old standby of detective agencies), **ring up and ask**.

For further tips, see the **FAQ on finding email addresses**: http://www.qucis.queensu.ca/FAQs/email/finding.html

Find games, hints, and cheats

Try one of the big games sites like the **Games Domain**, **PCME**, or **Happy Puppy**, or search through **Usenet** as explained above. Stuck on a level? Look for a walk-through, or ask in Usenet.

Find a product review

Generally the best place to get product advice is from a **newsgroup** dedicated to the subject. For example, if you want to know if some new nuclear flea collar works, toss it around alt.fleabags Specialist sites and magazines are always a good source, so check our listings in the Web guide or see what's under the category in Yahoo. Or, if you're really lucky, you might be able to find something in Product Review Net (http://www .productreviewnet.com).

Find something in Gopherspace

Gopherspace (see p.81) is just like the Web, but more navigable. Individual Gophers are internally searchable from a menu entry. To search the menu titles in "all Gopherspace" use **Veronica**, the Gopher search engine.

Veronica's database is compiled by trawling Gopher-space every couple of weeks, and retrieving the menu titles. All Veronicas contain the same data although some might be slightly fresher. Veronica searches produce a menu of Gopher items, which in turn point to Gopher data sources. You can find Veronica on the "Other Gophers" menu on Minnesota's Gopher server at: gopher://gopher.tc.umn.edu

Some of the **Web's search engines and guides**, particularly Lycos and Yahoo, cover Gopher as well as the Web. So you'll often find Gopher addresses interspersed among their Web addresses. **Lycos**, in fact, may actually be more useful than Veronica, since it retrieves sample text, not just menu titles.

The Gopher of all Gophers has to be **Gopher Jewels** at: http://galaxy.ienet.net/GJ/ This provides a catalog of Gopher resources and contains over 2000 pointers by category.

Find the latest news, weather, finance, sport, etc.

Apart from hundreds of newspapers and magazines, the Net carries several large **news-clipping archives** assembled from all sorts of sources. Naturally, there's an overwhelming amount of technology news, but there's also an increasing amount of services dedicated to what you would normally find in the newsstands – and it's often fresher on the Net. Occasionally there's a charge for access.

For pointers, check our Web Guide under News, Fashion, Finance, Weather, and so forth. Yahoo Daily News is a good place to start: http://dailynews.yahoo.com And for a list of news search services, see:http://searchenginewatch.com /facts/newssearch.html

Find out about a film or TV show

See the Film and TV section of our Web Guide or try the entertainment section of any major directory for leads to specialist sites. The **Internet Movie Database**, for example, is exceptionally comprehensive and its recent acqusition by bookstore Amazon.com means you should be able to order up videos of most movies, too.

Find commercial support and services

Apart from being user-friendly, the major justification for joining an **Online Service** has traditionally been the quality of the content and the user support forums. **AOL** and **CompuServe** once had the market cornered in things like travel booking services, online banking, financial data, and product support. They're still leading players but the Net is reaching out, and often surpassing their standards. And now as the Online Services are moving their content onto the Web on a pay-to-view basis, even if you only have regular Net access you can still get the best of both worlds.

Use the guides like Magellan, Yahoo, and LookSmart to point you toward **specialist databases**, **services**, **and companies** in your area of interest. Or try one of the **business directories** from our Web Guide. The most professional outfits also buy banner advertising on popular sites like search engines. So you probably won't have to find them. They'll find you.

Some companies offer **product support** channels through their Web sites, but if you want advice from other users, go to Usenet.

Find the latest software

Most people start software searches using an **Archie program** to query one of the Archie databases that accumulate FTP listings in the same way as search engines trawl the Web. We don't. Nor do we use the Web version, which you'll find in the Internet Search Tools section of the Web Guide. It's too hard. For one, you have to know the program's exact file name, or at least part of it. Half the time you're not even sure of the program's name. Imagine you've heard about a beta program called Net Drill, Netdriller, Nedrilla, or something, that caches

DNS queries locally. How are you going to find that with Archie when its program name's nedrrlb3.exe?

A much easier route is to try one of the **specialist file directories** like **Stroud's** or **TUCOWS**, and look under an appropriate category. Failing that, try coining **search terms** like "caches DNS" or "Netd*" and feeding them into the search engines, Usenet archives, and technical news clipping services like InfoMarket. As a bonus you'll likely find a description or review to tell you whether it's worth getting.

Once you've found a file, if it's proving slow to download, feed the file name into one of the **FTP engines** like **Filez**, **Shareware.com**, or **FTP Search**, to find an alternative FTP site from which to download it.

Find a mailing list

Tracking down a **mailing list** is a cinch. Subject search any of the directories in the Mailing List section of our Web Guide's **Searching the Net**. If that's not satisfactory, try the same search in a **Usenet archive** and check the FAQs from groups with hits.

Find help

If all else fails – and that's pretty unlikely – you can always turn to someone else for help. Use DejaNews to find the most appropriate newsgroup(s). Summarize your quest in the subject heading, keep it concise, post, and you should get an answer or three within a few days. Alternatively, try a mailing list.

Finding the right web address

It won't be long before you encounter a **Web link** or
address that won't work. Don't get too perturbed – it's
common and usually not too hard to get around. We
already know that many of the URLs in our Web Guide
will be wrong by the time you try them. Not because
we're careless. They just change. For example, in the
five months between the last edition of this book's first
and fifth printings, almost 100 sites needed addresses
updating. That's the way of the Net. The most useful
thing we can do is show you how to find new addresses.

Error codes

When something goes wrong, your browser will pop up
a box with a message and **error code, or display a page
with an error message** – that or nothing will happen, no
matter what you try. To identify the source of the problem, get familiar with the types of errors. Different
browsers and servers will return different error messages, but they'll indicate the same things. As an
exercise, identify the following errors:

Incorrect host name

When the address points to a **nonexistent host**, your
browser should return an error saying "Host not
found." Test this by keying: http://www.rufgide.com

Illegal domain name

If you specify an **illegal host name** or **protocol**, your
browser will tell you. Try this out by keying
http://wwwrufguide and then http://www.ibm.com (noting the
single slash before the www).

File not found

If the **file has moved, changed name**, or you've over-looked **capitalization**, you'll get a message within the page from the server telling you the file doesn't exist on the host. Test this by keying a familiar URL and slightly changing the path.

Busy host or Host refuses entry

Occasionally you won't gain access because the host is either **overloaded with traffic**, or it's temporarily or per-manently **off-limits**. This sometimes happens with busy FTP servers, like Netscape's. It's a bit hard to test, but you'll come across it sooner or later. You might also make a habit of accessing foreign sites when locals are sleeping – it's usually quicker.

When no URLs work

Now that you're on speaking terms with your browser, you're set to troubleshoot that problem URL. When you get one, first check that you have a **working connection** to the Web. Try another site (www.ibm.com should be one of the more reliable addresses).

If it works, you know the problem's with that URL (more on which below). If you can't connect to any Web site, **close and then reopen your browser**. It might only be a software glitch. Otherwise, it's most likely a prob-lem with your Net connection or proxy server (if you're using one).

Check your mail. If that looks dodgy, log off and then back on again. Check it again. If your mailer connects and reports your mail status normally, you know that the connection between you and your provider is okay. But there still could be a problem between it and the Net or with your proxy server. Check you have the right proxy settings and if so, disable them. If it still doesn't work, **ring your provider** and see if there's a problem at their end or diagnose it yourself.

To do this, test a known host – again, a good choice would be www.ibm.com – with a **network tool** such as **Ping**, **TraceRoute** or **NetMedic** (see p.73) or try logging in to an FTP site. If this fails, either your provider's connection to the Net is down, or there's a problem with your **Domain Name Server**. Get on the phone and sort it out.

If you've verified that all connections are open but your browser still won't find any URLs, then the prob- lem must lie with your **browser set-up**. Check its settings and reinstall it if necessary. Ensure there are no winsock.dll conflicts. And finally, make sure you have the right browser for your operating system. For exam- ple, 32-bit browsers won't work properly with Windows 3.x. Time to get a new operating system . . .

When one URL doesn't work

If only **one URL fails**, you know that either its address is wrong or the host at its end has problems. Now that you're familiar with error messages you can deduce the source and fix that address.

Web addresses disappear and change all the time, often because the address has been simplified, for example from http://www.netflux.co.uk/~test/New_Book/htm to http://www.newbook.com

If you're lucky, someone will have had the sense to leave a **link to the new page** from the old address but sometimes even that pointer gets out of date. Since the Web is in a constant state of construction, just about everything is a test site in transit to something bigger and more glorious. Consequently, when a site gets seri- ous, it might relocate to an entirely new host and forget the old address. Who said the life of a professional surfer was easy?

Finding that elusive URL

The error messages will provide the most helpful clues for **tracking elusive URLs**. If the problem comes from the host name, try **adding** or **removing the www part**. For example, instead of typing http://roughguides.com try http://www.roughguides.com Other than that you can only guess. It may just be that the host is busy, refusing entry, or not connecting, so try again later.

If you **can connect to the host but the file isn't there**, there are a few further tricks to try. Check capitalization, for instance: WorldWideMusic.htm instead of worldwidemusic.htm Or try **changing the file name extension** from .htm to .html or vice versa, if applicable. Then try **removing the file name** and then each subsequent directory up the path until finally you're left with just the host name. In each case, if you succeed in connecting, try to locate your page from the links presented or by browsing through directories and hotlists.

If you haven't succeeded, there's still hope. Try **submitting the main key words** from the URL's address or title to **HotBot** or **AltaVista**. Failing that, try searching on related subjects, or scanning through one of the subject guides like **Yahoo** or **Magellan**.

By now, even if you haven't found your original target URL, you've probably discovered half a dozen similar, if not more interesting pages, and in the process figured out how to navigate the Net.

Chat

There's a side to the Net that's been variously described as the online equivalent of CB radio, a coffee shop, a night-club and even an opium den. A locale where you can hold live keyboard, and more recently voice and video, conversations with people all over the world. Part of that mechanism is called Internet Relay Chat (IRC) and with other live Net chat techniques it's developing into a cheap alternative to long-distance telephone calls. It is hosted across thousands of channels, mostly on the wider Internet though AOL and CompuServe also have live chat forums, with occasional celebrity guest interviews.

The **AOL** and **CompuServe** chat forums are pretty straightforward – you get screen instructions for each session, and you will find interviews flagged on the menu pages. **Microsoft's comic chat** is easy, too, and quite cute. **IRC on the Net** is somewhat more complex and less controlled, and it's this we address, mainly, in the following pages. At the end of this chapter, you'll also find some notes on using **Web chat** (accessed through your browser) and the growing area of **Internet telephony**, which may yet pose a threat to the corporate telcos with its international calls at local rates.

About IRC

IRC, since starting in Finland in 1988, has played a part in transmitting timely eye-witness accounts of every subsequent **major world event** – including the Gulf War, the

LA riots, the Kobe earthquake, the Oklahoma bombing, and the Olympics. During the Gulf War, for example, IRC channels formed to dissect the latest news as it came in from the wire services. But, as you'll soon discover, politics, crises, and sport are not the only things discussed.

Unlike Usenet or email, on IRC your **conversations are live**. What you key into your computer is instantly broadcast to everybody else on the channel that you are taking part in, even if they're logged into a server on the other side of the world.

Some **channels** are clearly dedicated to **particular topics**, for example, #cricket, #quake, and #worldcup, but most are merely **informal chat lines**. Who knows, your perfect match could be waiting for you in an online chat channel like #hot-to-trot. Okay, so maybe not, but IRC has brought the odd couple together. A few have even held their wedding ceremonies online. If you ever get to attend one, be sure to throw some rice, like this: ՠՠՠՠՠՠՠՠՠՠ.

So, if you want to find out where the real pointy-heads play, read on.

> What's IRC? A veritable online Love Boat,
> say Mr. and Mrs. A. Hunt at:
> http://www.andyhunt.demon.co.uk

Requirements

What you enter into an IRC channel is sent immediately to everyone else in that channel, wherever they are. The only way that can happen is through **full Internet access**, or through a **local chat server**. However, you don't need a particularly fast connection nor a powerful computer. Ideally, you don't want to be paying **timed online charges** either, because it's another medium where, once you're hooked, you'll end up squandering hours online.

Many chatsters have free direct connections through university or work, so they can afford to leave their line open all day. That's one of the reasons why you'll often find **idle occupied channels**. When you enter a channel and "**beep**" **an occupant**, if they're in the vicinity of the terminal, they should answer. It's also possible they could be chatting or lurking in other channels, reading email, on the Web, or playing an online game, so give them time to respond.

A caution

Of all the Internet's corners, IRC is the one most likely to trip up newbies – mainly because you can't hide your presence. For example, on Usenet, unless you jump in and post, no-one will know you've visited. However, the second you arrive in an IRC channel **you'll be announced** to all and your nickname will remain in the names list for as long as you stay.

Chatting sleuths may be able to find out who you are behind your nickname and possibly tell whether you're a newbie from your settings. And some devious vermin might try to persuade you to enter commands that could hand over control of your computer. **Never enter an unfamiliar command at the request of another user**. If someone is bothering you privately, protest publicly. If no-one defends you, change channels. If they persist, get them kicked out by an operator. Think we're exaggerating? Then try a Web search on "hacking IRC."

Getting started

Net software bundles don't always include a standard IRC program. If that's your case, fire up FTP and download the latest **GUI client** (see our "Software Roundup" on p.425). Homer (http://www.blue-cow.com) is the most popular on Macs, and mIRC (http://www.mirc.co.uk) rules on PCs.

Once installed, read the help files and work through any tutorials. That might sound a bit pedestrian but in this case it's necessary. GUI IRC clients have an array of cryptic buttons and windows that are less intuitive than most Internet programs. And before you start randomly clicking on things to see what they do, **remember people are watching you**.

Additionally, before you can start, you must **configure your client** to connect to a specific IRC server's address, and enter your nickname, real name, and email address. If you're worried about embarrassing yourself, try an alias. Some servers, however, refuse entry if their reverse lookups detect discrepancies.

The servers

There are hundreds of open IRC hosts worldwide; many of them linked together through networks such as Undernet and Efnet. To ease the strain on network traffic, start with a **nearby host**. The best place to get a fresh list of servers, or indeed any information about IRC, is from the alt.irc newsgroup. But the quickest would be from: http://www.irchelp.org/irchelp/networks/

For starters, just choose a host from your client's menu or try: undernet.org on port 6667.

IRC commands

IRC has **over 100 commands**. Unless you're really keen, you'll only need to know a few. However, the more you learn, the more you can strengthen your position. You can almost get away without learning any commands at all with GUI clients, but it won't hurt to know the script behind the buttons, and you may even prefer it. Your client won't automate everything, so each time you're online test a few more. The "Help" file should contain a full list. If not, try: http://shoga.wwa.com/~edge/irc.html or: http//www.undernet.org

There are far too many commands to list here, but those below will get you started. Note that **anything after a forward slash (/) is interpreted as a command**: if you leave off the slash, it will be transmitted to your active channel as a message and you'll look like a dork.

Commands are NOT case sensitive.

/AWAY \<message>	Leave message saying you're not available
/BYE	Exit IRC session
/CLEAR	Clear window contents
/HELP	List available commands
/HELP \<command>	Return help on this command
/IGNORE \<nickname>\<*>\<all>	Ignore this nickname
/IGNORE \<*>\<email address>\<all>	Ignore this email address
/IGNORE \<*>\<*>\<none>	Delete ignorance list
/JOIN \<#channel>	Join this channel
/KICK \<nickname>	Boot this nickname off channel
/LEAVE \<#channel>	Exit this channel
/LIST \<-MIN n>	List channels with minimum of n users
/MOP	Promote all to operator status
/MSG \<nickname>\<message>	Send private message to this nickname
/NICK \<nickname>	Change your nickname
/OP \<nickname>	Promote this nickname to operator
/PING \<#channel>	Check ping times to all users
/QUERY \<nickname>	Start a private conversation with this nickname
/TOPIC \<new topic>	Change channel topic
/WHO*	List users in current channel
/WHOIS \<nickname>	Display nickname's identity
/WHOWAS \<nickname>	Display identity of exited nickname

Step by step through your first session

By now, you've configured your client, chosen a nickname you'll never use again, and are raring to go. The aim of your first session is to connect to a server, have a look around, get a list of channels, join one, see who's on, say something public, then something private, leave the channel, start a new channel, make yourself operator, change the topic, and then exit IRC. The whole process should take no more than about ten minutes. Let's go.

✦ Log on to a server and wait to be accepted. If you're not, keep trying others until you succeed. Once aboard, you'll be greeted with the MOTD (message of the day) in the server window. Read the message and see if it tells you anything interesting.

✦ You should have at least two windows available. One for input, the other to display server output. Generally, the two windows form part of a larger window, with the input box below the output box. Even though your client's point and click interface will replace most of the basic commands, since you probably haven't read its manual yet, you won't know how to use it. So instead just use the commands.

✦ To see what channels are available, type: **/LIST** You'll have to wait a minute and then a window will pop up, or fill up, with hundreds of channels, their topics, and the number of users on them. To narrow down the list to those channels with six or more users, type: **/LIST MIN 6** Now you'll see the busiest channels.

✦ Pick a channel at random and join it. Channel names are always preceded by #, so to join the lard channel, type: **/JOIN #lard** and then wait for the channel window to appear. Once the channel window opens, you should get a list of the channel's occupants, in yet another window. If not, type: **/WHO*** for a full list including nicknames and email addresses.

✦ Now say something clever. Type: **Hi everyone, it's great to be back!** This should appear not only on the screen in your channel window, but on the screen in every other person's channel window. Wait for replies and answer any questions as you see fit.

✦ Now it's time to send something personal. Choose someone in the channel and find out what you can about them first, by typing: /WHO followed by their nickname. Your client might let you do this by just double clicking on their nickname in the names window. Let's say their nickname is Tamster. To send a private message, just type: **/MSG Tamster Hey Tamster, I'm a clueless newbie, let me know if you get this so I won't feel so stupid.** If Tamster doesn't reply, keep trying until someone does. Once you're satisfied you know how that works, leave the channel by typing: **/LEAVE** Don't worry, next time you go into a channel, you'll feel more comfortable.

✦ Now to start your own channel. Pick any name that doesn't already exist. As soon as you leave, it will disappear. To start a channel called lancelink, just type: **/JOIN #lancelink** Once the window pops up, you'll find you're the only person on it. Now promote yourself to operator by typing: /OP followed by your nickname. Others can tell you have channel operator status because your nickname will appear with an @ in front of it. Now you're an operator – you have the power to kick people off the channel, change the topic, and all sorts of other things that you can find out by reading the manual as recommended. To change the topic, type: **/TOPIC** followed by whatever you want to change the topic to. Wait for it to change on the top of your window and then type: **/BYE** to exit IRC.

That's it really, a whirlwind tour but enough to learn most things you'll need. Now before you can chat with other chatsters, you'll need to speak their lingo.

The language of IRC

Just like CB radio, IRC has its own **dialect**. Chat is a snappy medium, messages are short, and responses are fast. Unlike CB, people won't ask your "20" to see where you're from but they will use **short-forms**, **acronyms**,

and smileys (:-). Acronyms are mixed in with normal speech and range from the innocuous (BTW = by the way) to a whole panoply of blue phrases. Don't be too shocked. It's not meant to be taken seriously. And don't be ashamed to use plain English, Urdu or whatever, either. You'll stand a better chance of being understood.

For just a taste of what you might strike, see "Net language" on p.464.

IRC netiquette

IRC attracts a diverse bunch. You're as likely to encounter a channel full of Indian expats following a ball-by-ball cricket commentary as a couple of college kids flirting. So long as no-one rocks the boat too much, everyone can coexist in harmony. Of course, there's bound to be a little mayhem now and then, but that usually just adds to the fun of the whole event.

However, some actions are generally frowned upon and may get you kicked from channels, or even banned from a server. These include dumping large files or amounts of text, harassment, vulgarity, beeping constantly to get attention, and inviting people into inappropriate channels. Finally, if you make a real nuisance of yourself, someone might be vindictive enough to track you down and make you regret it.

What's on

Although most of what goes on in IRC is spontaneous, it also plays host to loads of organized events, including **celebrity interviews and topical debates**. The big ones tend to hide behind the Online Service curtain but the Net still attracts its share. For a calendar of what's planned across all forms of Internet chat, including the structured Web-based alternatives, like Talk City (http://www.talkcity.com), see Today's Chat Schedule: http://www.yack.com

For a directory of themed, regularly inhabited, and most popular channels across almost 30 networks, see: http://www.liszt.com.net/chat/

Who's on

If you'd like to know when your friends are online, get them to grab **ICQ** from: http://www.mirabilis.com or **AOL Instant Messenger**, which comes with Communicator 4.0x or from: http://www.aol.com/aim/

These "**buddy lists**" are threatening email as the preferred tool for quick messages – which often lead to impromptu chat sessions if you're both online. But they can be a major source of distraction when your friends buzz you as you're trying to work. Email puritans also mourn the dearth of deeper discourse.

Web chat and Comic chat

Like almost every other aspect of the Internet, Chat too has moved onto the Web. About the only good thing you can say about **Web chat** it is that it doesn't require a special IRC client. All you need is your **Web browser**. Web chat is not usually as instant as IRC, as you have to wait a little while for the page to refresh to follow responses. However, if it's done through a Java or ActiveX applet, it can be just like the real thing.

For a rundown of the most popular Web chat channels, see: http://www.100hot.com/chat/

Comic Chat

Microsoft's Chat is definitely worth a quick look. You take on a cartoon character persona, and star

in a cute comic strip that's created on the fly. Even if chat's not your scene, it should keep you amused for several minutes.

You'll find it bundled with IE4.0x, or available as a standalone from: http://www.microsoft.com/ie/chat/

And if it really takes your fancy, here's where to find power tips: http://www.dido.com/chat/

IRC games

Many IRC channels are dedicated to **games**. You can sometimes play against other people, although more commonly you're up against programs called "**bots**." Such programs are written to respond to requests in a particular way, and even learn from the experience.

To find out more about IRC games, send:
info irc-games to listserv@netcom.com or see:
http://phobos.cs.ucdavis.edu:8001/~mock/irc.html and
http://www.yahoo.com/Recreation/Games/Internet_Games/

Internet telephony

The concept of using the **Internet as an alternative to the telephone network** is getting some quarters quite frisky – mainly because it can **cut the cost of calling long distance** to that of a local call (at each end). But it's an area that's well and truly in its teething phase. Although it works, don't expect the same fidelity, or convenience, as your local regular phone network.

To make a Net call, you need a **soundcard**, **speakers**, and a **microphone** – standard multimedia fare. If your soundcard permits duplex transmission, you can hold a regular conversation, like an ordinary telephone, otherwise it's more like a walkie-talkie where you take turns to speak. As for your modem, generally 14.4 Kbps is ample to the task but the higher the bandwidth at each end, the better your chance of decent sound quality.

Phone programs

There are plenty of **Net phone programs,** including: **Net-Meeting,** which comes with Internet Explorer; and **Conference**, part of the Netscape Communicator bundle. Some, like **Internet Phone**, are similar to IRC – you log into a server and join a channel. Others, such as **Web-Phone**, are more like an ordinary phone and start a point-to-point connection when you choose a name from a directory. It's worth trying a few to see what works best for you.

Microsoft **NetMeeting** is as good as any. It has **real-time voice and video conferencing**, plus things like collaborative application sharing, document editing, background file transfer, and a whiteboard to draw and paste on. Plus it's free. **Conference** will do the job, but it's a few rungs below NetMeeting both in features and performance. You'll find a variety of these clients in our "Software Roundup" (see p.425).

Video conferencing

You might like the idea of being able to see who you're talking to, but even with ISDN connections and snazzy graphics hardware, **Internet video conferencing** is more like a slide show than real-time video. But if it means seeing live footage of a loved one across the world, perhaps it's worth it, even at 14.4 Kbps.

The most popular clients are **NetMeeting** and **CU-SeeMe** (http://www.cu-seeme.com). Again, see our "Software Roundup" (p.425) for a wider selection.

Chat worlds

There's no doubt Virtual Reality can look quite cute, but there's not much call for it. The best applications so far

seem to be among the plethora of **chat worlds**, **virtual cities**, **and avatars**. These tend to work like IRC, but with an extra dimension or two. So rather than channels, you get rooms, playgrounds, swimming pools, and so forth. To switch channels, you might walk into another building or fly up into the clouds. You might be represented by an animated character rather than a text nickname and be able to do all sorts of multimedia things like build 3D objects and play music.

This all sounds pretty futuristic and it's certainly impressive at first, but whether you'll want to become a regular is another matter. Some interesting ones include **World's Chat**, **The Palace**, and **VizScape**. Once again, you'll find these programs listed in our "Software Roundup" (p.425).

If it's action and hi-tech graphics you're after, however, ditch chat, and head straight to the world of **Online Gaming**. Read on . . .

Online Gaming

Computers are entirely brainless. It doesn't take much skill to get through games like Quake, Duke Nukem and Command & Conquer in single player mode - just loads of practice. But over the Internet, playing against real people – even strangers – such games take on a whole new dimension. And things become way more serious. In fact, once you've played in multi-player mode, you'll never want to play alone again.

When home computers first appeared in the late 1970s, they weren't good for much else but games like Pong and Breakout. Back then gaming consoles and PCs sometimes let two players compete though joysticks or at either end of the keyboard. As computers became more useful in the 1980s, gaming took a back seat to business software, and game designers focused on players taking turns rather than playing together. Today, multi-player racing and martial-arts games dominate the arcade while at home, players compete on the same games by **connecting two personal computers** together. These machines needn't be in the same room. Or even in the same country. So, serious gamers no longer loiter in arcades. Not when they can have more fun at home.

Multi-player capability is becoming standard in most new games, and not just in the action genre. Almost any computer game that can be played by two or more people can be played online – from Snakes and Ladders up. Current hot numbers include: Age of Empires, Commanche

3, Caesar's Palace Virtual Casino, ChessMaster 5000, CivNet, Command & Conquer, Diablo, Hornet FA-18, Jedi Knight, Marathon, Monopoly, Myth, NetStorm, Panzer General, Quake II, Tomb Raider II, Total Annihilation, Unreal and You Don't Know Jack. And some like Netwar, Ultima Online and SubSpace can only be played online.

Come on in – we won't hurt you

To bring in another player to a computer game, you'll need to connect to their machine. The simplest way is via a **serial link**. Just run a null modem cable between your serial ports. It's a fast connection, and quick to set up, but restricts it to two players at cable's length apart. The same can be done over a **telephone line**, using modems or ISDN terminal adapters. Again it only links two players and is limited by the speed of the modem.

To conscript more victims, you need a proper network. A **local area network (LAN)** is best. That's where you connect all the machines via network cards and cables.

It doesn't cost much to set up at home, though everyone will have to bring their machines round. Easier still is to use a LAN at work. Just be sure to invite your boss to take the flak if you crash the network.

A far easier way to find new opponents, or someone to play you at 4am, is to chime into a public network – such as the **Internet**. This can be done from a number of different angles. **Commercial services** such as:

Mplayer (http://www.mplayer.com),

Engage (http://www.engagegames.net) and

Dwango (http://www.dwango.com) provide Internet accessible game servers. You log in via your ISP or Online Service, sometimes paying a premium above your regular Internet access charges. In turn your ISP may give priority to your gaming traffic to help smooth play.

Then there are **dial-up networks** set aside solely for gaming, sometimes with Internet access thrown in on top. For example:

E-On (http://www.e-on.com),

Wireplay (http://www.wireplay.co.uk),

Thrustworld (http://www.thrust.co.uk),

Internet Gaming Zone (http://www.zone.com) and

Ten (http://www.ten.net). Almost all **Online Services** and many **ISPs** also have local gaming servers set aside for exclusive customer use.

Another recent trend is for game software houses to set up their own **game servers** as part of the product package, like **Battle.net** (http://www.battle.net) for Diablo, **Bezerk** (http://www.bezerk.com) for You Don't Know Jack and **Bungie.net** (http://www.bungie.net) for Myth.

It's also possible, though trickier, to play **across the Net** directly, without logging into a special server, by configuring the game to find all the players' Internet (IP) addresses.

The problem with Internet gaming

Although it's undoubtedly the easiest way to meet other players, the Net has its drawbacks for games that require split second reactions. **Latency** is the biggest issue. That's the length of time it takes data to reach its destination. If it takes too long on a fast game like Quake, it becomes unplayable. Then there's **packet loss**. That's where segments of data fail to reach the other end and must be retransmitted. This has the same effect as high latency.

Game designers are now writing latency correction algorithms, which attempt to predict likely moves. The first, built into QuakeWorld (see opposite), works better than you might imagine. However players with lower latency times, usually those close to the server, will always be at a distinct advantage, giving the game an inbuilt bias. On the plus side, those who play on their ISP's server or on a non-Internet dial-in server are hardly affected by latency.

IPX and Kali

Network games that use the Internet's TCP/IP protocols are virtually **plug and play** on the Internet. However, older games such as Warcraft 2, Descent, Command & Conquer, Doom 2, and Duke Nukem 3D rely on the Local Area Network protocol, **IPX**.

The most popular way around this is to use an IPX to IP emulating program like **Kali** to sit between the game and the Internet. This way almost any network game can be used over the Internet by logging into a Kali server or even directly between two PCs. More about Kali, the world's largest Internet gaming network with over 350 servers in 54 countries, can be found at: http://www.kali.net

QuakeWorld

id Software's **Quake** was the first major game designed
primarily for online play. Over a network, it's usual to
switch off the 'monsters' and fight with or against other
players. You can compete independently or in teams, in
some cases with a mission to capture the enemy's flag.
Serious Quakers form clans, complete with their own
custom-designed outfits, called skins. Clan members
compete side by side against other clans or individuals.

QuakeWorld is a special version of online Quake with
several enhancements such as enabling players to com-
pensate for latency lags. It's fun, but with up to 32
players, can get crowded at times. That's where **Quake-
Spy** comes in handy. It's a program which works with
Quake to find the closest server with the lowest latency
and the ideal number of opponents.

Quake II comes with its own Netplay support for up to 64 players. For more see http://www.bluesnews.com and http://www.stomped.com

Where to find the real twist tops

Remember those ancient **text-based games** where you'd stumble around imaginary kingdoms looking for hidden objects, uttering magic words, and slaying unicorns? Believe it or not, they're still going strong on the Net. Admittedly, they've come a long way, and blended with the whole Dungeons and Dragons caper, but they're still mostly text. That's "mostly," because a few are starting to appear with **graphical interfaces**.

What sets them apart from conventional arcade games is the community spirit. Within each game, participants develop **complex alter egos** enabling them to live out their fantasies and have them accepted within the group. But it can also become an obsession where the distinction between an alter ego and the self becomes blurred, and players retreat into the reassurance of the game. If they're dialing in from a home account, it can also become an expensive one. In other words, it's about as geeky as it gets. If that sounds your bag, see http:www.cis.upenn.edu/~lwl/mudinfo.html and the newsgroup hierarchies: alt.mud and rec.games.mud

Somewhat up the evolutionary ladder graphically, but along similar lines, **Ultima Online**, the latest in the Ultima fantasy series, throws you into a continuous, evolving virtual world, complete with day and night. The idea is to create not only a battleground, but a social community for thousands of players. Again, unlike strictly competitive games, the object is to play a role and belong rather than win. See http://www.owo.com

For more information

Specialist gaming magazines, like
Netgamer (http://www.netgamer.net),
Computer & Netplayer (http://www.ogr.com) and
Computer Gaming World (http://www.zdnet.com/cgwuk/) are
often the best place to find out what's hot in online gaming. Not just because gaming companies send them
software evaluations early, but because they invariably
come with a free CD ROM full of games. Although you
can generally get game programs off the Net sooner,
with some games weighing in at over 20 Mb, it's a worthy save in download time. Especially when you'll flick
most of them out after a few minutes.

On the Net, the best source of news and downloads are
the main **games Web sites** (see p.304).

Creating Your Own Web Page

It won't take long exploring the Web before you'll get the itch to have a go yourself, and publish your own Web page. You don't need to be anyone particularly important, or a company with something to sell. You just need three things: something to say, some way to convert it into HTML, and somewhere to put it. Finding a location isn't too hard, or expensive. The logical place would be your Access Provider's server. Better providers usually include at least 2 Mb storage as part of a subscriber account. If not, we'll show you where to get it free. Though, if you're serious you should get your own domain name and shop around for the best deal on server space.

Once you have the space, you can publish anything you like from the way you feel about your hamster to your Mad Cow conspiracy thesis. Or you can use it to publicize yourself, push causes, provide information, sell your products or entertain. But before you leap out of the closet and air your obsessions or money-making schemes, do check you're not breaking any laws of decency or trade. Your Web space provider will know.

```
External Editor   □ Wrap                                    Line 12 of 188

</HEAD>
<BODY BGCOLOR="#FFFFFF">

<CENTER>

     <A HREF="../index.html" TARGET="_parent">
     <IMG SRC="../images/logos/rg-log.gif" WIDTH="412" HEIGHT="81" BORDER="0">
     </A></CENTER><P><CENTER>

</center>
<IMG SRC="../images/logos/net.gif" ALIGN="RIGHT" WIDTH="282" HEIGHT="76" BORDER="0"><
<P>
The <B>Third Edition</B> of the Rough Guide to the Internet will make you an internet
<B>Find</B> anything, anywhere, <B>send</B> email, <B>browse</B> sports, news and tra
<P><HR NOSHADE SIZE="1"><CENTER>
<FONT SIZE="+1" FACE="HELVETICA, ARIAL">
```

Putting your thoughts into HTML

Dozens of programs claim to simplify the procedure of **converting text into HTML**. These days most attempt to make it a **WYSIWYG** (What You See Is What You Get) desktop-publishing affair. However well they succeed, you'd still be advised to spend an afternoon **getting to grips with how HTML works**. The good news is that, unlike computer programming in general, it's dead easy. But, it is rather tedious. It basically boils down to writing the page in plain text, adding formatting codes, called tags (see section below), inserting instructions on how to place images, and creating links to other pages.

There's a small catch in that, like all Net protocols, HTML is under constant review – particularly by Microsoft and Netscape. As such, although a drawn-up standard exists, the latest **HTML enhancements** don't always work equally well on all browsers. Yes, as ever with the Net, the whole affair is quite a muddle.

Editing packages

The quickest way to get familiar with how HTML operates is to **create a simple page from scratch**. You won't need any complex compiling software – a text editor, or word processor, will do. However, an **HTML editor** can help by automating much of the mark-up process so you don't need to learn all the tags.

The competition between HTML editors is intense, but your choices narrow down fast if you know what kind of Web pages you want to create. Some editors excel at converting word-processed documents and spreadsheets, others specialize in basic page-creation using step-by-step wizards; some score best on image manipulation and mapping; others are competent all-rounders, with easy toggling between code views and page views. Experiment at first with one of the free, fairly basic, editors bundled with the full editions of either **Netscape** or **Microsoft's browsers**. Alternatively, you could get by (just) with desktop publishing afterthoughts like **Office 97's Internet assistants**.

Professional HTML edit programs incorporate site maintenance software which automates uploading, identifies old, key and orphan pages, spots dead links, and generally eases the daunting job of managing huge sites. Small site owners don't need and won't want to shell out for these extra capabilities. But if your online publishing ambitions extend beyond a home, contact and links page, investigate the following packages: **Dreamweaver** (http://www.macromedia.com), **GoLive Cyber-Studio** (http://www.golive.com), **Microsoft FrontPage** (http://www.microsoft.com), and **Net-Objects Fusion** (http://www.netobjects.com).

As things stand, WYSIWYG editing does not give you full control and you will inevitably end up grappling with raw code at some stage. So if you're serious about your Web pages, resign yourself to learning the basics of HTML. The rest of this chapter is designed to give you enough of them to start experimenting.

Tags

Next time you're online, have a look at the HTML which makes up any Web page. Choose **"View Source"** from your browser menu to see the raw code. The first thing you'll notice is that the text is surrounded with comments enclosed between less-than and greater-than symbols, like this: <BOLD> My Home Page </BOLD>

These comments are known as **tags**. Most, but not all, tags come in pairs and apply to the text they enclose. A forward slash signals the end of their relevance, like: </BOLD>.

THE CODE

Want to create a simple Web page? Easy. Save a blank page in a text or HTML editor with the suffix .html (eg test.html), then type in the following:

```
<HTML>(identifies the document as an HTML file)
<HEAD><TITLE>(the title goes in here)</TITLE></HEAD>
<BODY>(everything else goes in here)</BODY>
</HTML>(defines the end of the document)
```

That's it. You've created a Web page. Note that it has two parts: a **head** and a **body**. The head contains the title, which is displayed on the top bar of your browser window, as well as other more obscure bits of code. The body defines what appears within the browser window.

Everything following is a refinement.

Backgrounds and colors

You can define styles and formats for the entire body of a document within the <BODY> tag. For example, <BODY BGCOLOR="#00E4FF"> changes the page's **background color** to #00E4FF, the RGB (Red, Green, Blue) code for Aqua. HTML editors work out these numbers for you. Newer browsers also recognize literal words such as 'blue', 'red', and 'purple' – but not everyone who visits your site has a newer browser.

You can also **change the color** of four types of text within the body tag: the standard text, the text that links to other documents, the linking text that has been visited already, and linking text that has just been clicked. Just insert any or all of TEXT="a", LINK="b", VLINK="c", or ALINK="d" respectively within the <BODY> tag, where a, b, c, and d are your chosen RGB color codes. To **display a background graphic**, insert BACKGROUND="(image file location here)". You can apply all sorts of fancy effects. However, don't go overboard, as loud backgrounds often make the text unreadable.

Playing with text

To **change text size**, use <FONT SIZE=n>(insert text here)</FONT>, where n (-7 to +7) is the increment above or below the base font size. You can also change sizes with the **heading** tags, where <H1> is the largest heading size and <H6> is the smallest. Unfortunately your control here is limited: the actual size text appears when read depends on the viewer's browser and the way its settings have been configured.

Standard HTML ignores multiple spaces, tabs, and carriage returns. To get around that you can **enclose text** within the <PRE></PRE> (preformatted text) tag pair. Otherwise, any consecutive spaces, tabs, carriage returns, or combinations will produce a single space. It's more conventional to **end paragraphs** with <P>, which creates two line breaks. To create **single or multiple line breaks** you have to use <BR>.

Browsers automatically **wrap text** so there's no need to worry about page widths. To **center text** use: <CENTER>(text here)</CENTER> and to **indent** from both margins use: <BLOCKQUOTE>(text here)</BLOCKQUOTE>

Three simple but effective ways to **emphasize text** are to use bold, italic (though beware this can be hard to read on the Web), or colored type. To **bold** text, enclose within <B>(text here)</B> or <STRONG>(text here)</STRONG>

To **italicize**, use: <I>(text here)</I> or <EM>(text here)</EM>. To change **color**, use <FONT COLOR="RGB">(text here)</FONT>, where RGB is the RGB color code.

Viewing your page

To **see how your page would look on the Web**, open it up as a **local file** in your browser. Look under the File menu for "Open" or "Open page." Alternatively, drag and drop it into your browser window. And then to **see changes while editing**, hit "Refresh."

Images

Placing **graphics** on a Web page is easy. Planning and creating them is an art form. The smaller they are in bytes and the fewer you use, the quicker your page will load. So it's wise to reduce their file size first using an **image editor** like Paint Shop Pro (http://www.jasc.com) or a specialized file reduction program like SmartSaver (http://www.ulead.com). With practice, you can **reduce byte size** considerably without overly sacrificing quality.

The simplest way to **display an image** is to place it within the <IMG> tag, like this: <IMG SRC="(image location

here)"> This will display it full size and bottom-aligned with adjacent text. The picture will appear faster if you insert dimensions between IMG and SRC. You also insert page layout commands here.

For example,

<IMG HEIGHT=300 WIDTH=400 ALIGN=TOP VSPACE=60 HSPACE=70 BORDER=100 SRC="image.gif"> would set the dimensions of your image.gif to 300 high by 400 wide, align its top with the tallest item in the line, give it a border of 100 and separate it from the text by 60 vertically and 70 horizontally. All measurements are in pixels.

Alignments

You can specify all manner of **alignments** including:

ALIGN=right
: Aligns image with left margin. Text wraps on right.

ALIGN=left
: Aligns image with right margin. Text wraps on left.

ALIGN=texttop
: Aligns top of image with tallest text in line.

ALIGN=middle
: Aligns the baseline of text with middle of image.

ALIGN=absmiddle
: Aligns the middle of text with middle of image.

ALIGN=baseline
: Aligns the bottom of image with the baseline of the current line.

ALIGN=bottom
: Aligns the bottom of image with the bottom of the current line.

Plain text versions

It is generally accepted as good practice to include an **alternative text version** for browsers with images switched off. To do this, insert ALT="description of image" anywhere between IMG and SRC. This is crucial if the image describes a self-contained link.

Lines

A **horizontal rule** can be created using <HR> or, in more detail, <HR WIDTH=X% ALIGN=Y SIZE=Z>, where X is the percentage proportion of page width, Y is its positioning (CENTER, LEFT, or RIGHT) and Z is its thickness. The default is 100 percent, CENTER and 1. Or you could insert an image of a line or bar.

Lists

HTML offers three principal types of **lists: ordered, unnumbered**, and **definition**.

Ordered lists

Ordered lists are enclosed with the <OL></OL> pair. Each item preceded by <LI> is **assigned a sequential number**. For example:

<OL> On the command, "brace! brace!":
   On the command, "brace! brace!":
   <LI> Extinguish cigarette
   1. Extinguish cigarette
   <LI> Assume crash position
   2. Assume crash position
   <LI> Remain calm
   3. Remain calm
</OL>

Unnumbered lists

Unnumbered lists work similarly within the `<UL></UL>` pair, except that `<LI>` **produces a bullet:**

```
<UL>Suspected carcinogens
  Suspected carcinogens
  <LI>Television
  • Television
  <LI>Red gummy bears
  • Red gummy bears
  <LI>Toast
  • Toast
</UL>
```

Definition lists

Definition lists are enclosed within the `<DL></DL>` pair. The `<DT><DD>` pair **splits the list into levels:**

```
<DL>
  <DT>Best screenplay
  Best screenplay
  <DD>Eraserhead II, Son of Henry
        Eraserhead II, Son of Henry
  <DT>Best lead actor
  Best lead actor
  <DD>Chow Yun Fat, Duke Nukem
        Chow Yun Fat, Duke Nukem
</DL>
```

Links

The whole idea of HTML is to add a third dimension to documents by **linking them to other pages**. This is achieved by embedding **clickable hot-spots** to redirect browsers to other addresses. A hot-spot can be attached to text, icons, buttons, lines, or even images. Items containing hot-spots usually give an indication of where the link goes, but the address itself is normally concealed. Many browsers reveal this address when you pass your mouse over the link.

You can embed hot links to anywhere on the Net. Here's how to:

Create a link to another Web site

`<A HREF="http://www.roughguides.com">Rough Guides</A>`
Clicking on "Rough Guides" would load the Web page at:
http://www.roughguides.com

Create a link to a local page

`<A HREF="trap.html">Step this way</A>`
If the file trap.html is in the same directory or is mapped as a local file, clicking on "Step this way" will launch it.

Embed links in images

`<A HREF="fish.html"><IMG SRC="fish.gif"></A>`
`<A HREF="bigfish.gif"><IMG SRC="fish.gif"></A>`
In both cases, the locally stored image fish.gif contains the hot-spot. The first case launches the local Web page fish.html while the second would display bigfish.gif, which could be a different image – for example a more detailed version of fish.gif

Invite mail

`<A HREF="mailto:bigflint@texas.net">GPF Browne</A>`
On most browsers, clicking on "GPF Browne" would bring up the viewer's email program, with the send mail dialog box already addressed to bigflint@texas.net

Route to a newsgroup

```
<A HREF="news:alt.elvis.sighting">Find Elvis</A>
```

Clicking on "Find Elvis" would bring up articles in the alt.elvis.sighting newsgroup.

Commence a Telnet session

```
<A HREF="telnet://pctravel.com">PCTravel</A>
```

If the browser is configured to launch a Telnet client, clicking on "PCTravel" would initiate a Telnet session with pctravel.com

Burrow through to a Gopher

```
<A HREF="gopher://gopher.scs.unr.edu">Veronica</A>
```

Clicking on "Veronica" would transfer you to the Gopher at gopher.scs.unr.edu

Log in to an anonymous FTP server

```
<A HREF="ftp://ftp.bennett.com/paul/packet.exe">Packet Plus</A>
<A HREF="ftp://ftp.microsoft.com/">Microsoft</A>
```

Clicking on "Packet Plus" would commence the download of packet.exe while clicking on "Microsoft" would bring up a listing of the root directory of ftp.microsoft.com

But wait, there's more

Once you're comfortable with HTML logic, you can glean advanced techniques by **analyzing other Web pages or plundering their code**. Just find a page you like and from your browser menu, call up View Source. You can cut and paste selections into your own pages, or save the file and tweak it with a text or HTML editor.

That's about all you'll need to know in about 90% of cases, but if you're adventurous there are no bounds to the things you can do with a Web page. At the first level there are dozens more (fairly straightforward) tags to create **tables, frames, forms, blinking text,** and assorted tricks. Then there are multimedia options like **audio, video, animation,** and **virtual reality**. And at the top level there's **form processing** and **interactive pages**.

As you move up the levels of sophistication, you'll start to move out of the standard HTML domain, into more complex **scripting and programming languages** like **Java Script, ActiveX, Java, PERL, CGI,** and **Visual Basic**. You may also need access to the special class of storage space reserved for Web programs, known as the **cgi-bin directory**.

If you see a feature you like, and you can't work out how it's done by looking at the source code, ask the site's Webmaster, or search the Web for a good DIY document. There are plenty of books on the subject, but beware: the technology's moving so fast that they date instantly.

Java

Amongst the most over-hyped things to hit the Web in the past few years is **Java**, It's not a mark-up code like HTML, but a hard-core programming language designed to be interpreted by any computer. That makes

it perfect for the Web as you can place an **applet** (Java program) on your site and activate it from your Web page. Newer versions of Netscape Navigator and Internet Explorer have in-built Java interpreters, so visitors don't need any extra software to view it. As for writing applets yourself; if you think C++ is a laugh, it's probably right up your alley. Good luck.

Java Script

JavaScript, a Netscape innovation, extends the Java concept to HTML. You don't need any special compilers, because it sits entirely within the source of the Web page. That means you can pinch the code from other pages, just like regular HTML. It can add tricks, which are usually, just that: tricks. But if you want to, say, create personalized messages for each visitor to your site, display a clock, or spawn twenty pop up windows, then look at Developer.com (http://www.developer.com), Javascripts (http://www.javascripts.com) and WebCoder (http://www.webcoder.com). Just keep in mind that most of your visitors would rather you didn't.

Free Web space

Want up to 10 Mb of entirely free Web space within minutes? Then see:

Free Web space (http://www.freewebspace.net),
Fortune City (http://www.fortunecity.com),
Tripod (http://www.tripod.com),
GeoCities (http://www.geocities.com) or
The Globe (http://www.theglobe.com).

You'll get all the space you'll need plus free homebuilding tools to make the process of editing and uploading pages a breeze. It's all a bit too good to be true.

Be king of your own domain

Say you run a shop called Top Clogs and you'd like to flog your clogs over the Web. Well don't even consider

an address like: http://members.tripod.com/~clogs/topclogs.htm
If you want to be taken seriously you'll want nothing
short of: http://www.topclogs.com

To get that you'll need to **register the domain name**
and get two domain name servers to direct traffic to
wherever your site's located. How much it will cost, and
how hard it will be, depends on whether you want a full
top level domain like topclogs.com or a cheaper local one
like topclogs.com.nl And whether you do it yourself through
Internic (http://www.internic.net), a third party such as your
Access Provider, or a **name specialist** like NetNames
(http://www.netnames.com).

If you're combining the deal with Webspace, check out
the bandwidth thoroughly. You don't want to be stuck
on a slow server. But before you make any plans check
into Websitez (http://www.websitez.com) and **make sure your
name's not already taken**.

Your own Web or FTP server

Once your computer's connected to the Net, it can also
act as a **Web** or **FTP server**, just by running the right
software. You can even run your own server on a regular dial-up account, though of course your pages or files
will only be accessible while you're online. And if you're
using PPP, you'll have a different IP address each time
you log in, so you won't be able to pass it on until you're
online. This is functional enough if you just want to
demo a couple of Web pages to a colleague or friend.
However, if you want a serious Web presence, you'll need
a permanent connection to run your own server.

Servers are remarkably simple to install – read the
help file and you'll be up within half an hour. But take
the time to set up your **security options** to allow only
appropriate access to the appropriate directories. That

means things like making your Web pages read-only and your FTP incoming write-only. Otherwise you might get hacked. You'll find server software detailed in the Software Roundup (see p.425).

How to publicize your site

Once you've published your page and transferred it to your server, the real problems begin. You'll need to **get people to visit it**.

Before you crank up the publicity campaign, consider how you'd find such a site yourself and whether, if you stumbled across it, you'd bother stopping or returning. Most of all, decide whether publicity now would be good, or if you want to keep the site under construction awhile before you take out the full-page adverts in *The New York Times*.

On a basic level, most people will arrive at your site by taking a **link from another site** or by **typing in the URL**. That means if other pages link to yours, or people can find your address written somewhere, you'll stand a chance of getting traffic. Look around the Web for sites of parallel interest to your own and send them email suggesting **reciprocal links**. Most will oblige.

The best publicity machines of all are the **search engines and directories**. Before you submit your URL to them (and you should), find out how they work. This means, for example, establishing if they accept brief reviews, if they scan your page for key words, or if they index your site in full. See Search Engine Watch (http://www.searchenginewatch.com) for how they tick.

Whether you register or not, the biggest search engines should eventually find your site. You can skew their results in your favor by putting the appropriate key words and phrases (meta tags) in the head of your HTML pages in the following format:

    <META NAME="KEYWORDS" CONTENT ="key words and
    phrases here">

To test your meta tags, try: http://www.webpromote.com

To save time tracking down all the various engines, several services such as Submit-it (http://www.submit-it.com), Broadcaster (http://www.broadcaster.co.uk) and Submit Spider (http://www.suzton.com/SubmitSpider/) will **send your details to multiple engines and directories** at once. And if what you're doing is **new**, ask Yahoo to create you a new category, and then try Emap's What's New pages (http://www.emap.com/whatsnew/). Once you've done all that, Web Position Agent (http://www.webposition.com) and Rank-This! (http://rankthis.webpromote.com) can tell you how you're ranked.

Next, generate some off-Web interest. Announce your site in appropriate **newsgroups and mailing lists**. You can get away with posting the same message periodically in Usenet, and as many times as you like if it's part of a signature file, but don't post to a mailing list unless you have something new to say.

Don't forget about the old world, either. **Include the URL** on your stationery, business cards, and in all your regular advertising. And flash it in front of everyone you can. Finally, if it's really newsworthy, send a press release to whatever media might be interested. And just quietly, it mightn't hurt to throw a party, invite some journos, and wave some free merchandise about.

But before you tell anyone, install a **hit counter** and **statistics service** (see: http://www.countmaster.com and http://www.dbasics.com/counter/). Then sit back and watch them roll in.

Where to next?

For more about HTML, Web programming, and publicity try the following sites:

Web Developer's Virtual Library (http://www.stars.com), CNET's Builder.com (http://www.builder.com), Developer.com (http://www.developer.com) and WebMonkey (http://www.webmonkey.com).

You should find everything you need either on or linked to these sites, while for HTML editors see our "Software Roundup" (see p.425). And to check your site's health, for example, how it looks in different browsers and whether all the links work, drop in to the Web Site Garage (http://www.websitegarage.com).

On the Road

Wherever you travel, if you can get to a phone line, you can get to your email. Unlike a phone number, fax number, or postal address, you can take your email address anywhere, picking up and sending your mail as if you were at home. Read on and we'll show how the Internet can liberate you from your desk.

Going Portable

Anyone who's serious about work mobility has a **laptop (notebook) computer**, often as a desktop replacement. After all, almost anything you can do on a desktop you can do on a portable. And although at present, they're still more expensive than their bulkier equivalents – and lag slightly in chip, video, and sound technology – that margin is rapidly closing. When shopping around, here are a few things to look out for:

Weight: No matter how small a laptop might seem in the shop, it's a different experience carrying it over your shoulder for a few hours. Get one that's light.

Power: If you plan to use it on a plane, in your car, or anywhere away from a power socket, go for long battery life and consider a spare. Also ensure your power adapter supports dual voltage (100-240 V and 50/60 HZ). It's becoming standard on notebooks, but still double check before you buy. A built-in transformer is an added bonus, as it cuts space and weight.

Modem: Another space saver is a built-in modem, or failing that, one that plugs into the PCMCIA slot. Neither need an external power source so that cuts down on leads as well. If you can, get one that is flash-upgradable to higher speeds.

There's also a new breed of PC cards that combine a **mobile phone and modem**. Something most travelers don't consider is whether their modem is approved internationally. Technically, you could be breaking the law if you're caught using a non-approved modem. If you're trotting the globe, check out 3Com's Global Modem PC Cards. They have built in digital line guards, tax impulse filtering, widespread approval and software to tweak your modem to the tastes of almost every country's telephone network. See: http://www.3com.com

Network card: Modems are convenient but nowhere near as fast or as cheap as hooking into a corporate network. If you're on business, visiting a branch office, ask the IT manager to fill in your network settings. Now, that's luxury. But only practical if you plan to spend extended time there. Otherwise it's the back to the phone jack.

Warranty: Having a notebook go down with all your mail and data onboard is one of life's least rewarding experiences. If you can have a replacement shipped to you anywhere in the world the minute you have problems you'll never regret having paid a bit extra.

Scaling down

If the risk of having your $5,000 technological triumph shorted by tropical rain, or filched from your backpack, makes your skin creep, look at taking something smaller and/or cheaper. Exactly what, depends on how small or cheap you want to go, and why you need it. There are plenty of options, but many are little more than expensive novelties.

You can reduce size and weight without losing features, by moving towards **sub-notebooks** and **palmtops** that can run Windows 95 programs. But they'll cost as much as, if not more than, their larger equivalents. If price is the key, or you just need a powerful organizer, consider something like the **Psion Organiser**, **3Com Palm Pilot**, or **Apple MessagePad**, which combine basic office programs with Net connectivity, and can upload later to your main machine.

Scaling down further, you can collect your email, and surf the Web (just), with a **Nokia 9000 mobile phone**. Or, if you only need to receive mail, see what your local paging services have to offer. These, however, only work within one country.

An address that moves with you

Once you have a **reliable fixed email address**, no matter where you roam, people can reach you. Put it on your business card and say, "If you want a swift reply, email me." You might shift house, business, city, or country, but your email address

Road Trip

need never change. So, take care when choosing your address as it might become your virtual home for years to come. For more on email addresses, see email chapter, p.117. Here's how to use the various types on the move:

POP3 and IMAP
Almost all ISP mail accounts these days are **POP3** (ask your provider if you're unsure), which means that if you

can get onto the Internet, you should be able to collect your mail.

If you're taking **your computer** with you, it's doubly easy. You mightn't even have to change your mail settings – only your dial-up configuration, and possibly your outgoing mailserver.

To collect mail on **another computer**, you need to enter your **user name**, your **incoming mail server** address, and your **password**, when prompted. To send email you also need to enter your **identity** (who you want your mail to appear it's come from) and your **return address** (your email address). Although you can often use your regular **outgoing mailserver** address, you'll get a faster response if you use the one maintained by the ISP through whom you're dialing. So if the machine you're using has one set, leave it be.

If your connection's slow or difficult, you can **configure your mail program** to download the first 1 Kb or so of each message and then select which you want to read. Alternatively, if your mailserver supports **IMAP** (a superior form of POP mail which allows you to manage mail on the server – again, ask your provider), you can download just the headers. So when you're up in a plane paying 14¢ per second to download at 2400 bps you can leave all those massive mail list digests for later.

Another way to be efficient on the move is to maintain a alternative address for **priority mail**.

Webmail

With **Webmail accounts** like **Hotmail** and **RocketMail**, you can send and collect email on any machine with access to the Web. If you don't already have an account, stop by their sites (see p.117) and you'll be granted one, free, right away.

What makes Webmail so different, is no matter what

computer you're on, you won't need to change any settings; you just log into your account using a Web browser. Plus, you can scan through your headers first and only retrieve what interests you. HotMail also provides a way to read your POP3 mail on the Web.

A few ISPs – for example **UUNet Pipex** in the UK – also provide a Web interface for their email accounts. So you can just dial into their Web page, from any machine, enter your email address and password, and read your mail.

The problem with Webmail is that you need Web access, which can make things slow or impossible over low bandwidth connections. It also has zero prestige – if that's an issue.

CompuServe's global connection

CompuServe's biggest drawcard is its globally scattered **dial-up points**. You can dial in direct to a CompuServe number in pretty much any country in the world.

Hats off to CompuServe, too, for providing an extra and bizarre way to collect your mail. You can call a toll-free number, punch in your account number and PIN, and have your **mail selectively read back to you over the phone**. This service also doubles as an international phone calling card. In CompuServe, GO Globalconnect.

Converting CompuServe to POP3 mail

Apart from being impersonal and hard to remember, the biggest problem with CompuServe's numbered mail is that you can't collect it through an Internet mail program like Outlook Express or Messenger. So not only do you miss out on the latest mail advances like HTML and encryption, it's not easy to pick up from another machine. Thankfully, that's been solved with its parallel introduction of POP3 mail.

Converting your account requires changing your email number to a personal name, activating a new POP3 account, and redirecting your old account if required. Just follow the instructions at GO Popmail or http://www.csi.com/communications/ That will you give you two addresses: one ending in compuserve.com, the other in csi.com If you wish, you can continue to collect the former as before.

AOL mail

Like CompuServe, AOL has heaps of **international points of presence**, but you can only collect using **its own software**. Nevertheless, you **don't have to dial AOL** itself. If you go to Setup and change the Network setting under the Location from AOLnet to TCP/IP, you'll be able to access AOL over any full Internet connection. That's easy enough if you have your own machine, or you can get to one that has AOL. However if you're traveling outside the US, it would be wise to carry an AOL install coaster, just in case.

Telnet

Many universities and workplaces don't maintain POP3 mail accounts. If that applies to you, you might have to use **Telnet** to log in. Once you get over the indignity of not being able to point and click, it's not so bad. You can access Telnet in Windows 95/98 by opening Run on the Start menu and typing telnet

Collecting this way will involve logging into your mail server over the Net, supplying identification, then **typing commands** into a UNIX mail program. You can also read your POP3 email by Telnetting to your mailserver on port 110, entering user then your user name, pass then your password, and list to list your messages. To read messages selectively, type retr followed by the message's number. This can be handy when you're operating over a very low bandwidth or limited by software, for example with a palmtop. Ask your ISP or systems manager for further instructions.

How to stay connected

Keeping in touch needn't mean expensive long-distance calls home to your provider. It's possible to travel the world on a single **ISP account**, dialing locally wherever you are. Depending on your deal and where you travel between, that should work out considerably cheaper – though if you only need to dial in every few days, then calling long distance with a discount calling card may be both practical and economical. Only you can tell what suits you best, but these are your most likely options:

Cybercafés and Net terminals

When you're traveling without hardware, you have to use someone else's machine. If you can't get to one through a friend or work, look for somewhere to rent

Internet time. That's most commonly available through so-called **cybercafés**. These are basically coffee shops or bars, with a few Net-connected computers up for public use. You generally pay by the half hour.

If you're new to the Net, they're the ideal place to test-drive it under supervision. Or if you're after a temporary account on your travels they can point you to a provider. Most of all though, they're an easy access point to do your email, and coincidentally meet other wired travelers.

Whether you're using a cybercafé or someone else's computer, the procedure is the same. Look for a **mail program**. There should be one attached to the Web browser. If not, chances are they use Eudora. Open the settings, and fill out your details as described earlier (under "POP 3" – see p.220). Then set it to "leave mail on server," and "CC" yourself everything you send. That way when you get back to your main machine, and download for the first time, you'll have a record of all your correspondence. Once you've finished, delete all your mail (don't forget the "sent" box), and change the settings back.

To **find a cybercafé** before you leave, try the following directories:

Internet Café Guide (http://www.netcafeguide.com),
Traveltales (http://www.traveltales.com),
Cybercafés of Europe (http://www.xs4all.nl/~bertb/cybercaf.html), and **Yahoo** (http://www.yahoo.com)

Or even easier, just ask at any backpacker's guest house once you arrive. Even if there's only one cybercafé in town, you can bet it will be close to the main tourist district. And keep your eye out for **Netbooths** in places like airports, major hotels, or shopping malls. They're like public phones, except with a computer screen instead of escort ads.

National ISPs

Most of the **ISPs in our directory** (see p.487) have national coverage or at least multiple dial-up points across a country. But this doesn't mean they'll have local call access everywhere – it may be restricted to major urban areas. Before you sign with a provider, ensure it covers your territory at local call rates. Many ISPs, particularly in the US and Australia, have a national number charged at a higher rate. Check that first and do your sums. All our listed UK providers have local call access throughout Britain.

International ISPs

Several **Online Services** and **ISPs** have international points of presence (POPs). These include:

AOL: Although AOL has POPs in more than 100 countries, many are serviced by third-party networks. Outside the UK, North America, Australia, and select European cities, you'll be hit with a surcharge. For full details, log onto AOL and type Global

APC: Set up mainly to link non-governmental organizations and social activists worldwide, APC is represented by GreenNet in the UK, IGC in the US, and Pegasus in Australia. APC members in more far-flung places like Ethiopia might not have full Internet access, but you could get your mail forwarded if you plan ahead. See: http://www.apc.org/dial.html

CompuServe: Nothing will get you up and running faster when you land in a new city than a CompuServe account. Like AOL, though, it relies on variety of networks once you stray a little. And once again, pricing varies between countries. It's never going to be as a cheap as a local ISP. But you can treat it like any ISP, forgo its software and dial through, say, Windows 95 Dial-up networking.

However at the time of writing not all countries offer full IP, and some require a different dial-up script. If you intend to visit any such countries you'd better keep a CIM installation CD handy. Then it's just a matter of picking the network from a drop-down menu. Of course, if it's not full IP you won't be able to browse the Web, or pick up your POP3 mail. But you will be able to use compuserve.com mail. Best to do your research before you set out. You'll find all you need to know at: GO Phones

EUNet: The leading Europe-based ISP, EUNet maintains local POPs in most of Europe, the former USSR, North Africa, and North America. Charges are US$40.00 for the first 90 minutes then 12¢ per minute thereafter. See http://traveller.eu.net

IBM Internet Connection: Big Blue subscribers get full reciprocal Internet access in over 50 countries – though charges vary between regions. Outside the US, it's aimed more at the corporate user so don't expect a cheery welcome. See http://www.ibm.net

Microsoft Network: Just click on the icon in Windows 95/98 for details of MSN's full Internet access in worldwide centers including the US, UK, Australia, France, Germany, Canada, and Japan. Or see http://www.msn.com

Netcom: Local call access is offered throughout much of North America, and the entire UK, plus global roaming through GRIC. (see below). More details at http://www.netcom.com and http://www.netcom.net.uk

Prodigy: With ventures in China, Africa, and Latin America you'd expect reciprocal access from Prodigy, however as yet it hasn't been announced. At this stage, it's restricted to North America. If you're venturing into the regions above, though, it might be worth calling to see if you can secure a local account before you leave. See http://www.prodigy.com

UUNet: UUNet/Pipex Dial subscribers can pay extra for a month (or more) reciprocal international access – in selected cities in North America, Europe, Australia and Asia. For more, see http://www.dial.pipex.com/services/roaming/

Global roamers

Another way of ensuring international access is to join an ISP that belongs to a **global roaming group**. This means you can dial into any ISP in the group. However you'll be billed by the minute for the convenience. That is fine for email but if you plan to surf the Web abroad, it might be better value signing up with a local. See GRIC (http://www.aimquest.com) and the i-Pass Alliance (http://www.ipass.com) for their lists of participating ISPs, or to access i-Pass members without a home account, see HomeGate (http://www.homegate.net).

Jacking in

No matter what your account, you'll get nowhere fast if you can't **get your modem talking** to the phone system. This is where it can get a bit technical, especially when you're abroad, so be prepared to roll up your sleeves. Here's what you should know:

Foreign plugs

If you think the variety of power plugs is crazy, wait until you travel Europe with a laptop and modem. There are six different varieties of phone jacks in Germany alone. Nevertheless, thanks to wired travelers, the US **RJ11 plug** is becoming somewhat of a world standard.

Trouble is, some countries use this plug but connect the two wires to different pins. So, before you set out, get a **lead/adapter** that plugs into your modem at one end with a US-wired RJ11 plug/socket at the other. As long as you travel with this setup, you'll have no trouble finding an adapter at a local airport, electrical store, or market. Or if you'd like to prepare in advance, grab a plug bundle such as TeleAdapt's Laptop Lifeline (http://www.teleadapt.com).

Dial tone detect

It's a rare modem that's smart enough to recognize every foreign dial tone, and if it's been instructed to **wait for a tone before dialing**, you mightn't get anywhere. If dial tone errors persist, or your modem refuses to dial, switch this setting off. It's usually as simple as checking a box in your dialer. If not, you'll need to insert the **Hayes command X1** into the modem's initialization string. Refer to your modem manual for more on initialization strings.

Then there is the question of **pulse or tone**? Pick up a phone and dial. If it sends beeps, set it to tone dialing. If it makes clicking sounds, set it to pulse.

Manual dialing

Sometimes you need to dial with a **phone in parallel**. For example, if you have to go through an operator or calling card company, or if the phone system won't recognize your modem's tones. If that's the case, **turn the dial detect off** and set it to dial a short number, say 123. Have it ready to dial with one key press or mouse click. Now, dial your provider with the phone. When the other modem answers, press, or click, to fire off your dialer. As soon as you hear the two modems handshaking, hang up the phone and you'll be away.

Public phones

In the US, Australia, and Asia (though rarely at present in Europe), an increasing number of phones at airports, convention centers, and hotel lobbies have **modem ports** – generally RJ11 sockets. Other public phones can be used by means of an **acoustic coupler**, which you just strap over the handset. Roadwarrior (http://www.warrior.com) sells a beauty that transfers up to 28.8 Kbps, while TeleAdapt's model peaks at 24 Kbps.

If the handset has a carbon microphone, give it a tap first to loosen the grains, but don't expect better than 2400 bps. However you connect, you'll need to dial manually (see p.228).

Planes

Don't set your hopes too high on surfing the Net at 35,000 feet. Yes, with the wide-scale introduction of **satellite telephony** in planes, it's possible. But, at present it's limited to a speed of 2400 bps, with 9600 bps some way on the horizon. At up to US$10.00 per minute, you'd only use it for the most urgent email.

Digital PBX

Most offices and hotels run their own **internal PBX phone systems**. What matters to you is whether the extensions are hooked to the exchange using **digital** or **analogue** techniques. If it's digital, your modem won't like it. At worst, it could cause damage. If you strike a digital system, look around for an alternative line. Try the fax line, for starters. Otherwise, you might need to use an acoustic coupler or a device like TeleAdapt's **TeleSwitch** or Road Warrior's **Modem Doubler** to tap you in between the handpiece and the phoneset.

Hard wiring

More often than not, hotel phones are wired directly into wall sockets. If you don't have an acoustic coupler, you'll have to tap in. In that case, before you set out, pick up a **telephone line tester** and a **short patch cord** with an RJ11 female socket at one end and a pair of alligator clips on the other. You can get both from TeleAdapt, Road Warrior, or any good computer store. If you can't get a patch cord it's easy enough to make – just find an extension lead, cut off the male end and crimp clips to

the right two wires (usually the red and green, but use your line tester for confirmation). You'll find clips at any electronic store.

When you're ready to operate, fish around for something to unscrew that will expose wires. Inside the mouthpiece is sometimes a good bet. Once you've tapped in, check the polarity with the line tester. Keep trying wires until you get the green light. That's all there is to it. Just plug in to your new extension and dial.

Dropouts

If you keep losing your connection, it could be something simple. First check that "**call waiting**" is switched off. Those beeps that tell you someone's waiting will knock out your modem every time. Next, **unplug any phones that share the same line**. Some phones draw current from the line every few minutes to keep all those numbers stored in memory.

It could also be the **secret police** bugging your line. Don't laugh, it happens in certain countries. And after all, if your hotel cleaner spots you hunched on the floor tapping in messages, jacked in through a nest of clips and wires, you probably will look a bit suspicious.

Mostly, however, it's just a noisy line and there's nothing you can do.

Tax impulsing

A few countries – Austria, Belgium, Czech Republic, Germany, India, Spain, and Switzerland, among them – send metering pulses down the line to measure call times. Unless your modem is approved in these countries, the pulses will slow down or knock out your connection. A solution is to fit a filter, such as TeleAdapt's **TeleFilter**, between your modem and the line.

Faxes and voicemail

Although thanks to email, the fax's days are clearly numbered, many still cling to this antediluvian protocol. But what do you do if your fax is in Houston, and you're in Hochow? **Jfax** (http://www.jfax.com) has the answer. It can allocate you a phone number in one of several cities worldwide. Any fax sent to this number is converted to an email attachment and redirected to your email address. It can also take voicemail messages, forwarding them on as highly-compressed audio files.

Most **Online Services** offer this, or a similar, service, as do several large ISPs such as **UUNet** (http://www.uu.net) and **PSInet** (http://www.psi.net).

Further info

As the world wakes up to this new era of computer mobility, you'll see loads of new products and new opportunities.

For **general news** read
Mobilis (http://www.volksware.com/mobilis/) and
On the Road (http://www.roadnews.com).

For tips on how to **connect worldwide**, see
Help for World Travelers (http://www.kropla.com).

For **adapters, insurance, advice, and support** see
TeleAdapt (http://www.teleadapt.com) and
Road Warrior (http://www.warrior.com).

And for more on **portable computers** see
Notebook User (www.notebookuser.com),
Lapland (http://www.ccia.com/~wsw/lapland/), and the
Portable Computing Center
   (http://www.enteract.com/~epbrown/).

PART TWO

The Guide

World Wide Web Sites

Usenet Newsgroups

Software Roundup

World Wide Web Sites

No-one knows exactly how many addresses are accessible from the World Wide Web. Several hundred million, probably. But that's not just Web pages. Its tentacles also reach into Usenet, Gopher, Telnet, and FTP, through links embedded into the pages. The Web itself, though, is the most popular part. It's a little like having your own library, chocked with magazines, music, business catalogs, academic journals, and fanzines from just about every obsessive, enthusiast, and wacko out there.

Technically, Web site addresses start with the prefix http: – anything else, although accessible from the Web, really belongs to another system. What sets the Web apart is its hypertext navigation. Any Web page can link to any other Web page, whether it's on the same system or on the other side of the world.

Almost all Web sites contain links to similar sites as well as to some of general interest. It's entirely up to the whim of whoever owns the site. For example, at the Virtual Pub, you'll find original content as well as links to other beer-related sites. Take one of those links, and you'll most likely arrive at another site with links to even more related sites. So even though there are only about 1100 sites reviewed in the following pages, they'll lead you to millions more.

FINDING WHAT YOU WANT

The keys to finding your way around the Web are the **Internet search tools and directories**. They're listed first. See "Finding It" (p.160), for how to use them.

HOW TO GET THERE

To reach a site, carefully enter its **address** (taking note of capitalization) into your browser's **URL, Location, or Address** window. Technically, Web addresses are preceded by http:// but this is not always written out, as few modern browsers require it. So if you find yourself in front of something archaic or obscure, you might need to add the http:// at the front.

HOW TO FIND A SITE AGAIN

When you see something you like, save its address to your **bookmarks**, **favorites**, or **hotlist**. To find it later, simply click on its name in the list. Or you could read it offline by saving the page to disk or switching to Offline mode. For instructions, see p.75.

WHEN IT'S NOT THERE

Some of the following sites will have disappeared, or changed address, but don't let that deter you. For advice on how to track them down, see p.176. The easiest way is to enter the title, and/or related subjects, as keywords into one of the search engines such as HotBot, Altavista, or Northern Light. Once you've mastered the Internet Search Tools and Directories, you'll be able to find anything. So, wax down your browser and get out there!

WEB SITES DIRECTORY

Most human life has found its way onto the World Wide Web, so it doesn't easily lend itself to **categorization**. We've adopted the following headings to make our listings easier to navigate. However they do tend to blur into each other at the slightest opportunity. So, if you're into music, you might want to explore "Music," "Entertainment," "Ezines," "Shopping," and "News, Newspapers, and Magazines." If you're up for fun, check under "Comedy," "Entertainment," "Weird," "Ezines," "Games," and so on. To search the Net by **subject or keyword**, try out some of the tools in our "Search Tools and Directories" section.

THE ROUGH GUIDE TO THE INTERNET – ON THE NET

We've posted the whole of this Web Guide section on the Net itself at the Rough Guides' home site. So rather than type each of these addresses individually, simply browse this chapter, get an idea of what you'd like to see, go online, then type: http://www.roughguides.com/net/ and follow the links from there.

PART ONE: SEARCH TOOLS AND DIRECTORIES

First, the sites you need to get you started and help you find your way around the Web.

THE SEARCH POWERHOUSES

The web sites detailed below are the most comprehensive search engines and directories online. They'll enable you to find just about anything you might want. Get to know them all in depth, compare their services, and come to your own conclusions about which is best for what. Save their addresses in your "bookmarks" or "favorite sites" as you're sure to return often.

Probably the best **search engine** choice is Altavista when you're in a hurry as you can expect results in the first few hits; HotBot **is good** for serious searches; then Northern Light for extra depth.

For **directories**, Yahoo has the greatest breadth; Lycos 5% and Magellan are big but subjective; and What's New tends to be the freshest.

Most of these sites have international versions, personal editions, free Web mail, and a host of other services tacked on – most of them fed from other sites.

Altavista
http://www.altavista.digital.com
Web and Usenet searches, plus translations. Huge, fast, multilingual, and discriminate.

DejaNews
http://www.dejanews.com
Largest archive of Usenet articles. Best for profiling users, reading old articles, and finding the right group to join.

Excite

`http://www.excite.com`

Web search database that's gone somewhat downhill. Requires fine key-word tweaking to get relevant results. Also maintains a reasonable site directory with some ratings. Comes in several international editions all padded out with a plethora of services like TV listings, news, weather, stock quotes, people finding, email lookup, flight booking, maps, and yellow pages.

HotBot

`http://www.hotbot.com`

First-class Web search, sponsored by **HotWired**, with several useful search options. Particularly adept at finding instances of people's names on sites. Supremely discriminate and easy to tune, and gives 100 results per time. Also accesses content from several top directories – but you might, for example with Usenet, do better by going straight to source.

InfoSeek

`http://www.infoseek.com`

Search the Web, Usenet, various newswires, and Web FAQs plus loads of other services similar to Excite. The Web search is fast and gives accurate results, but not enough of them. Appears to be paying more attention to its ever-improving Web site directory.

LookSmart

`http://www.looksmart.com`

Massive, though orderly, Web directory from the Readers Digest. Every link includes a comment.

Lycos

`http://www.lycos.com`

Various services, like news, city guides, and maps. Its Web search, Lycos Pro, is highly discriminate due to a fancy Java front end but it's flawed by a puny database. Still, if you can weave through Web directory hell to Point's Top 5% of the Web (whatever that means), it's worth seeing what it rates as the strongest sites in each genre.

Magellan

http://www.mckinley.com

Another massive directory that reviews and rates sites. But don't bother with its Web search.

Northern Light

http://www.nlsearch.com

Search a large Web database and/or special collection of newswires, journals, books and magazines. Results listed and sorted into sensible folders.

Yahoo

http://www.yahoo.com

The closest the Net has to a central directory. Big and easy to navigate by subject, though light on reviews. Loads of specialist stuff like national and metropolitan directories, weather reports, kids guides, yellow pages, sport scores, plus outstanding news and financial services. And don't overlook the local area Yahoos, which often include a few sites not in the main directory. Use liberally.

OTHER DIRECTORIES AND SEARCH AIDS

Argus Clearinghouse
http://www.clearinghouse.net

Directory of specialist Web directories that's hardly exhaustive, but meticulously maintained. Crack open the most interesting categories and bookmark anything that might be useful later. You never know.

Ask Jeeves
http://www.askjeeves.com

Ask questions in plain English for replies that are often more intriguing than useful. Searches several engines, plus its own database simultaneously.

Brittanica Internet Guide
http://www.ebig.com

Reviews and rates sites by category. Not that big, but still a good place to find some of the Web's main attractions.

Disinformation
http://www.disinfo.com

Archives the dark side of politics, religious fervor, new science, and the current affairs you seldom read about in the dailies.

Electric Library
http://www.elibrary.com

Simultaneously searches databases of newspapers, magazines, newswires, classic books, maps, photographs, and major artworks.

EuroSeek
http://www.euroseek.net

Multilingual European Web search and directory.

Gopher Searching
gopher://gopher.scs.unr.edu

Find text stored in Gophers using Gopher Jewels or Veronica. Primarily used by technological retards.

HumanSearch
http://www.humansearch.com

A search engine with a difference: you submit a query to humans (Rhode Island students), who get on the case.

IBM InfoMarket
http://www.infomarket.ibm.com

Dredges a wide selection of places that search engines miss like technical journals, newsletters, newspapers, newswires and corporate databases.

Internet Sleuth
http://www.isleuth.com

Front end to search over 2000 Web and specialist databases, more than one at a time. However it's usually more efficient to search the sites directly. So use this listing to find them.

Internet Tools
http://www.itools.com

All-in-one search, publicity forms, currency rates, parcel tracking, dictionaries, pronunciation aids, and you name it.

MetaCrawler
http://www.metacrawler.com

Bug several Web search engines at once. Limited to 30 results per engine, which in many circumstances renders it useless.

The Mining company
http://www.miningco.com

Site directory with purportedly 'expert' guides. Adds a nice personal touch.

New Rider's Official Yellow Pages
http://www.mcp.com/nrp/wwwyp/

Online edition of that plump yellow Web guide.

Regional Directories
http://www.edirectory.com

Nearly every country, and for that matter US state, has at least one Web directory all to itself. You won't find them all here, but it's still a mighty big list.

Springboard
http://www.springboard.com.au

Telstra's directory to everything Australian. See also:
http://www.yahoo.com.au and http://www.sofcom.com.au

Starting Point
http://www.stpt.com

Another general directory which aims at best of genre.

UKOnline
http://www.ukonline.com

Make this your first stop for everything British. Particularly
noteworthy for its massive Psion software archive and
superb travel section. Essential reference for bargain flights
and transport timetables.

What's New
http://www.whatsnew.com

New sites listed as they're released from captivity. Search
archives by category or country.

Women.com and WWWomen
http://www.women.com
http://www.wwwomen.com

Rival guides to the Web's man-free zones.

WWW Virtual Library
http://www.w3.org/vl/

Hotch-potch consortium of subject-specific directories
scattered all over the Web.

Yell
http://www.yell.co.uk

The biggest UK-specific Web guide plus a company A–Z, film
finder, and the UK Yellow Pages business phone directory.
And don't forget: http://www.yahoo.co.uk

BUSINESS AND PHONE DIRECTORIES

Athand
http://www.athand.com

PacBell's guide to more than a million Californian businesses. With detailed maps, reviews, and contact details, plus a sharp way to shop for a shack.

Big Book
http://www.bigbook.com

Lists over 16 million US businesses, plus street maps, reviews, and free home pages.

Big Yellow
http://www.bigyellow.com

Millions of US business listings, plus links to international business directories and people finders.

Electronic Yellow Pages
http://www.eyp.co.uk

UK business phone directory.

Scoot
http://www.scoot.co.uk

Search for a British, Dutch or Belgian business by product, name, business type, and/or location. Returns all the contact and payment details, plus Web pages if available.

Switchboard
http://www.switchboard.com

Trace people and businesses in the US.

Telstra Yellow Pages
http://www.yellowpages.com.au

Australian business phone directory complete with street maps.

EMAIL SEARCH

As soon as you get an email address, submit it to these directories if you want it made public. Most of their databases are drawn from Usenet visitors, so they're in no way complete, but still worth trying. They also integrate with related services like people finders, free email addresses, and who's online with Internet phones.

Bigfoot
http://www.bigfoot.com

FourI I
http://www.four11.com

Internet Address Finder
http://www.iaf.net

WhoWhere?
http://www.whowhere.com

LISTS AND PICKS

100 hot Websites
http://www.hot100.com
> The hundred most visited Web sites each week, overall or by category. Not necessarily accurate, but close enough.

Cool Site of the Day
http://cool.infi.net
> CSOTD still comes up with something fresh each day, but that wasn't what made it so popular. Before Beavis and Butthead Inc took over it used to be about giving Web designers new ideas. If that's what you're after try CSOTD founder Glenn Davis' Project Cool: http://www.projectcool.com

Cruel Site of the Day
http://www.cruel.com
> Something horrid daily.

Internet Chartshow
http://www.emap.com/chartshow/

Top 10 new sites of the week, as chosen by EMAP Online.

Netsurfer Digest
http://www.netsurf.com/nsd/

Subscribe to receive weekly site updates and reviews.

Top TenLinks
http://www.toptenlinks.com

Vote to create top ten site lists under various categories.

Top 50 UK Web Sites
http://www.top50.co.uk

The top 50 busiest British sites, maybe.

Useless Pages
http://www.go2net.com/internet/useless/

The sludge festering at the bottom of the Net.

Web100
http://www.web100.com

Reviews and ranks the Web's 100 'top' sites in several categories.

Wired Cybrarian
http://www.wired.com/cybrarian/

Wired's selective directory of essential references.

World Charts
http://www.worldcharts.com

Lists the 100 most popular each week in games, showbiz, music and the Web.

DISCUSSION DIRECTORIES

Forum One
http://www.forumone.com

Search over 180,000 Web-based discussion groups.

Liszt
http://www.liszt.com

Find a mailing list, chat channel or newsgroup on your
favorite topic.

Publicly Accessible Mailing Lists
http://www.neosoft.com/internet/paml/

Thousands of specialist email discussion groups organized
by name or subject, with details on traffic, content, and how
to join.

Reference.com
http://www.reference.com

Search Usenet, thousands of mailing lists, and Web forums.

SOFTWARE GUIDES

Andover.Net
http://www.andover.net

Not just one, but several, of the Net's finest file directories
that includes reviews and links to most of the best Windows
shareware in Dave Central and Slaughterhouse; a fair sized
image library and tools for Web design in Mediabuilder; and
the right source code for the job at FreeCode.

Archie
http://pubweb.nexor.co.uk/public/archie/servers.html

Find a file on an FTP site, if you know its exact name.

Browser Watch
http://www.browserwatch.com

All the latest on browsers and plug-ins.

Cool Tool of the Day
http://www.cooltool.com

A new Windows or Mac program of merit each day.

Download.com
http://www.download.com

The latest notable downloads in all categories, for PC and
Mac, from CNET.

Filez
http://www.filez.com

File search engine for most platforms. Includes descriptions.

FTP Search
http://ftpsearch.ntnu.no

Powerful, but complex, Norwegian FTP search engine.

Hotfiles
http://www.hotfiles.com

Mac and PC shareware reviewed by ZDNet.

InfoMac HyperArchive
http://hyperarchive.lcs.mit.edu/HyperArchive/HyperArchive.html

HTML dip into the InfoMac Macintosh software pig trough.

Jumbo Shareware
http://www.jumbo.com

Mammoth shareware archive for all platforms.

The Mac Orchard
http://www.macorchard.com

Daily-updated, user-reviewed Internet Software for Macs. See also: http://www.mactimes.com/puremac/

Shareware.com
http://www.shareware.com

Search several major file archives for all platforms.

SoftSeek
http://www.softseek.com

PC downloads reviewed.

Stroud's Consummate Winsock Applications
http://www.stroud.com

Mostly Windows Internet applications posted and reviewed as released. Still rates amongst the best but it misses quite a lot and many of the reviews are looking dated.

TUCOWs
http://www.tucows.com

Another highly regarded Windows Internet applications archive with mirrors all over the world.

Version Tracker
http://www.versiontracker.com

Keep your Mac up to date.

Walnut Creek CDROM
http://www.cdrom.com

Download direct from this massive shareware archive or get it all at once on CDROM.

Winfiles
http://www.winfiles.com

The latest Windows (including CE) applications, drivers, bug fixes and tutorials.

INTERNET STUDIES

CommerceNet
http://www.commerce.net

Industry consortium that promotes and researches Net commerce.

Forrester Research
http://www.forrester.com

Few research firms are as switched on to new media as Boston-based Forrester. Consequently its views on the Internet don't always come free. Those that do are here.

GVU's WWW User Survey
http://www.cc.gatech.edu/gvu/user_surveys/

The biggest and oldest periodic Web user survey. Its latest results show a marked change in profiles, reflecting the Net's convergence with the mainstream.

MIDS
http://www.mids.org

Examines the composition, content, and users, of the Net and other networks in the matrix of computers worldwide that exchange electronic mail. In graphs, maps, or text.

NUA Internet Surveys
http://www.nua.org/surveys/

Leading Internet survey results as they're announced.

Traveloco Global Node Monitor
http://www.traveloco.com/nodes/

See how far the Internet has spread. One site from every country domain around the world.

Values and Lifestyles
http://future.sri.com

The VALS program is digging deeper into the psychographic profiles of Net users with each new questionnaire. Complete the survey and discover whether you're regarded as an Actualizer, Fullfilled, an Achiever, an Experiencer, a Believer, a Striver, a Maker, or a Struggler. Marketeers, like astrologers and royals, need to class people to help justify their existence.

OTHER INTERNET STUFF

Blacklist of Internet Advertisers
http://math-www.uni-paderborn.de/~axel/BL/

How to deal with electronic junk mail and pesky advertisers buzzing your favorite newsgroups. And then if you're still feeling militant, see: http://www.cauce.org

FAQ Consortium
http://www.faqs.org

The place to find all the Frequently Asked Questions from Usenet newsgroups. Look here before you post.

Free Email Addresses
http://www.emailaddresses.com
http://www.geocities.com/SiliconValley/Vista/8015/free.html

Get 'em while they're hot.

Free Webspace
http://www.freewebspace.net

More than a hundred sites offer free homepage storage. Here's a guide to what's on offer.

GeoCities
http://www.geocities.com

Build your own free "homestead" in the virtual city that suits your style. Done through forms so you needn't know HTML and comes complete with a POP3 email address. Tripod is quicker to set up and gives you a shorter address, but doesn't include email: http://www.tripod.com

GIF Wizard
http://www.gifwizard.com

Reduce your Web-bound GIF images instantly.

Hackers.com
http://www.hackers.com

Crawl through the Net's very underbelly. Hackers, crackers, phreakers, and warez traders – it's business as usual here in Geek Alley.

Hotmail
http:/www.hotmail.com

Get a free address from the biggest Webmail donor within a few minutes.

HTML Converters
http://union.ncsa.uiuc.edu/HyperNews/get/www/html/converters.html
Convert almost any document to a Web page.

Internet Traffic Report
http://www.internettrafficreport.com

Monitor the state of the world's main Internet arterials.

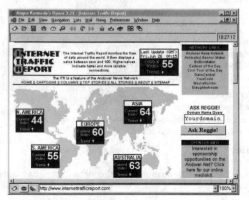

MailBank
http://www.mailbank.com

Rent a cheap personalized Web/email address combination from a range of more than 10,000 domains.

MailStart
http://www.mailstart.com

Collect your POP3 mail instantly simply by entering your email address and password. Perfect for cybercafés.

Mozilla.org
http://www.mozilla.org

Stop by Netscape's rehab clinic and see what punk hackers can do with the classic browser now its source code is out in the public domain.

Name Registration
http://www.internic.net
http://www.netnames.com
http://www.worldnic.com

If you'd like to register your own domain name, try Internic first, but if that all seems too hard then try a third party specialist. Check here first to see if your choice has been taken. The look-up takes seconds. Regional domains, which end in a country code, are usually cheaper. See:
http://www.uninett.no/navn/domreg.html

NetMind
http://www.netmind.com

Alerts you when a Web page changes. As does:
http://www.getreminded.com

Newsgroups in Oxford
http://www.lib.ox.ac.uk/internet/news/

Automatically compiled hypertext list of Usenet groups, FAQs, and reviews.

NewzBot
http://www.jammed.com/~newzbot/

If you're behind a firewall at work or your ISP's Usenet coverage is lacking, try an open news server. This list is generated by a bot that looks for open ports. But if it's open unintentionally, and they notice a marked increase in traffic, they may shut the door. Also provides a way to read Usenet postings via the Web.

Scambusters
http://www.scambusters.org

Bulletins exposing the sharks who prey on gullible Net newbies.

Search Engine Watch
http://www.searchenginewatch.com

Don't believe any search engine's hype about it being the biggest or freshest. Don't even believe what you read in magazines. Here's the truth.

Six Degrees
http://www.sixdegrees.com

Network the Net, by submitting all your friends' email addresses.

Top Hosts
http://www.tophosts.com

Directory, and ratings, of commercial Webspace hosting services.

Web page design
http://www.builder.com
http://www.webmonkey.com
http://www.developer.com
http://www.stars.com

Everything from building your first page to professional site management.

World Wide Web Consortium
http://www.w3.org

Read all the hard core technical specs on the Web's next generation.

PART TWO: WEB SITES
SUBJECT GUIDE

First off, a disclaimer. This isn't a definitive guide to the best Web sites. That just isn't possible any more: there are too many sites, and besides, it's a matter of personal tastes and interests. However, the range here should be broad enough, and each site should house enough links to eventually get you where you want to go. So, get clicking!

ART AND PHOTOGRAPHY

24 hours in Cyberspace
http://www.cyber24.com

Collective output of over 1000 photographers and 100 photojournalists documenting the impact of the digital revolution on 8 February 1996, everywhere from the Sahara to Times Square.

A Life Garden
http://alifegarden.com

Adopt a virtual organism and set it loose in a hostile critter-eat-critter environment. Not unlike:
http://www.technosphere.org.uk

Americans for the Arts
http://www.artsusa.org/clearinghouse/

US government sponsored index to the arts, focusing mainly on how to get your mitts on the gravy.

ArtAIDS Link
http://www.illumin.co.uk/artaids/

Internet equivalent of the AIDS patchwork quilt. Upload your own tribute to this ever-growing mosaic of love, loss, and memory.

The Art Connection

http://www.art-connection.com

See what's for sale in a selection of London's top commercial galleries.

Art Crimes: Writing on the Wall

http://www.graffiti.org

Diverse collection of international graffiti art, showcasing the works of youths with little to say, speaking their minds.

Big Fire Anime

http://www.bigfire.com/bigfire.htm

Monstrous archive of Japanese cartoon art and software. See also: http://otakuworld.com

Chankstore Freefonts

http://www.chank.com/freefonts.html

Download a wacky Chank Diesel display font free each week.

Clip Art

http://www.clipart.com
http://www.clipartconnection.com

Somewhere down the artistic spectrum beneath Pierrot dolls, velvet prints, muzak, and butt photocopies lies clip art. For some reason, this soulless dross is often used to inject life into documents and overhead transparencies. To make your next presentation look thoroughly canned, dig in here.

Comics Page

http://www.comics-page.com

Even with a fast, fat connection, reading comics on the Net can be pretty tedious. But if you're into them as a communications medium, or art form, there's ample here.

Core-Industrial Design Resources

http://www.core77.com

Industrial design exhibits, jobs, chat, and tips on how to get yourself seen.

Dancing Baby

http://www.viewpoint.com/features/baby/

Here's where that dancing baby
movie came from and where you'll
find more in the series.

Dysfunctional Family Circus

http://www.spinnwebe.com/dfc/

Write your own twisted Family
Circus captions.

The Font Fairy

http://ourworld.compuserve.com/homepages/kayhall/

Stuff your sack with free fonts.

Font Net

http://www.type.co.uk

As with almost everything Neville Brody – uber-
designer of **The Face**, **Arena**, and **Actuel** – touches, his Web
debut oozes style at every turn. But there's substance as well
in the form of various font samples and **Fuse** magazine
posters, along with persistent urging to buy FontWorks' type
products.

Grokware Flowfazer

http://www.grokware.com/Flowfazer.html

Generate swirly psychedelic patterns in a Java window and
then find out what became of Todd Rundgren.

Internet Type Foundry Index

http://www.typeindex.com

Typeface news, plus a directory of font and design resources.

Joke Wallpaper

http://www.jokewallpaper.com

Corny backgrounds for your desktop.

King Features

http://www.kingfeatures.com

You should know most of King's comics because just about
every city in the world has a newspaper that runs its daily
strips. If you like Juliet Jones, Popeye, Zippy, The Phantom,
Blondie and that lot, you can dip back into the archives and

bring yourself up to date. For Dilbert, Peanuts, Tarzan and the rest of the United Media family, see:
http://www.unitedmedia.com/comics/

Life
http://www.pathfinder.com/Life/

View **Life** magazine's picture of the day, then link through to some of the world's most arresting photographs. Don't expect to have much change left from an hour.

Ping Datascape
http://www.artcom.de/projects/ping/

Add to a 3D flight through the Web. Conceived as a TV test pattern but seems to have come off the rails.

Pitchford's Panoramas
http://www.pitchford.com

QuickTime VR whizzkid Dave Pitchford's 360 degree snapshots of his jaunts from Sydney to Sarajevo. Straight up they'll look like regular photos. But just watch what happens when you drag them around with your mouse. Alas, from now on your family album's going to look a tad flat.

Production Book Online
http://www.pb.com.au/pb/

More than 18,000 pages of Australian advertising, film, TV, and multimedia contacts.

Red Meat
http://www.redmeat.com

Dark comic humor from deepest Middle America.

The Secret Garden
http://www-personal.umich.edu/~agrxray/

Stunning gallery of X-rayed flowers.

Sensorium
http://www.sensorium.org

Bizarre Japanese geek art projects like listening to the sound of the Internet as a living organism by assigning musical tones to protocol requests.

SITO
http://www.sito.org

Photos, drawings, tattoos, ray-traces, video stills, record covers, sculpture, art links, and more.

Spumco's Wonderful World of Cartoons
http://www.spumco.com

Animated Shockwave movies from the creators of Ren & Stimpy.

Stelarc
http://www.merlin.com.au/stelarc/

No-one hangs naked from a hoist suspended only by flesh-piercing hooks (while onlookers from the Net control their robotic third arm) with more grace than Stelios Arcadiou.

Stereogram pages
http://www.ccc.nottingham.ac.uk/~etzpc/sirds.html

Create your own Magic Eye pictures or download others' spotty 3D creations. Soon you'll induce migraines at will.

Stick Figure Death Theater
http://www.calvert.com/sfdt/sfdt.html

Stickcity citizens meet their sticky ends. Like a minimalist Itchy & Scratchy.

Synergy Grid
http://www.sito.org/synergy/panic-grid.html

Find out how to create collaborative image grids or use the infinite grid selector to tailor a multi-layered psychedelic collage to your favorite of only 12,288,000,000 possible configurations.

World Wide Art Resources
http://wwar.world-arts-resources.com

Biggest index of everything arty from the mandatory real world galleries, online exhibits and artists' pages to the more obscure tentacles like embroidery, belly dancing, and clock collecting. It's impeccably categorized, mostly reviewed, and maybe all the preparation you need before attempting to wade through a sticky web of slow-loading fuzzy pictures.

Year in the Life of Photojournalism
http://www.digitalstoryteller.com/YTL/

Tag along with several professional voyeurs and see what they do in their day to day.

BANKING

Many banks offer online services, though few as yet allow access to records via the Internet. It's more common to install special software and dial into their modem banks.

DigiCash
http://www.digicash.com

DigiCash is right on the verge of introducing an acceptable "smart" currency for Net transactions. After years of playing with toy money, real banks are taking interest. Here's where it all started.

MasterCard International
http://www.mastercard.com

Like Visa, DigiCash, and First Virtual, MasterCard appears
well poised to profit from developments in electronic
payments, smart cards, and online transactions. You'll get a
somewhat rosy idea of where it's all heading by delving
through these pages, plus whatever MasterCard information
you could possibly want – other than your balance.

Online Banking Report
http://www.netbanker.com

Use this as a starting point to shop for a true Internet bank
or track down your own bank's site.

Visa International
http://www.visa.com

Will Visa achieve "One World, One Currency – Visa"? Who
knows, but they certainly have an edge in electronic
banking. As this site drums home.

World Bank
http://www.worldbank.org

The World Bank mainly tries to help developing countries
reduce poverty and sustain economic growth. If you're
perplexed by how it can give away so much money and still
stay afloat, you might come away a little more enlightened.

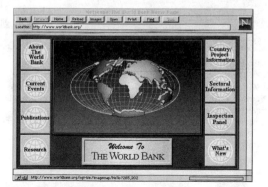

BOOKS AND BOOKSTORES

Amazon Books
http://www.amazon.com

Not only the world's most successful online bookstore, but often cited as the Web's biggest success story, even though it's not shown a profit to date. Featuring over 2.5 million discounted titles, many reviewed by visitors, and all searchable by author, title, and keywords. Delivery, gift-wrapped to please, is swift, both within the US and internationally, and the introduction of a CD and video store means you can pack a shopping trolley with multi-media treats.

Atomic Books
http://www.atomicbooks.com

John Waters, director of cult movie classics, **Pink Flamingos**, and **Female Trouble**, frequents this Baltimore shop in search of "insane books about every kind of extreme." Thanks to a Web linked storecam you can spy such clientele as you order online. For more of the same, see:
http://www.fringeware.com/shop/

Banned Books Online

http://www.cs.cmu.edu/Web/People/spok/banned-books.html

See which books have been banned or come under attack, and why, by reading the contentious extracts. Many titles are now considered classics.

Barnes and Noble

http://www.barnesandnoble.com

The world's biggest bookseller – it issued legal proceedings against Amazon to prove the point – on the Web. All titles are discounted for online sale, for dispatch to anywhere in the world. Like Amazon, it has loads of literary tidbits and links to what the press are saying.

Bibliofind

http://www.bibiliofind.com

This is the Web at its best: a search tool that pulls together some six million old, used and rare books offered by 2000 US booksellers – and all orderable online. It claims with some justice to be the most interesting bookstore on the Net.

Blackwells

http://bookshop.blackwells.co.uk

Order online from one of the world's leading (UK-based) academic booksellers.

The Bookpl@ce

http://www.thebookplace.com

Apart from stocking over 1.5 million books, the most notable thing about UK high street chain Dillons' online shop is that its search engine indexes descriptions as well. You might find that useful if you're looking for the best title on some obscure topic.

Bookwire

http://www.bookwire.com

Literary goldmine charged with bundles of reviews, publishing news, bestseller lists, an author tour calendar, and links to other such nooks Netwide.

Borders
http://www.borders.com

Borders are Barnes & Noble's chief rivals in terrestial bookselling. Their stores are funky places, with good staff picks on both books and music, as well as the usual superstore range and discounts. The online site follows a similar formula. Like Amazon, it allows seamless ordering of books, CDs and videos, and ships internationally.

Dymocks
http://www.dymocks.com.au

Order direct from Australia's best-stocked chain.

Etext Archives
http://www.etext.org

Hundreds of thousands of words, ranging from the complete works of Shakespeare to the script of a lost episode of Star Trek. Plus links to similar archives of religious, political, legal, and fanzine text.

Eland Books
http://www.travelbooks.co.uk

A small press – and a neat example of how such publishers can rival the big boys online. Read short extracts from any of Eland's travel narratives, then order the rest . . .

Elsevier Science
http://www.elsevier.nl

Elsevier claims to be the world's leading supplier of scientific information. On board is an exhaustive list of its journals, publications, and multimedia products, plus news, reviews, and ordering channels.

Future Fantasy Bookstore
http://futfan.com

Order fantasy, horror, science fiction, and mysteries, by email.

The Internet Public Library
http://ipl.sils.umich.edu

Links to thousands of online books, magazines, journals, and newspapers.

Kaiser Books

http://kbc.com

Books or magazines, on or off the Net, you'll find a way to get them from here. If not in the book and magazine marketplace, then maybe amongst the hundreds of links, or from a shop in the secondhand bookstore directory.

Literary Kicks

http://www.charm.net/~brooklyn/LitKicks.html

Shrine to the Beats with a mass of fine audio and text on Kerouac, Corso, Ginsberg, Cassady, and all who came into their Beat orbit.

Loompanics

http://www.loompanics.com

Get your hands on some subversive, strange, and sometimes downright nasty gems of anarchic and alternative writing.

Macmillan USA

http://www.mcp.com

Goes further than most publishers, putting searchable contents pages and full chapter samples for many of its thousands of books online. What's more, you can download copies of any software included with computer titles, here or from its FTP site.

Online Books

http://www.cs.cmu.edu/Web/books.html

Complete texts lie tucked away in obscure archives all over the Net. Here's an index of about a thousand titles as well as links to almost 100 specialist repositories.

Penguin Books

http://www.penguin.com   http://www.penguin.co.uk

What's new, and catalogs, from Penguins on both sides of the Atlantic. Featured books include extracts and a number of authors get their own mini-sites.

Poetry Society

http://www.poetrysoc.com

UK halfway house for budding poets and victims. Americans will find more reasons to rhyme at: http://www.poets.org

Project Gutenburg
http://promo.net/pg/

Fifty years or so after authors croak, their copyrights pass into the public domain. With this in mind, Project Gutenburg is dedicated to making as many works as possible available online in plain vanilla ASCII text. Not all the books are old, however – some, such as the computer texts, have been donated. As great as that sounds, in practice you might prefer the convenience of hard copy.

Pure Fiction
http://www.purefiction.com

For pulp worms and writers alike. Packed with book previews, author interviews, and hundreds of links to the sort of stuff you need to get off the ground and punch out your first bestseller. See also: alt.books.purefiction

Thomas Pynchon Home Page
http://www.pomona.edu/pynchon/

Archives of Pynchon-l, the fiery mailing list that inspired the book **Lineland**, plus all the literary fandom you'd expect from one of Net culture's most popular authors.

Shakespeare
http://the-tech.mit.edu/Shakespeare/

The Bard's complete works online.

Sun Tzu's The Art of War
http://zhongwen.com/bingfa.htm

Discover Sun Tzu's **The Art of War** in English, or Chinese script. At 2400 years old, it's believed to be the world's oldest military treatise. Like other Chinese wisdom such as the teachings of Confucius, much of it still rings true and its adages can be applied to any conflict. So much so, that it became the Yuppies' surrogate bible. Oh well, battles do have their casualties.

Tech Classics Archive
http://classics.mit.edu

Searchable archive of hundreds of translated Greek and Roman classics.

UK Online Bookshops

http://www.bookshop.co.uk
http://www.bookpages.com
http://www.alphabetstreet.com

Pretty much the same deal as Amazon, but with a better
range of British releases. Naturally, the freight works out
cheaper too, if you're shipping within Europe.

Urban Legends

http://www.urbanlegends.com

Repository for dubious yarns compiled from alt.folklore.urban

Waterstones

http://www.waterstones.co.uk

Britain's best browsing bookshop chain has the elegant,
content-rich site you'd expect, including a pick of the
newspaper book reviews, archives of its in-house magazine,
and a rare book search for out of print stock.

The Yarn

http://www.theyarn.com

In this story, you'll be faced with two options at the end of
each chapter. Your choice will either lead you to a new
chapter or you'll be invited to contribute your own. It makes
for some wild plot twists.

BUSINESS

Advertising Age
http://www.adage.com

Newsbreaks from the ad trade.

Barcode Server
http://www.milk.com/barcode/

Find out how bar codes work, then generate your own.

Business Index
http://www.dis.strath.ac.uk/business/

It may look low key, but start here, and you'll be no more
than a few clicks away from almost any business-related site.

Companies Online
http://www.companiesonline.com

Get the score on over 100,000 public and private companies.

Corporate Grantmakers
http://fdncenter.org/grantmaker/corp.html

Companies who might spare you a fiver.

Direct Marketing World
http://www.dmworld.com

How to junk mail and influence people.

Entrepreneurmag
http://www.entrepreneurmag.com

Get rich now, ask us how.

FedEx
http://www.fedex.com

Federal Express has revolutionized the way carriers haul
freight, take orders, and service customers. Now it's moved
online, you can book shipping, track parcels, or compare
rates with UPS at: http://www.ups.com

Friends and Partners
http://solar.rtd.utk.edu/friends/home.html

US–Russian joint venture to help create a better understanding between the old foes. There's economics, education,
geography, music, weather, and health, plus a literature

section which contains the full text of **The Brothers Karamazov** and **Anna Karenina**. It's all meant to encourage trade.

Guerilla Marketing
http://www.gmarketing.com/main.html

How to get ahead by metaphorically butchering your competitor's families and poisoning your customer's water supply.

IBM Patent Server
http://www.patents.ibm.com

Sift through US patents back to 1971, plus a gallery of obscurities. Ask the right questions and you might stumble across tomorrow's technology long before the media. For UK patents see: http://www.patent.gov.uk

Internet Magazine's Marketing Hotlist
http://www.internet-sales.com/hot/

UK godfather of new media, Roger Green's one-stop guide to working the Web like a pro.

MediaFinder
http://www.mediafinder.com

Media profile and contact directory. Lists newspapers, magazines, mailing lists, catalogs, newsletters and more, sorted by subject focus.

MoneyHunter
http://www.moneyhunter.com

How to milk funds for your online white elephant.

Who's Marketing Online
http://www.wmo.com

What's new in Web marketing trends, including new site reviews from an ad campaigner's perspective.

COMEDY

Archive of Useless Facts
http://www.lsds.com/key/facts/

Just the sort of stuff you didn't want to know, but are glad you do.

Biggest List of Humor Sites on the Net
http://www.bigron.com

Bit of a lucky dip. Take a link, strike it lucky, and you'll get to laugh.

Bonk Industries
http://www.telegate.se/bonk/

Surreal dig at corporate propaganda.

Citizen's Self-Arrest Form
http://www.uoknor.edu/oupd/selfarr2.htm

Time to give yourself up, son.

Comedy Channel
http://www.aentv.com/home/chcomedy.htm

Live and archived stand-up routines in Real Video.

Complaint Letter Generator
http://www-csag.cs.uiuc.edu/individual/pakin/complaint/

Someone getting on your goat, but stuck for the right words? Just mince their details through here for an instant dressing down.

Dobe's Punny Name Archive
http://www.eskimo.com/~dobe/

Thousands of unwise baby names.

Doonesbury Electronic Town Hall
http://www.doonesbury.com

Need your daily dose of Gary B. Trudeau online? Or a little background, or some archival strips of Zonker Harris or Boopsie? This is their official home.

Funny – The Comedy Directory
http://www.funny.co.uk

Small, but selective, guide to the top Web humorbases.

Humor Database
http://www.humordatabase.com

Thousands of jokes searchable by age, topic, keyword, or popularity.

HumourNet
http://www.humournet.com/HumourNet/

Home of the HumourNet mailing list. Join to exchange funnies or read the archives here.

LaughWeb
http://www.intermarket.net/laughweb/

Bundles of jokes sorted into categories, and rated by readers.

Pranksta's Paradise
http://www.ccil.org/~mika/

Larks and laughs at the expense of others compiled from the Usenet archives of alt.shenanigans

Pythonline
http://www.pythonline.com

Terry Gilliam-illustrated Monty Python mayhem, juvenilia, and humor, plus where they all are now.

Rec.humor.funny Home Page
http://www.netfunny.com/rhf/

Archives of the rec.humor.funny newsgroup, updated daily.

Surrealist Compliment Generator
http://pharmdec.wustl.edu/cgi-bin/jardin_scripts/SCG/

It mightn't make a shred of sense, but hey, at least it's positive.

Tony's Illustrated Guide to Unpleasantness
http://www.geocities.com/SouthBeach/Marina/1743/

Refresher course in insults.

Uploaded
http://www.loaded.co.uk

Monthly emissions from the journal of British lad culture.

COMPUTING

Sites below are just a tiny fraction of this area. Pretty
much every PC brand has a Web site where you can
download software, get support, and find out what's
new. It won't be hard to find. Usually it's the company
name or initials between a www and a com. So you'll find
Dell at: http://www.dell.com, Texas Instruments at:
http://www.ti.com, Hewlett Packard at: http://www.hp.com,
Hitachi at: http://www.hitachi.com and so forth. Consult
Yahoo if that fails.

Adobe
http://www.adobe.com

Information, support, and download areas for Adobe's
desktop publishing software.

Apple
http://www.apple.com

Essential drop in for all Mac users and developers for the
latest product info and system updates.

CNET
http://www.cnet.com

Daily technology news and features (some in RealAudio),
plus reviews, games, and downloads, along with schedules,
transcripts, and related stories from CNET's broadcasting
network. Worth reading weekly as a lightweight way to keep
up with what's what in computing.

Easter Egg Archive
http://www.eeggs.com

Would you believe there's a flight simulator in Excel 97, a
basketball game in Windows 95, and a raygun wielding alien
in Quark Xpress? They're in there alright, but you'll never
find them on your own. Here's how to unlock these types of
secrets in scores of programs.

Free-Help
http://www.free-help.com/fh_main.htm

Ask an expert to sort out your computer problems.

IBM

(1) http://www.ibm.com   (2) http://www.ibm.net

Key the first address for IBM's corporate world, products, and international operations. The second for IBM Global Network contact details, plus a helpful set of tutorials and links to get you started on the Net.

Internet Product Watch

http://ipw.internet.com

Directory of Internet product announcements.

Inquiry

http://www.inquiry.com

Answerbase for computer professionals. References thousands of IT journals and product sheets.

Macintouch

http://www.macintouch.com

Specializes in Mac software fixes.

MacNN – the Macintosh News Network

http://www.macnn.com

Mac news with links to software updates and most of the best Mac resources.

Microsoft

http://www.microsoft.com

If you're running any Microsoft product, and the chance of that seems to be approaching 100%, drop by this disorganized scrapheap regularly for upgrades, news, support, and patches. That includes the latest free tweaks to Windows, Office, and particularly all that falls under the Internet Explorer program. Grab the lot, and watch your system directory blossom.

Modem Help

http://www.modemhelp.com

Solve your dial-up dramas for modems of all persuasions including cable, ISDN and xDSL. And be sure to check your modem maker's page for driver and firmware upgrades, especially if it's X2 or K56flex. See also: http://www.56k.com

Need to Know
http://www.ntk.net

The news you need to know when you already know too much, plus a chickenscratch through what's coming up in UK TV.

Newslinx
http://www.newslinx.com

Subscribe to get the top Net technology stories, aggregated from around 50 sources, delivered to your mailbox daily.

PC Mechanic
http://www.pcmech.com

Step-by-step instructions on how to build, or upgrade, your own computer. It's easier than you think.

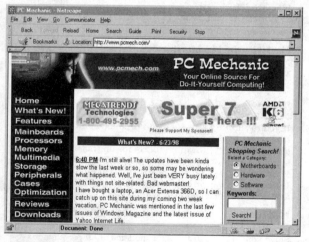

PC Webopaedia
http://www.pcwebopedia.com

Superb Illustrated encyclopedia of computer technology with loads of helpful links.

Silicon Graphics
http://www.sgi.com

All the corporate and product guff you'd want from SGI, along with some impressive demonstrations of what its high-end graphics workstations can do.

Slashdot.org
http://slashdot.org

News for those who've entirely given up on the human race.

Software.net
http://www.software.net

The time can't be far off when it will be standard practice to ship commercial software via the Net. So far only about 3000 of its 30,000-odd packages are downloadable here, while the rest are conventionally boxed for Fedex delivery.

Symantec
http://www.symantec.com

Free software, online updates and support on Symantec/Norton's award-winning range of virus, disk management, communications, and Java utilities.

Tidbits
http://www.tidbits.com

Macintosh newsletter, from Adam Engst, author of the seminal doorstopper, *Internet Starter Kit*.

Tom's Hardware Guide
http://www.tomshardware.com

How to overclock your processor, tweak your bios, and upgrade your storage capacity to attract members of the opposite sex. More courtship rituals at: http://www.anandtech.com

Windows Annoyances
http://www.annoyances.org

Fixes and replacements for many Windows 95, 98 and NT "features" and omissions.

Yahoo! Computing
http://www.yahoo.com/Computers/

The grandpappy of all computing directories.

ZDNet
http://www.zdnet.com

Computing information powerhouse from Ziff Davis, publisher of PC Magazine, MacUser, Computer Gaming World and scores of other IT titles. Each magazine provides content such as news, product reviews, and lab test results; plus, there's a ton of prime Net-exclusive technochow. By far the best place to start research for buying anything even vaguely computer-related.

EMPLOYMENT

America's Job Bank
http://www.ajb.dni.us

Links to over 1800 US State Employment Service offices and 100,000 vacancies. A state project that's free for all.

CareerMosaic
http://www.careermosaic.com

Search for jobs with corporate heavyweights in several countries. As with most job sites, there's plenty of advice on résumés, career trends, and salaries. Each client outlines its employment conditions and corporate guff.

Careers Online
http://www.careersonline.com.au

Generate a résumé online, get career advice and see what's on offer in the Australian hard labor market.

Cool Works
http://www.coolworks.com

Seasonal jobs in US resorts, national parks, camps, ranches and cruise lines.

E*Span
http://www.espan.com

Thousands of jobs and seekers frustratingly concealed behind a restrictive search interface.

EagleView
http://www.eagleview.com

Post your details to hundreds of Fortune 500 companies.

Hot Jobs
http://www.hotjobs.com

Technical jobs worldwide. Easier to search than most.

Jobs at Microsoft
http://www.microsoft.com/Jobs/

Get hard cash for your soul.

Jobsearch
http://www.jobsearch.co.uk

Browse or search for British jobs across a wide spectrum of fields.

Jobsite UK
http://www.jobsite.co.uk

Professional openings gleaned from a variety of employers and agencies.

Monster Board
http://www.monster.com

Search for professional employment in several countries. Like E*Span, the content's there but it's cumbersome.

Price Jamieson
http://www.pricejam.com

Easy to browse international listings mainly in new media, marketing, and communications, updated at least weekly.

Reed

http://www.reed.co.uk

Top-notch service from the UK's largest employment agency,
covering such diverse vocations as nursing, computing,
catering, accounting, driving, charity, insurance, and project
management.

The Riley Guide

http://www.dbm.com/jobguide/

Messy directory of job-hunting resources around the world
and tips on how to use them.

TopJobs

http://www.topjobs.co.uk

Technical positions vacant across the UK and Europe.

ENTERTAINMENT

!sdrawkcab

http://smeg.com/backwards/

Enter a URL and surf the Web backwards.

Aloud

http://www.aloud.com

Book UK music, festival and event tickets online. For theatre
tickets, see: http://www.whats on.com

Avenger's Handbook

http://www.ekran.no/html/revenge/

Much of this armory of nastiness is compiled from the
archives of the Usenet group alt.revenge – the definitive
meeting place for suburban terrorists. Like vicious
programs, things to do before you quit your job, school
pranks, and oodles of treacherous anecdotes about getting
even. John Steed would never stoop this low.

Card Central

http://www.cardcentral.net

You can send free multimedia greeting cards from hundreds
of sites. Instead of mailing the actual card, they usually send

a PIN number, which is used to retrieve the message. This directory lists quite a few, but you'll find dozens more in Yahoo under "Greeting Cards."

ContestGuide
http://www.contestguide.com

Enter loads of competitions. See also: http://www.contestworld.com and http://www.intervid.co.uk/prize/

Celebsites
http://www.celebsites.com

Stalk your favorite celebrities online.

Centre for the Easily Amused
http://www.amused.com

Hundreds of sites where thinking's banned.

Dialect Translator
http://www.shortbus.net/dialect.html

Translate your text into Valley Girl, Swedish Chef or Jive.

Driveways of the Rich & Famous
http://www.driveways.com

Asphalt on the senses.

Events Online
http://www.eventsonline.co.uk

Search or browse UK music, film, stage, arts, TV, kids, and comedy listings.

Famous Birthdays
http://www.famousbirthdays.com

See who shares your birthday, and estimate how many more you should expect.

Guess the Dictator/Sitcom Character
http://www.smalltime.com/nowhere/dictator/

Assume a character, and answer yes/no questions until the computer figures you out.

Happy Birthday
http://www.happybirthday.com

Create a free birthday wish page and learn how to say happy birthday in 150 languages. Here's how to say it to someone who's deaf: http://www.bconnex.net/~randys/birthday.htm

Hidden Mickeys
http://www.hiddenmickeys.org

Subliminal Mickeys hidden around Disneyland? Must be something in the drinks. And all those rumors you've heard, well here's which ones are true: http://www.snopes.com/disney/

I Ching
http://www.facade.com/Occult/iching/

If the superior person is not happy with their fortune as told by this ancient Chinese oracle, they can always reload and get another one.

Kissogram
http://www.kissogram.com.au

Send not just animated kisses, but wiggling butts, pouting drag queens, hatching eggs and more. Not all in the best taste but then what did you expect?

Lockpicking
http://www.indra.com/archives/alt-locksmithing/

They laughed when I told them I was learning to burgle, but when they came home . . .

Net Casino
http://www.casino.com

Apply for an offshore debit card, then flush it down the Net.

Peeping Tom
http://www.coolbase.com/peepingtom/

Spend a night peeping through the Net's many cameras, then rest content that you've sat with pioneers at the very cutting edge of technology. Tick that off the list and get on with life.

Penn and Teller
http://www.sincity.com

While, regrettably, Penn and Teller's input here is fairly minimal, it has enough links to other magic and entertainment sites, including other P&T exhibits, to make it worthwhile.

Sony
http://www.sony.com

News, support, product blurbs, media clips, previews, and colorful allsorts from Sony's huge stable of movies, music, broadcast, publishing, video, Playstation, and electronic toys. It's like ten major sites under one roof, with hundreds of corners to explore. See for yourself.

Tarot Information
http://www.facade.com/Occult/tarot/

Choose from several different packs to find out what your future holds. For a second opinion, link up to the master site and try your luck at the **I Ching**, Biorhythm, Bibliomancy, Stichomancy, or Runes predictions. If you suspect it's all a great pile of randomly generated nugget, the Cindy Crawford Concentration exercise will surely set you straight.

The 80s Server
http://www.80s.com

And you swore they'd never come back. Meanwhile, the decade before still won't go away:
http://www.rt66.com/dthomas/70s/70s.html

Text to speech converter
http://www.bell-labs.com/project/tts/voices.html

Enter your profanity, hit return, and it will speak the phrase back for the mirth of all within earshot. Try spelling phonetically for greater success. Or maybe you'd prefer it in Morse beeps: http://www.babbage.demon.co.uk/morse.html

Ticketmaster

http://www.ticketmaster.com

Book event tickets online.

Trading Card Dealers

http://www.wwcd.com/scdealer.html

Find that elusive baseball, football, or phone card.

UK National Lottery

http://lottery.merseyworld.com

Stats, winning numbers, draw details, numerical analysis: everything you need to know about the UK lottery, except the one thing that matters.

Uri Geller's Psychic City

http://www.urigeller.com

Test your ESP, fail dismally, and then find out why you need the services of the champion cutlery curler himself.

Virtual Presents

http://www.virtualpresents.com

Why waste money on real gifts when, after all, it's only the thought that counts?

Virtual Voodoo Doll

http://www.virtualdesign.com/v2/onlinedemos/voodoodoll/voodoo.htm

Torture a Java Voodoo doll and then email it to your victim.

Zodiac Forecasts

http://www.bubble.com/webstars/

Have the UK *Daily Mail*'s Jonathan Cainer read your stars. And then see how it compares with:

http://www.efd.lth.se/~e91ju/astrologi/astrofaq.html

EZINES

It's a fine distinction as to what's a Net magazine (ezine) and a magazine posted on the Net; those below are largely the former. The best lists of electronic journals and ezines are the Ezine List: http://www.meer.net/~johnl/e-zine-list/ and Inkpot's Zine Scene: http://inkpot.com/zines/ See also "News, Newspapers and Magazines."

Addicted to: Stuff
http://www.morestuff.com
Quirky ezine where readers share obsessions.

Anorak
http://www.anorak.co.uk
Irreverent daily review of the UK tabloids and broadsheets.

Blender
http://www.blender.com
Download the issue, install it, then fire it up online. If you've seen the CD version, it's more of the same. A fairy floss skim across the surface of pop culture cynicism, with brainless games, trivialities, and interactive tricks, all cushed up in that retro Jetsons' look.

Chick Click
http://www.chickclick.com
Coalition of the most notable independent grrl-powered Web sites including; Disgruntled Housewife, GrrlGamer, Smartypants, Mousy, Amazoncity, Riotgrrl, DJDazy, Hellfire and Bimbionic. You'll know straight away if it's your scene.

Erack
http://www.erack.com
Selections and exclusives from UK newsstand titles: **Q, Select, New Woman, FHM, Carworld, Maxpower, Motorcycle World** and **Empire**.

FiX Magazine
http://www.widemedia.com/fix/
One of London's longest running monthly ezines. Also claims to be the "world's widest." Figure that one out yourself.

Fray

http://www.fray.com

Personal, provocative, and potentially disturbing, Fray melts haunting graphics over strong prose on criminals, drugs, work, and hope.

FutureNet

http://www.futurenet.co.uk

Daily news, plus features from the UK magazine publisher's many titles such as **net**, **arcane**, **Mountain Biking UK**, **EDGE**, **Comedy Review**, **First XV**, **Total Guitar**, **Total Football**, and the acclaimed **Needlecraft**.

Geek Girl

http://geekgirl.com.au/geekgirl/

Assorted raves compiled by Australian cyberfemme Rosie X.

Giant Robot

http://www.giantrobot.com

Selections from the print popzine that scoops into Asian treats like **Ultraman**, **CYF**, sumo, manga, and larger-than-average robotica.

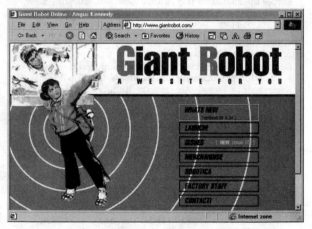

J Pop
http://www.j-pop.com

Japanese pop culture features on the likes of manga, anime, games, and Pizzicato 5.

Maxi
http://www.maximag.com

For the woman who doesn't take no for an answer, but then again probably wouldn't ask in the first place.

The Onion
http://www.theonion.com

News satire to die for.

Phrack Magazine
http://www.phrack.com

Renowned hackers' quarterly. Never far from controversy.

Psyche Journal
http://psyche.cs.monash.edu.au

All the latest goss on stuff like vagueness, semantics, the language of thought, delineating conscious processes, and contrastive analysis. Piece of cake.

Salon
http://www.salonmag.com

Daily news and cultural chop-ups with columns from renowned US writers like Camille Paglia, David Horowitz, and James Carville.

Slate
http://www.slate.com

Thoughtful, though dry, news, culture and arts analysis that's recently decided to charge. It's owned by Microsoft, but don't hold that against it.

The Smoking Gun
http://www.thesmokinggun.com

Celebrity shame dug up from police records complete with the photocopied sources.

The Straight Dope
http://www.straightdope.com

Cecil Adams' answers to hard questions. Find out how to renounce your US citizenship, what Kemosabe means, and the difference between a warm smell of colitas and colitis.

Suck
http://www.suck.com

In a smug class all by itself, and arguably the only ezine that ever mattered. Worth reading daily, if not for its cocked eye on all that's wired and painfully modern, then at least for Terry Colon's cartoons.

Swoon
http://www.swoon.com

Dating, mating, and relating. Courtesy of Condé Naste's **Details**, **GQ**, **Glamour**, and **Mademoiselle**.

Underwire
http://underwire.msn.com

Light features from women writers on things like marital politics, table manners, fitness, health, relationships, and car care. You might wonder if you really need to get onto the Net to read this sort of stuff.

Urban Desires
http://www.desires.com

Modern city stories of technology, food, sex, music, art, performance, style, travel, politics, and more.

Utne Online
http://www.utne.com

Selected articles from the progressive US alternative press digest, **The Utne Reader**, biweekly Web-only content and a busy gender-discriminatory café area for word bashing.

Z Times
http://www.zpub.com/z/

Monthly time-capsules as viewed from the Web.

Zug
http://www.mediashower.com/zug/

Irreverence, Henry-Root-style email pranks.

FASHION

1-800-SURGEON
http://www.surgeon.org

Well, if it doesn't scrub up in the mirror you can always put a knife to it.

Angel of Fashion Award
http://www.fashionangel.com/angel.html

Unless you have a chubby connection, fancy fashion sites can be pretty frustrating. And if they're not kept up to date, they hardly qualify as fashion. Angel singles out groundbreaking sites for praise and supplies links to many others.

Clear Plastic Fashions
http://clearplastic.com

For those with nothing to hide.

Clothes Care
http://www.clothes-care.com

Point and click image consultancy, stain removal tips, and soap suds ads.

Designer City
http://www.designercity.com

London fashion and lifestyle monthly with input from **Cosmo** and **Esquire**.

Elle International
http://www.elle.com

Scraps from the 27 international editions of **Elle**. They barely resemble their glossy paper counterparts but still sport enough swish types in bright duds to make you feel undershopped in any language.

Fashion Net
http://www.fashion.net

More fashion links than you could poke a chapstick at.

Fashion UK
http://www.widemedia.com/fashionuk/

Another minimal, but fresh, vanity monthly out of London.

Is Fashion Silly?
http://www.pittimmagine.com

Peephole at the Italian fashion industry.

The Lipstick Page
http://www.users.wineasy.se/bjornt/Lip.html

Cosmetic appliances for fun and profit.

Sneaker Nation
http://sneaker-nation.com

Trainer confessionals and brand reassurance.

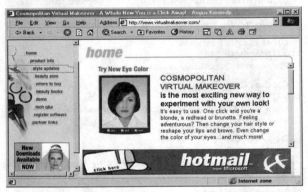

Virtual Makeover
http://www.virtualmakover.com

Order the demo, scan in your photo, and try on the latest hairdos.

FILM AND TV

It's a rare TV station that doesn't have a Web site today and most have very good ones with all kinds of extras like live sports coverage and documentary follow-ups. We won't need to give you their addresses because they'll be flashing them at you at every opportunity. In any case, you'll find them all at: http://www.ultimatetv.com/tv/ If you'd like personalized listings, perhaps delivered by email, try: http://www.sofcom.com.au/TV/ (Australia); http://www.clicktv.com (Canada); http://www.toaster.co.uk (UK); or http://www.gist.com (USA). Consult Ultimate TV or Yahoo for other regions.

All Movie Guide
http://www.allmovie.com

Colossal, but easy to navigate, sound and screen directory, complete with reviews and synopses.

Cinemachine
http://www.cinemachine.com

Movie review search engine. Redirects to the original source.

E! Online
http://www.eonline.com

Daily film and TV gossip, news, and reviews.

Encyclopedia Brady
http://www.primenet.com/~dbrady/

The collected antics of "three very lovely girls," their stepbrothers, and folks.

God of Actors
http://www.geocities.com/Athens/8907/factor.html

Valuable insight into the John Woo regular who makes Arnie look like Richie Cunningham. Widely regarded as the "coolest man alive."

Hergé and Tintin
http://www.du.edu/~tomills/tintin.html

The official Tintin site in English or French.

Hollywood Reporter
http://www.hollywoodreporter.com

Tinsletown tattle, previews and reviews daily, plus a flick biz
directory.

Internet Movie Database
http://www.imdb.com

You'll be hard pressed to find any work on or off the Net as
comprehensive as this exceptional relational database of
screen trivia from over 100,000 movies and a million actors.
It's all tied together remarkably well – for example, within
two clicks of finding your favorite movie, you can get full
filmographies of anyone from the cast or crew, and then see
what's in the cooker. Unmissable.

The Love Boat
http://www.asb.com/usr/indtvprd/loveboat/lbp1.htm

Come aboard they're expecting you.

Movies.com
http://www.movies.com

Preview forthcoming Touchstone and Hollywood Pictures. All
with short synopses, minute-long sample clips, interviews,
stills, and assorted press releases.

Mr Cranky
http://internet-plaza.net/zone/mrcranky/

He mightn't know a thing about films but he sure knows
what he doesn't like.

Reel
http://www.reel.com

Claims it's the world's biggest movie store. With more than
80,000 titles for sale and half that for rent, maybe it's right.

Secret Chimps Worldwide
http://digartz.com/link/evorevo.htm

There was a time when it looked like all actors might be
replaced by chimpanzees. So, what went wrong? After all the
nature of Monkey is irrepressible:
http://www.geocities.com/Tokyo/Towers/8153/

Shock Cinema
http://members.aol.com/shockcin/main.html

Picking over celluloid scavenged from Mr. Subtlety's dumpster.

Showbizwire
http://www.showbizwire.com

Top music, theatre, celebrity, film, television, video, and entertainment industry stories aggregated from about 50 major sources as they're released. More music at: http://www.musicnewswire.com

The Simpsons Archive
http://www.snpp.com

In barefaced defiance of Fox's "cease and desist" order, fans persist in garnishing the Web with the unofficial sights and sounds of Springfield. Meanwhile, Fox's own at: http://www.foxworld.com/simpindx.htm, hardly compares.

Soap Links
http://members.aol.com/soaplinks/

Keep up with who's doing what to whom, whom they told, and who shouldn't find out, in the surreal world of soap fiction. There's more at: http://www.soapdigest.com

Time For Teletubbies!
http://www.bbc.co.uk/education/teletubbies/tubbies.htm
http://www.pbs.org/teletubbies/

Discover the official recipe for tubby custard.

Treklove - the Un-Aired Star Trek Episode
http://www.lunaticlounge.com/treklove/

Go boldly where TV wouldn't touch.

Tromaville
http://www.troma.com

Here's your lucky break. Troma, home of class films like
Toxic Avenger, **Chopper Chicks** from **Zombie Town**, **Space
Freaks from Planet Mutoid**, **Subhumanoid Meltdown**, and
Fatguy goes Nutzoid, needs acting outcasts and writers for
its Troma Army Bizarre productions.

Ultimate TV
http://www.ultimatetv.com

More on everything televisual than is mentally healthy.
Places to vent your gripes, broadcasting addresses,
schedules, job vacancies, and links to fan pages of just about
every show ever made. By the time you get through this lot,
you'll be too plum-tuckered for the neon bucket itself.

Universal Studios
http://www.mca.com

What's in store from the MCA/Universal movie and music
stable. All sorts of fun promo gimmicks, such as being able
to interview the stars by email and download clips.

Variety
http://www.variety.com

Screen news fresh off the PR gattling gun.

X-Links Central
http://www.geocities.com/Hollywood/6050/xfsites.html

The X-Files remains up there with Star Trek in attracting Net
obsessives, despite mockery from respective leading actors
David Duchovny and William Shatner and copyright bullying
from Fox (the network, not Mulder). Here's a path to over a
thousand such X-shrines.

FINANCE

ASX Quote Weblink
http://www.weblink.com.au

Australian stock market quotes and historical charts.

Charles Schwab
http://www.schwab.com

NY brokerage that leads the pack of rats in online money juggling.

DataChimp
http://www.datachimp.com

Plain English primer in the mechanics behind financial maths.

Electronic Share Information
http://www.esi.co.uk

UK share quotes, fundamentals, and online trading.

Global Strategist Game
http://www.global-strategist.com

Sprinkle a pretend portfolio around various investments. Whichever player ends up with the biggest pie, bags the kitty.

Interactive Investor
http://www.iii.co.uk

Award-winning British portfolio management warehouse.

Motley Fool
http://www.fool.com

Investment forums, market tipping, quotes and sound advice. Stands above the rabble.

OilWorld
http://oilworld.com

All the gas on petrochemicals.

PAWWS Financial Network
http://pawws.secapl.com

Free North American quarter-hourly updated stock quotes, charts, fundamentals, and news. Pay to get more meaty stuff like online brokerage, portfolio management, real-time quotes, research, and all the other services you would expect from a stock shark.

QuoteCom
http://www.quote.com

More free trading data, news and charts, plus a multitude of subscription services.

RateNet
http://www.rate.net

Tracks and ranks finance rates in over 11,000 US institutions in 175 markets. Also links to thousands of banking sites and investment products.

Shareholder Action Handbook
http://www.bath.ac.uk/Centres/Ethical/Share/

When you buy shares in a public company, you get certain voting rights. By putting the entire text of the Shareholder Action Handbook online, it's hoped you'll exercise those rights to the benefit of your community.

Silicon Investor
http://www.techstocks.com

Outstanding selection of free technology stock quotes, charts, forums, advice, and sentiment surveys. To bet on the Net's success, start your research here.

Stockmaster
http://www.stockmaster.com

Quotes and rankings on major US stocks, funds, and Indices.

Wall Street Journal Interactive
http://www.wsj.com

Not only is this online edition equal to the print, its charts and data archives give it an edge. That's why you shouldn't complain that it's not free. After all, if it's your type of paper, you should be able to afford it, bigshot.

Yahoo! Finance
http://quote.yahoo.com

Business wires, charts, quotes, forex rates wrapped around the Net's mother lode of finance links.

FOOD AND DRINK

All India Food Page
http://www.gadnet.com/foodx.htm

Simple directory of Indian recipes and restaurant sites.

Beer Info Source
http://www.beerinfo.com

None of the usual beer yarns like waking up in a strange room stark naked with a throbbing head and a hazy recollection of pranging your car. Here, beer is treated with the same dewy-eyed respect usually reserved for wine and trains.

Beershots
http://micro.magnet.fsu.edu/beershots/

Beers of the world put under a microscope. Literally!

Birdseye Recipe Search
http://www.birdseye.com/search.html

Cast your line into the Fish Finger king's own recipe database or trawl through hundreds of other Net collections.

Chile-Heads
http://neptune.netimages.com/~chile/

Dip into chili recipes, chemistry, botanical facts, gardening tips, and general peppering. Find out what's the hottest pepper, what makes it so hot, how your body reacts, and identify that mystery one in your kebab.

Chocolate Lover's Playground
http://www.godiva.com

Mouth-watering cocoa recipes and meanderings into chocoholism. You can satisfy your cravings online, but only within the US. See how your favorite bar rates at:
http://www.hhhh.org/cloister/chocolate/

Cocktail
http://www.hotwired.com/cocktail/

Guzzle your way to a happier home.

Cook's Thesaurus
http://www.northcoast.com/~alden/cookhome.html

Find substitutes for fatty, expensive or hard-to-find ethnic ingredients.

Crazy Vegetarian
http://www.crazyveg.com

Light-hearted, meatless nutrition raps.

CyberChocy
http://www.caliebe.de/e/cyberchocy.htm

Design your own label, and they'll wrap it around a Ritter Sport bar and ship it anywhere worldwide. Can't spare ten dollars? Then send a virtual one instead:
http://www.virtualchocolate.com

DineNet
http://menusonline.com

Thousands of US restaurant menus, plus maps to aid fulfillment.

Epicurious

http://www.epicurious.com

Web-only marriage of Condé Nast's **Gourmet**, **Bon Appetit**, and **Traveler** magazines, crammed with recipes, culinary forums, advice on dining out around the world, and ways to stave off hunger with panache.

Fillet

http://www.fillet.com

Weekly tales of food snobbery and quiet drunkenness.

Greengrocer.com

http://www.greengrocer.com.au

Local fruit and vegetable delivery success story run from a houseboat in Sydney Harbour. If that's a bit distant for you, similar services include the US-wide, FedEx-delivered Netgrocer (http://www.netgrocer.com), and Tesco (http://www.tesco.co.uk) which covers select parts of the UK.

Internet Chef

http://www.ichef.com

Over 30,000 recipes, cooking hints, kitchen talk, and more links than you could jab a fork in.

Kim Chee

http://www.kim-chee.com

Learn to love the Korean spicy cabbage dish even if it makes you smell like a rendering plant.

Kitchen Link

http://www.kitchenlink.com

Points to more than 7,000 galleries of gluttony.

Over the Coffee

http://www.cappuccino.com

Enough coffee trivia, mail order firms, reviews, anecdotes, and links to similarly minded sites to keep you pleasantly caffeinated for life.

The Real Beer Page

http://realbeer.com

Here's the place to tune your brew. Apart from links to almost everything drunken and disorderly, it hosts several hypertext home-brew recipe books, including the entire Cat's Meow series, and a gallery of 228 labels in 128 shimmering colors. Yet real pros might prefer:

http://www.probrewer.com or http://www.breworld.com

Restaurant Row
http://www.restaurantrow.com

Key in your dining preferences and look for a match from hundreds of thousands of foodbarns worldwide.

Singapore Unofficial Food
http://www.sintercom.org/makan/

Vibrant guide to eating out in Singapore, plus oodles more than noodles to cook at home.

Spice Guide
http://www.spiceguide.com

Encyclopedia of spices covering their origins, purposes, recipes, and tips on what goes best with what.

Tasty Insect Recipes
http://www.ent.iastate.edu/Misc/InsectsAsFood.html

Dig in to such delights as Bug Blox, Banana Worm Bread, Rootworm Beetle Dip, and Chocolate Chirpie Chip Cookies (with crickets).

Tea Health
http://www.teahealth.co.uk

Types of tea, tried and tasted, and a turnpike to all that's tea taken truly. See also: http://www.teatime.com

Tokyo Food Page
http://www.twics.com/%7erobbs/tokyofood.html

Where and what to eat in Tokyo, a sushi decoder, plus a few recipes and tips like how to detect parasites in your uncooked mullet. From the author of "What's What in Japanese Restaurants."

Top Secret Recipes
http://www.topsecretrecipes.com

At least one commercial recipe, like KFC coleslaw, revealed each week. Many are surprisingly basic.

The Ultimate Cookbook
http://www.ucook.com

Plans to put hundreds of popular cookbooks online.

Wine Net
http://www.wineguide.com

Slick directory of wineries, retailers, publications, and general grape gratification.

GAMES

For more on online gaming, see our **"Online Gaming"** chapter (pp.193–199).

Blues News
http://www.bluesnews.com

The best place to keep up with Quake advances.

Connect 4
http://www.cyberus.ca/~pomakis/c4/

Challenge the beast to connect four, or any number for that matter. For tips on how to beat the system, read Victor Allis's masters thesis on expert play.

Crime Scene
http://www.crimescene.com

Help two detectives analyze forensic evidence and track down suspects in an ongoing murder investigation. Move along folks, nothing to see here.

Dave's Video Game Classics
http://www.davesclassics.com

Know someone who grizzles on about old school arcade games like Pleides, Lunar Rescue, Donkey Kong, and Xevious? Sentence them to ten minutes here.

Godzilla vs Tamagotchi
http://www.jitterbug.com/gvt/gvt.shtml

Do your bit to stamp out virtual pets.

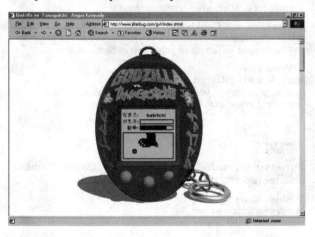

Grrl Gamer
http://www.grrlgamer.com

Team up with other game grrls and prepare to kick dweeb boy butt right across their own turf. More reinforcement at:
http://www.gamegirlz.com

Kasparov vs Deep Blue
http://www.chess.ibm.com

If Kasparov ever takes on Deep Blue again, here's where to watch it live. Apart from that, it chronicles the historical triumph of machine over mortal with links that will tickle any serious chess aficionado. Or if you're up for a game yourself, head straight to: http://www.ichess.com

PC Game Finder
http://www.pcgame.com

Top games search engine that intelligently splits results by reviews, cheats, demos, and required hardware. Indexes most of the leading game lairs.

Playsite
http://www.playsite.com

Play popular table games like Chess, Backgammon and Go-moku against online opponents. It's all done through Java applets so you won't need any extra software, but it might crash your browser.

The Riddler
http://www.riddler.com

Use your Web scavenging, lateral thinking, literary, trivia, and other skills to compete across the Net for prizes.

Sega
http://www.sega.com   http://www.segasoft.com

Product news, tips, and support plus games to play online and a few PC demos like Daytona and Sega Touring Car to download.

Virtual Vegas
http://www.virtualvegas.com

Showgirls, VRML slot machines, Shockwave blackjack, Java poker, shopping, and a chat-up lounge. VVbucks are virtual, but occasionally the prizes are real.

Webgames
http://happypuppy.com/compgames/webgames/

Pit your wits against the computer or remote opponents on a whole variety of games.

You Don't Know Jack
http://www.toasted.com

This wacky trivia quiz computer game was all the rage a couple of years back. Now you can download the software free and compete against other players over the Net for cash.

PC GAMES

For reviews, news, demos, hints, patches, cheats, downloads, and other PC game necessities try:

Gamecenter
http://www.gamecenter.com

Games Domain
http://www.gamesdomain.com

Games Mansion
http://www.gamesmansion.com

Gamespot
http://www.gamespot.com

Happy Puppy
http://www.happypuppy.com

Online Gaming Realm
http://www.ogr.com

PCME
http://www.pcme.com

GOVERNMENT

Active Most Wanted and Criminal Investigations
http://www.gunnyragg.com/crimes.htm

Compendium of fugitive listings including the FBI's top ten most wanted, the US State Department's Anti-Terrorism Unit, and a war criminal directory.

Australian Government Entry Point
http://www.nla.gov.au/oz/gov/

Dig down to find any Australian State, Local or Federal
Government department as well as the political parties,
diplomatic posts abroad, courts and progress on the
campaign to kick out the crowd below.

The British Monarchy
http://www.royal.gov.uk

Official drone of the House of Windsor. Way more larks at:
http://www.royalnetwork.com

CCTA Government Information
http://www.open.gov.uk

Here's where to find any UK government authority. Just
open this colossal directory, scan down the list, make your
choice, and before long you'll be nodding off, just as if you
were actually there.

Central Intelligence Agency

http://www.odci.gov/cia/

Learn about the CIA's role in international affairs, its intelligence cycle, history and real estate. But that's not what you're after is it? You watch TV and read the **Weekly World News**. You want to know about political assassinations, arms deals, Latin American drug trades, spy satellites, conspiracy theories, phone tapping, covert operations, government-sponsored alien sex cults, and the X-files. This must be another CIA.

Declassified Satellite Photos

http://edcwww.cr.usgs.gov/dclass/dclass.html

Here's what you've been expecting from the Net: the first spy pictures taken from satellites, then dropped to earth by parachute. They're freshly declassified and plenty more will follow. Look closely and see Soviets knitting socks in preparation for a bleak winter. Or, if you'd prefer to commission your own, try: http://www.rsi.ca

DOE Openness: Human Radiation Experiments

http://tis-nt.eh.doe.gov/ohre/

The improbable annals of Cold War research into nuking human flesh to see what happens.

FBI FOIA Reading Room

http://www.fbi.gov/foipa/foipa.htm

FBI documents released as part of the Freedom of Information Act. Includes a few files on such celebrities as John Wayne, Elvis, Marilyn and the British Royals.

FedWorld

http://www.fedworld.gov

Locate US federal government servers, contacts, and documents.

Her Majesty's Treasury

http://www.hm-treasury.gov.uk

Another British spine-tingler. Read press releases, ministerial speeches, minutes, economic forecasts, and the budget, and decide whether your tax pounds are going to worthy causes.

Palestinian National Authority
http://www.pna.net
Official mouthpiece of Palestine on the Net with regular "progress" reports on the settlement process.

Police Officer's Directory
http://www.officer.com
Top of the pops cop directory with more than 1500 baddy-nabbing bureaus snuggled in with law libraries, wanted listings, investigative tools, hate groups, special ops branches and off-duty homepages.

US Census Bureau
http://www.census.gov
More statistics on the US and its citizens than you'll ever want to know. Search the main census database, read press releases, view the poster gallery, check the projected population clock, listen to clips from its radio broadcasts, then link to other serious info-head sites.

US Federal Government Servers
http://www.fie.com/www/us_gov.htm
Get to any US Fed department.

The White House
http://www.whitehouse.gov

Wild Bill might not really be at his PC when you choose to "speak out" through the White House's official suggestion form, but you never know, something just might filter through. It's easy to be cynical about this PR exercise, particularly the moribund guided tour, but it does show the doors of democracy are at least ajar. (Not to be confused with the hacker spoof http://www.whitehouse.net or (especially) http://www.whitehouse.com which is a hard-core porno site.)

HEALTH

Achoo
http://www.achoo.com

Like a Yahoo of health and wellbeing sites. Drill down until you get your medicine.

Alternative Medicine
http://www.pitt.edu/~cbw/altm.html

Part of the Net's ongoing research function is the ability to contact people who've road-tested alternative remedies and can report on their efficacy. Start here and work your way to an answer.

Ask Dr Weil
http://www.drweil.com

Time magazine felt Popdoctor Andrew Weil's eagerness to prescribe from a range of bewildering, and often conflicting, alternative therapies earned him front cover status. Naturally, it had nothing to do with his move from **HotWired** to **Time**'s Pathfinder complex. Here, he answers a medical question each day, Dr Ruth gives her usual get-fresh tips and Dr Holly Atkinson delves into women's troubles.

Biorhythm Generator
http://www.facade.com/attraction/biorhythm/

The Skeptic's Dictionary says biorhythms are a con. Generate your own and put it to the test.

Dr Squat
http://www.drsquat.com

Avoid getting sand kicked in your face through deep full squats. There's more in the Weightlifting FAQ at:
http://www.imp.mtu.edu/~babucher/weights.html

The Drugs Archive
http://www.hyperreal.org/drugs/

Articles, primarily accumulated from the alt.drugs newsgroup, that provide first-hand perspectives on the pleasures and dangers of recreational drugs. See also:
http://www.paranoia.com/drugs/

GYN101
http://www.gyn101.com

Swot up for your next gynecological exam. But if you're after honors go straight to: http://www.obgyn.net

Health on the Net
http://www.hon.ch
Medical search engine.

Healthfinder
http://www.healthfinder.gov

US Government-funded directory pointing to a qualified selection of health resources. Search by ailment, for a Web address or phone number.

HealthWorld
http://www.healthy.net

Health megasite styled as a cybervillage with its own university, library, nutrition clinic, self-help center, marketplace, and newsroom. Aimed at practitioners and patients alike with a healthy balance of the conventional to the alternative.

Interactive Patient
http://medicus.marshall.edu/medicus.htm

Determine whether you're really cut out for the quackhood with this doctor/patient simulation. First fire a few questions, make an examination, x-ray, diagnose, and prescribe a remedy. Then send a hefty bill, turn on the answerphone and shoot off to get blotto at the golf course.

Medicinal Herb Faq
http://sunsite.unc.edu/herbmed/mediherb.html

If it's in your garden and it doesn't kill you, it can only make you stronger. More leafy cures and love drugs at:
http://www.algy.com/herb/

Medline
http://www.healthgate.com/HealthGate/MEDLINE/search-advanced.shtml

If you're serious about medical research go straight to Medline, the US National Library of Medicine's database. It archives references and abstracts from some 3,500 medical journals and periodicals going back to 1966. You can get to it free from here, along with a raft of other biomedical resources.

Medscape
http://www.medscape.com

While this medical forum is primarily aimed at health pros and med students, it's equally useful to anyone concerned with their general well-being.

NursingNet
http://www.nursingnet.com

Springboard to medical discussion groups, professional bodies, and other nursing resources.

Online Birth Center
http://www.efn.org/~djz/birth/birthindex.html

Support for midwives and parents, especially anxious expectant mums. For more, see: http://www.babydirectory.com

Patient UK
http://www.patient.co.uk

Clutter-free British health directory.

Pharm Web
http://www.pharmweb.net

Pharmaceutical Yellow Pages.

Phys: In Fitness and in Health
http://www.phys.com

Assess and improve your fitness and diet. Net exclusives plus select features from Condé Nast's **Sports for Women**, **Mademoiselle**, **Glamour**, **Vogue**, **Allure** and **Self**.

Poisons Information Database
http://vhp.nus.sg/PID/

Directory of plant, snake, and animal toxin cures, information centers, and practitioners.

Reuters Health
http://www.reutershealth.com

Medical newswires, reviews, opinion, and reference.

Smart Drugs and Nootropics

http://www.damicon.fi/sd/

If nootropics really make you smarter, how can we afford not to take them? Read all sides and decide whether it's money well spent at offshore pill barns like:

http://www.smart-drugs.com

The Virtual Hospital

http://www.vh.org

Patient care and distance learning via online multimedia tools such as illustrated surgical walkthroughs.

The Visible Human Project

http://www.nlm.nih.gov/research/visible/

These unappetizing scans were once the talk of the Net. Namely because, though not mentioned here, the thinly sliced fillets came from the frozen body of an executed serial killer. And now the visible woman, interactive knee, and virtual colonoscopy appear on the menu. Want higher production values? Then see: http://www.medtropolis.com/vbody/

Yoga

http://www.timages.com/yoga.htm

Stretch yourself back into shape with a personalized routine.

KIDS (MOSTLY)

Animal Information Database
http://www.seaworld.org

Tune in to the Webcams at the right time and you'll catch J.J. the grey whale being fed, or any of thirty-two species of sharks doing the kind of big fish chomping stuff that makes surfers shiver. After that there's games, teaching guides, and quizzes about such other adorables as dolphins, dugongs, gorillas, lions, tigers, and walruses.

Bizarre Things You Can Make In Your Kitchen
http://freeweb.pdq.net/headstrong/

Rainy-day science projects and general mischief like volcanoes, stink bombs, cosmic ray detectors, fake blood, and hurricane machines.

The Bug Club
http://www.ex.ac.uk/bugclub/

Creepy crawly fan club with e-pal page, newsletters, and pet care sheets on how to keep your newly bottled tarantulas, cockroaches, and stick insects alive.

Children's Literature Web Guide
http://www.ucalgary.ca/~dkbrown/

Critical roundup of recent kids books, and links to texts.

Club Girl Tech
http://www.girltech.com

Encourages smart girls to get interested in technology without coming across all geeky.

Coloring.com
http://www.coloring.com

Select a picture segment, choose a color and then shade it in. You don't need to be Leonardo.

Cyberteens

http://www.cyberteens.com/ctmain.html

Submit your music, art, or writing to a public gallery. You might even win a prize.

Disney.com

http://www.disney.com

Guided catalog of Disney's movies, books, theme parks, records, interactive CD Roms and such. For a richer experience, try its commercial online service: http://www.dailyblast.com If you're with MSN, it's free, otherwise you can trial it for 30 days and then decide whether to pay.

Everything Cool

http://www.everythingcool.com

Budding ezine written by under 18s for under 18s.

Fantastic Fractals

http://library.advanced.org/12740/msie/

A fractal is a complex self-similar and chaotic mathematical object that reveals more detail as you get closer. Download the software, follow the instructions, and generate some funky graphics.

Funschool

http://www.funschool.com

Educational games for the preschool to first grade age group.

Greatest Places

http://www.greatestplaces.org

Which are the world's greatest places? See if you agree with these choices.

The History Net

http://www.thehistorynet.com

Bites of world history, with an emphasis on the tough guys going in with guns.

KidPub

http://www.kidpub.org/kidpub/

No drinks served here, just thousands of stories submitted by kids worldwide.

Kids' Space
http://www.kids-space.org

> Free hideout for kids to swap art, music, and stories with new friends across the world.

Learn2
http://learn2.com

> Figure out how to do all sorts of things from fixing a zipper to spinning a basketball. While the interests aren't strictly for kids, there's nothing here that's too hard for a whippersnapper.

Math Magic Activities
http://www.scri.fsu.edu/~dennisl/CMS/activity/math_magic.html

> Card, rope, and calculation tricks that require no mirrors or sleight of hand, just a basic understanding of maths.

Mr. Edible Starchy Tuber Head
http://winnie.acsu.buffalo.edu/potatoe/

> Create your own, customized Mr. Potato Head.

Name That Candybar
http://www.sci.mus.mn.us/sln/tf/c/crosssection/namethatbar.html

> So, how well do you know your chocolate bars?

Purple Moon
http://www.purple-moon.com

The drawcard here is the clubhouse where girls can collect treasures, create their own Web pages, and exchange postcards.

StarChild Review
http://starchild.gsfc.nasa.gov/docs/StarChild/StarChild.html

Educational funhouse for junior astronomers.

White House for Kids
http://www.whitehouse.gov/WH/kids/html/kidshome.html

Follow Socks through the White House to uncover its previous inhabitants, including the kids and pets. Then, write to the resident moggy and get the goss on what goes down in DC after dark.

Yahooligans
http://www.yahooligans.com

Kid-friendly Web guide intuitively organized into subject groups like dinosaurs, hobbies, and homework answers. Like big brother Yahoo, but without the dodgy and heavy stuff.

You Can
http://www.beakman.com

Answers to typical kid questions from the likes of "why poop is brown" and "why farts smell" to "why your voice sounds different on a tape recorder" and "why the TV goes crazy while the mixer is on."

The Yuckiest Site on the Internet
http://www.yucky.com

Fun science with a leaning towards the icky-sticky and the creepy-crawly.

LEGAL

Advertising Law

http://www.webcom.com/~lewrose/home.html

How far you can push your products has always been an iffy end of the law. And on the Internet, where any snake-oil merchant can set up shop for next to nothing, many business precedents are yet to be set. Here's help in finding the fine line between puffery and lies.

Bentham Archive of British Law

http://www.ndirect.co.uk/~law/bentham.htm

Independent synopsis of Criminal, Roman, European, and property law, plus UK legal threads and essential lawyer jokes.

Free Advice

http://www.freeadvice.com

US legal tips in over 100 topics.

Law Crawler

http://www.lawcrawler.com

Search the Web for legal info worldwide. Then try Findlaw: http://www.findlaw.com

LawGirl

http://www.lawgirl.com

Excellent copyright and entertainment law forums and primers. It's also run by one of those cybergrrl types if that means anything to you.

Lawrights
http://www.lawrights.co.uk

Helpful FAQs on various legal issues in England & Wales,
plus a free lawyer referral service.

The 'Lectric Law Library
http://www.lectlaw.com

Legal repository aimed at both laypeople and pros. Archives
reams of legal references plus guides to legal forms, phrases,
software, law schools, business formalities, and professional
bodies, as well as the latest case news.

Seamless
http://www.seamless.com

Exceptional local content plus a directory which seems to
adequately span the broad ambit of legal carrying-ons.

West's US Legal Directory
http://www.wld.com

Accused of grand theft, arson, or murder one? Then whip
through this database of over half a million US lawyers
who'd rather see you go free than go without their fee.

MUSEUMS AND GALLERIES

A-Bomb WWWMuseum, Hiroshima
http://www.csi.ad.jp/ABOMB/

Fiftieth anniversary commemoration of the Hiroshima and
Nagasaki bombs, interviews with survivors, and exhibits
from the Hiroshima Peace Park and Museum.

Central Intelligence Museum
http://laf.cioe.com/~dna/

Spy toys and an active imagination on parade.

The Exploratorium
http://www.exploratorium.edu

Museums generally haven't translated to the Web too
successfully but this showing from San Francisco's
Exploratorium is a notable exception. Some of its 650-odd

interactive exhibits have adapted quite well, making it an engaging and educative experience, especially for children.

Field Museum of Natural History, Chicago
http://www.fmnh.org

Page through the eras in the DNA to Dinosaurs exhibit, downloading movies and sound bites. Or get caught in the spell of Haitian Vodou art. Again, it's more for the kids.

Library of Congress
http://www.loc.gov

Research tools, exhibitions, library services, current bills under consideration, and an unparalleled multimedia showcase of American history. Described as one of the seven wonders of the Internet.

Museum of Modern Art NY
http://www.moma.org

If you only ever visit one modern art museum ... here's a sample of what to expect when you get there.

Museums Around The World
http://www.icom.org/vlmp/world.html

Directory of Web museums sorted by country.

The Natural History Museum
http://www.nhm.ac.uk

London's Natural History Museum was one of the Web's pioneering sites. It has a few science galleries that could be classed as exhibits in their own right, but most of the elaborate content simply teases. It won't save you a visit but it might convince you it's worth the trip.

UCMP Time Machine
http://www.ucmp.berkeley.edu/help/timeform.html

Jump aboard the University of California's Museum of Paleontology's time machine for a rocky ride through the geological eras.

WebMuseum
http://lot49.tristero.com/wm/

Famous art from Gothic right through to Pop, plus classical music samples, special exhibitions of medieval art, Cézanne,

and more to come, complete with commentary courtesy of the
Encyclopaedia Britannica. Used to be called Le Louvre, until
the French lawyers stepped in.

MUSIC

Music is one of the Web's strongest selling points and
the myriad band, label, and fan sites are fortunately well
served by directories like the Ultimate Band List (see
p.330). Our selections should be seen as little more than
starter options. Before you check in grab the latest version of RealPlayer – http://www.real.com – so you can listen
to music samples.

Addicted to Noise
http://www.addict.com

Monthly news and reviews with a heavy bias towards the
alternative rock end of the spectrum.

Algorithmic Music Stream
http://www.stg.brown.edu/~maurice/

Streaming RealAudio music generated on the fly by a cheeky
algorithm. Not exactly melodic, but not unlistenable either.

All Music Guide
http://www.allmusic.com

Massive music database spanning most popular genres, with
bios, reviews, ratings, and keyword crosslinks to related
sounds, sites, and online ordering. It's well-researched,
sufficiently critical, and surprisingly comprehensive.

AltVideos
http://www.areohvee.com

Indie music videos on demand via Microsoft NetShow or the
Vivo Active plug-in. They're impressive, but not TV quality.

Art of the Mixed Tape
http://www.artofthemix.org

"If you have ever killed an afternoon making a mix, spent the
evening making a cover, and then mailed a copy off to a

friend after having made a copy for yourself, well, this is the site for you." Kind of says it all.

Audio Review
http://www.audioreview.com

Audio equipment reviewed by end users. A fine concept but somewhat flawed by extreme opinions. Still, if you're not satisfied here, there's more than enough alternatives off the links page.

Buying records online

Shopping for music is an area where the Net not only equals, but outshines, its terrestial counterparts. Apart from the convenience of not having to tramp across town, you can find pretty much anything on current issue, whether or not it's released locally, and in many cases preview album tracks in RealAudio. You can often make price savings, too, depending on where you buy, whether you're hit with tax, and how the freight stacks up.

The biggest hitch you'll strike is when stock is put on backorder. Many operators boast a huge catalog simply because they order everything on the fly, thus putting you at the mercy of their distributors. The trouble is your entire order might be held up by one item. The better shops check their stock levels before confirming your order, and follow its progress until delivery.

As far as **where to shop** goes, that depends on your taste. In terms of sheer innovation, Tunes.com (http://www.tunes.com) stands out by profiling your preferences, recommending selections, linking to reviews, and serving up tons of RealAudio samples.

Aus Music Guide
http://www.amws.com.au

Massive directory of all that's shakin' down under.

Canonical List of Weird Band Names
http://home.earthlink.net/~chellec/

Just be thankful your parents weren't so creative.

You can't go too far wrong with most of the blockbusters either, such as:

Amazon	http://www.amazon.com
Borders	http://www.borders.com
CDNow	http://www.cdnow.com
CD Universe (US)	http://www.cduniverse.com
Music Boulevard (US)	http://www.musicblvd.com
IMVS (UK)	http://www.imvs.com

If you'd like to **compare prices**, check out

Aureva	http://www.aureva.com
Virtual Outlet	http://www.virtualoutlet.com
CompareNet	http://www.comparenet.com
Bottom Dollar	http://www.bottomdollar.com

Or, if you're after something more obscure, you'll find no shortage of options under the appropriate Yahoo! categories. Following are a few of our favorite specialist shops:

Dusty Grooves
http://dustygroove.com

Soul, Jazz, Latin, Brazil, and Funk on vinyl and CD.

Hard to find records
http://www.hard-to-find.co.uk

Record finding agency, which specializes in house, hip-hop, soul, and disco vinyl.

Record Finder
http://www.recordfinders.com
  Stocks deleted vinyl including over 200,000 45s.

TimeWarp
http://www.tunes.co.uk/timewarp/
  Jazzy grooves, Latin, hip-hop, funk and underground dance.

X-Radio
http://www.x-radio.com
  Acid jazz, downtempo, leftfield, techno and urban beats.

COOKING YOUR OWN CD

Fancy whipping up your own custom CD? Then try out a DIY compilation shop. Simply run through their catalog, preview what looks good, submit your track listing, and they'll burn it to disk. Expect this to catch on in a big way. For a glimpse of what's to come, see:

Cductive	http://www.cductive.com
My CD	http://www.my-cd.com
Custom Disc	http://www.customdisc.com
Supersonic Boom	http://www.supersonicboom.com
MusicMaker	http://www.musicmaker.com

CDDB
http://www.cddb.com
  Attach song listings to the CDs playing in your PC drive by installing a player that logs in and references this database.

CD Zapping
http://www.netcomuk.co.uk/~wwl/cdzap.html
  Put your flatmate's Verve CD out of its misery.

Cerberus Digital Jukebox
http://www.cdj.co.uk

It's more the eclectic selections from labels like Ninja Tune, Moving Shadow, and Pork, than magnitude, that rates this as a visit. Download the player, flip through the free samples, and decide whether you'd be willing to pay for more.

Classical Music on the Net
http://www.musdoc.com/classical/

Gateway to the timeless. To shop, see:
http://www.classicalinsites.com

Daily Mix
http://www.dailymix.com

Hip-hop news daily.

The Dance Music Resource

http://www.juno.co.uk

New and forthcoming dance releases for mail order, UK radio
slots, and a well stocked link directory. See also:
http://www.fly.co.uk

Dancetech

http://www.dancetech.com

One-stop shop for techno toys and recording tips.

The Daily .Wav

http://www.dailywav.com

Features at least one new TV/film sound sample a day. Fun
for assigning to computer events like new mail. That is until
they drive everyone around you up the wall. See also:
http://www.wavcentral.com

Dirty Linen

http://kiwi.futuris.net/linen/

Excerpts from the US folk, roots, and world music magazine.
Includes a US gig guide. See also Folk Roots:
http://www.froots.demon.co.uk

The DJ

http://www.thedj.com

Choose from over 70 RealAudio channels in a wide range of
genres.

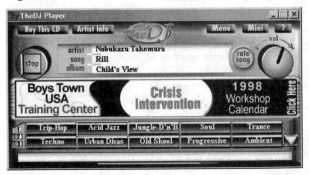

dotmusic
http://www.dotmusic.com

UK and worldwide charts, gossip, contacts, and profiles from top industry rags **Music Week**, **Record Mirror**, **MBI**, and **Gavin**.

ECM
http://www.ecmrecords.com

Sound samples and online ordering from the German-based jazz and contemporary classical label, home to the likes of Keith Jarrett, Jan Garbarek, Pat Metheny, and Arvo Part.

The Ever Expanding Web Music Listing
http://www.columbia.edu/~hauben/music/web-music.html

Monolithic directory split into academic, non-academic, user-maintained, geographically local, and artist-specific sites. Although it's no longer being updated, it's still a good source of links.

Firefly
http://www.firefly.com

Rate and slate a hundred or so records and films and have your taste buds diagnosed. Once processed, it can recommend selections you're likely to adore or abhor, and hook you up with your peers. Now that Microsoft has annexed this "passport" customer profiling technology it's likely to become more widespread.

Global Electronic Music Market
http://gemm.com

One-point access to over two million new and used record titles from almost two thousand sources.

The Grateful Dead
http://www.dead.net

Official place to speak no ill of the Dead. Thanks, Jerry – RIP.

Hyperreal
http://www.hyperreal.org

One-stop rave shop. Find out what's hip, where it's at, what's going down, and what's the best nourishment.

Independent Underground Music Archive
http://www.iuma.com

Get in touch with thousands of unsigned and indie-label underground musicians. All provide samples, biographies, and contacts. A cool and well-established site which has recently spawned its own net radio channel.

List of Music Mailing Lists
http://www.shadow.net/~mwaas/lomml.html

Obsess about your favorite pop tunes with other fans.

Michael Jackson Internet Fan Club
http://www.fred.net/mjj/

All you want (and more than you need) to know about little Mr. Epaulettes and his troops. "Only **factual truth** is presented on these pages."

Jazz Central Station
http://www.jazzcentralstation.com

Bulging global jazz multimedia digest in English or Japanese.

Kraftwerk Infobahr
http://www.analogue.org/infobahr/

Demos, live out-takes, MIDI files, interviews, lyrics, and the discography of pioneering Krautrockers.

Live Concerts
http://www.liveconcerts.com

Major gigs live in RealAudio.

London Techno Events
http://www.sorted.org/london/

What's spinning around London's techno circuit.

Lyrics Server
http://www.lyrics.ch

Search a massive lyrics database by title, artist, or text. Everyone from Aaron Neville to 999.

MIDI Farm
http://www.midifarm.com

Thousands of synthesized debasements of popular tunes, TV themes, and film scores. Cheesy listening at its finest.

MP3 Resources
http://www.mp3.com
http://mp3.box.sk

Internet music pirating has caused quite a stink. Not surprisingly when you can download full CD quality tracks compressed in MP3 format. Bear in mind that while it's legal to store them on your hard drive for 24 hours, after that you might breach copyright. Here's where to get started.

MTV
http://www.mtv.com

What's ironic about MTV's official home on the Web is it's all just a bit too much hard work. Maybe it's not really fair to complain. After all the content's there: news, charts, vid clips, interviews, reviews, and great ladles of its trademark popcultural blancmange. But you're forced into reading, waiting, and worse, having to think – and surely that's not part of the grand MTV plan.

Music Festival Finder
http://www.festivalfinder.com

Daily-updated listings of more than 1500 forthcoming Portaloo installations across North America. Covers all genres.

NME
http://nme.com

Weekly soundclipped record reviews, charts, features, news, gigs, demos, archives, and live chats from the world's most influential indie/pop tabloid. For more indie links and news, see: http://www.head-space.com/iworld/

Rap.Org
http://www.rap.org

Videos, sound clips, lyrics, clothes, gossip, and links to just about every other hip-hop haven.

The Residents
http://www.residents.com

The world's strangest neo-classical ensemble has performed anonymously, wearing giant eyeball heads, for a quarter of a century, so efficient at subterfuge that even their most avid fans remain bewildered. Take this one for instance.

Rolling Stones
http://www.stones.com

Originally set up to promote the Stones' Voodoo Lounge album, with ongoing video feeds, loads of sound files, interviews, and pictures. Carved its place in history by hosting the first live Internet concert broadcast which, although not a critical success, was a turning point in the Net's evolution from research tool to lifestyle accessory.

The Rough Guide to Rock
http://www.roughguides.com/rock/

What can we say? The world's coolest rock encyclopedia online? It's certainly the most democratic, having been developed on the Web, using fans as contributors, for the 1100-plus entries. Expect to see a relaunch soon, adding the option of buying any recommended CD, alongside a huge web of links out to fan- and band sites.

Shareware Music Machine
http://www.hitsquad.com/smm/

Tons of shareware music players, editors, and composition tools, for every platform. Yes, even Linux.

Sonic Net
http://www.sonicnet.com

Big name live cybercasts, streaming audio and video channels, chats, news and reviews. Subscribe to find out what's coming up.

Soul Links
http://www.cet.ac.il/personnel/yonin/soulinks.htm

If it's got soul, chances are you'll find it from here.

Sound Dogs
http://www.sounddogs.com

Over 60,000 sound effects for sale.

Sounds Online
http://www.soundsonline.com

Preview loops and samples, free in RealAudio. Pay to download studio quality.

SSEYO Koan System

http://www.sseyo.com

Fool around with Koan music, which reinvents itself on each listen. Proponents include Eno (of course) and Loop Guru.

SS7x7 Sound System

http://www.ss7x7.com

Mix your own ambient, jazz, and breakbeat tracks instantly in Shockwave.

Streetsound

http://www.streetsound.com

Warren of urban sound and style, ranging from the latest electro clips to a series of streetwear forums where hip-hop label lemmings disclose what brands they wouldn't be seen shot dead in.

Taxi

http://www.taxi.com

Online music A&R service. And guess what? You and your plastic kazoo are just what they're looking for.

The Ultimate Band List
http://www.ubl.com

Don't give up if your favorite pop ensemble, music mag, or
record shop isn't stowed in here. While it's probably the most
professional effort at an all-encompassing music directory,
it's nowhere near complete. Still, if you're after something
artist-specific, it's generally ace.

Timecast
http://www.timecast.com

What's new on the RealAudio and RealVideo airwaves. Get a
sound card, download the RealPlayer, and visit this crucial
site regularly.

Trouser Press
http://www.trouserpress.com

Entertaining and encyclopedic guide covering alternative
rock from the 70s to the present.

Unfurled
http://www.unfurled.com

Yahoo/MTV search engine collaboration that points to some
80,000 music sites plus reviews, events, and cybercasts.
Started off promisingly but appears to have lost momentum.

Vietnam Jukebox
http://www.war-stories.com/Oldies/Oldies.htm

Top of the Pops from 1960 through 1975. Only one catch –
they're all cheesy midis.

Virtual Pipes
http://www.geocities.com/Vienna/5704/fav.html

Wake up refreshed to the drone of 1000 midi bagpipers.

NATURE

Australian Botanical Gardens
http://www.anbg.gov.au

All the gear on Canberra's Botanical Garden's projects, flora, and fauna: tourist guides, flowering calendars, biodiversity studies, bird and frog call sound files, even fire procedures. It's a bit like stumbling into a government office to reams of papers strewn across the floor in unrelated piles – but in this case substance beats style.

British Trees
http://www.u-net.com/trees/home.htm

Apparently there are only 33 native British trees. Find out all about them here, though they might be easier to recognize if they threw in a few pictures!

Cool Dog Site of the Day
http://www.st.rim.or.jp/~ito/d/dogmark.html

You really have to wonder about someone who loves dogs this unconditionally.

The Electronic Zoo
http://netvet.wustl.edu/e-zoo.htm

Directory of fauna information that will lead you way up the virtual garden path before you find what you're looking for. Despite its name, it's not a virtual zoo with animations and recordings of animal sounds. However, when one arrives, you'll be sure to find it here.

The EnviroWeb
http://envirolink.org

Claims to be the largest online environmental information service on the planet.

Environmental Organization Directory
http://www.webdirectory.com

Primary production and green-minded sites sorted by focus.

F@rming Online
http://www.rpl.com.au/farming/

Gateway to predominately Australian agricultural resources.

Gardening.com
http://www.gardening.com

Includes an illustrated gardening encyclopedia, a problem solver to debug some 700 horticultural ailments, and a guide to hundreds of other ground breaking sites. See also: http://www.gardenguides.com

Global Bigfoot Encyclopedia
http://www.planetc.com/users/bigfoot/scott.htm

Identify the hairy hominids tramping down the bushes at the back of your house.

The Hamster Page
http://www.tela.bc.ca/hamster/

Definitive guide to online hamsters and their inevitable obituaries.

the Hamster page

Internet Directory for Botany
http://herb.biol.uregina.ca/liu/bio/idb.shtml

Search engine for serious plantlife research.

MooCow
http://www.moocow.com

Living under the influence of cattle as lifestyle accessories.

Natural History Bookshop
http://www.nhbs.co.uk

Browse or search the world's largest environmental bookshop.

NetVet
http://netvet.wustl.edu/vet.htm

A certain way to anything animalian. Choose from the NetVet Gopher, Electronic Zoo, Veterinary Medicine page of the WWW Virtual Library, or one of the several specialist directories.

Planet Ark
http://www.planetark.org/new/worldnews.html

Daily environmental news from Reuters.

The Virtual Garden
http://www.pathfinder.com/vg/

Splendid horticultural digest – a nibble of Time Warner's megalithic Pathfinder complex – that provides the most fulsome online guide to gardening. Includes several plant society and gardening magazines, databases, book excerpts, plant directories, and an electronic encyclopedia which helps pick the best plants for your patch.

NEWS, NEWSPAPERS, AND MAGAZINES

Now that almost every newspaper in the world from the **Washington Post** (http://www.washingtonpost.com) to the **Falkland Island News** (http://www.sartma.com) is discharging daily content onto the Net, it's beyond this guide to list more than a smattering of the majors, the pioneers, or the worthies. For comprehensive listings check AJR/Newslink, Crayon, Ecola's Newsstand, MediaInfo or the Ultimate Collection of News links in the pages following. See also our "Ezine" and "Music" listings.

ABC News
http://www.abc.net.au/news/

24-hour news as it breaks from the Australian Broadcasting Commission.

AJR/Newslink
http://www.newslink.org

American Journalism Review features and a well-stocked directory of newspapers, magazines, broadcasters' and journalists' resources.

The Australian
http://www.theaustralian.com.au

A fair helping of The Australian, bolstered by occasional bulletins and stories from other Murdoch rags such as the **Brisvegas Bugle**.

BBC News
http://news.bbc.co.uk

The sort of service you'd expect from the British broadcaster, but it can be hard work wringing out the text.

Christian Science Monitor
http://www.csmonitor.com

Daily print news and opinion, plus live and archived audio feeds from Monitor Radio.

Clarinet News
http://www.clarinet.com

High-quality subscription news service with a toe-hold into such big guns as Reuters, Associated Press, and Newsbytes. A single-user subscription costs about $40 per month, or cheaper if shared across a site. If your Access Provider subscribes, you'll get the **clari.** series free in Usenet or via this Web address. It also bolsters Newspage's industrial news: http://www.newspage.com

CNN
http://www.cnn.com

Up-to-the minute US and world news, weather, sports, showbiz, technology, food, and health updates in text, streaming audio and video.

Crayon
http://www.crayon.net

Create your own custom paper from hundreds of local, national, and international online sources, such as newspapers, site reviews, sports bulletins, weather reports, comics, and much more. It grabs the headlines. You click to retrieve the story. Looks a bit like the future of news. Try it – you'll be hooked.

Drudge Report
http://www.drudgereport.com

In case you slept through early 1998, this is the service that set off the Lewinsky avalanche. Drudge's knack of leaking media moonshine by free email bulletin, before the major press, has brought him widespread notoriety if not respect. Apart from providing forms to subscribe and submit scoops, the top page also serves as a front door to many of the best news sources on the Net.

Ecola's Newsstand
http://www.ecola.com/news/

Only paper-printed newspapers or magazines with actively updated English-language content and free access qualify for this list – that's over 6000. Search, browse, or check what's new.

The Economist
http://www.economist.com

Politics and business commentary, plus a small slab of the magazine free. The lot, if you subscribe.

The Electronic Daily Telegraph
http://www.telegraph.co.uk

Generous daily doses of news, sports, finance, entertainment, and pictures.

Electronic Newsstand
http://enews.com

Directory of over 2000 magazines' homepages, plus home to another 200 or so, with sample articles and subscription facilities. The UK press is better covered at:
http://www.britishmagazines.com

The Guardian Online
http://www.guardian.co.uk

Selections from the UK **Guardian**'s Thursday Online liftout,
snippets from the broadsheet, the entire weekly edition, jobs,
and cultural bits you won't find anywhere else. High quality,
but not a daily replacement.

The Hindu
http://www.webpage.com/hindu/

Daily online edition of India's national newspaper. Tons more
Indian press at: http://www.mahesh.com/india/media/

HotWired
http://www.hotwired.com

Part of the **Wired** magazine family, now focusing firmly on
the techie future. The site has delayed archives of the
magazine plus Wired News – an exceptional source of
breaking news of the new electric frontiers. Also a collection
of distinct ezines on Web design, Net culture, jobs, music,
and travel, including the full text of several Rough Guides.

Infobeat
http://www.infobeat.com

Personalized news, weather, sport, entertainment, snow
reports and reminders delivered to your mailbox free.

InfoSeek Personal
http://personal.infoseek.com

Live personalized news, stock quotes, comics, stars, weather, movie, and TV updates. Specify which topics, companies, people, sports, etc, you want to monitor and it will look after the rest. All the major search directories maintain something similar. You'll feel flooded.

MediaInfo
http://www.mediainfo.com/edpub/

Online publishing news, commentary, and advice from **Editor & Publisher** magazine. Also maintains an exceptional Web newspaper list.

Megastories
http://www.megastories.com

Backgrounds and behind-the-scenes reports on many of the world's big flare-ups like Northern Ireland and Algeria.

Multimedia Newsstand
http://mmnewsstand.com

Probably as good as anywhere to lodge subscriptions to any of over 600 popular magazines or to order videos. Little in the way of content though.

NewsHub
http://www.newshub.com

Technical, World, Tech PR, Health, Entertainment, Finance and other Headlines from several sources, updated every quarter hour. Click on the headline to go direct to the original story. Saves flipping through several sites.

News Index
http://www.newsindex.com

Search current news across a massive list of international online newspapers and news sources.

New York Times
http://www.nytimes.com

Pretty close to the entire current national edition and more in the archives. As is becoming the trend, you might have to pay to read some of the older stories.

PA NewsCentre

http://www.pa.press.net

24-hour live UK news, parliamentary proceedings, weather, sports, broadcast listings and ball-by-ball cricket.

Pathfinder

http://www.pathfinder.com

Whoah, this one from Time Warner's a monster, with something for everyone. With publications like **Time**, **People**, **Sports Illustrated**, **Life**, **Money**, **Fortune**, **Entertainment Weekly**, and **Vibe**, plus CNN, to draw from, that's to be expected. But it's not all rehashed features and samples. It's a publishing venture in its own right and more like what you'd expect from an Online Service. Modeled on Crapfinder: http://c3f.com/crapfind.html

PM Zone

http://popularmechanics.com

Popular Mechanics has been showing us "the easy way to do hard things" since the turn of the century. It provides a generous selection of stories, retrospectives, movies, Web tools, home improvement projects, and much more.

Ribcast
http://www.ribcast.com

Pay to have all your favorite Russian newspapers dumped onto your desktop using that trendy push technology.

Ringing World
http://www.luna.co.uk/~ringingw/

Sunday morning noise polluters of the world unite.

South Polar Times
http://205.174.118.254/nspt/home.htm

Whenever the temperature hits a hundred below, the gallant South Polars first squeeze into a sauna, then charge out into the snow starkers from the socks up. That's what they do for fun, in case you've ever wondered.

Sydney Morning Herald
http://www.smh.com.au

Streamlined news, columns, sports, computers, and the Metro, on the Net before the **Herald** hits the street. Plus archives, opinion polls, and links to the **Financial Review** and Melbourne's **The Age**.

The Times (London)
http://www.the-times.co.uk   http://www.sunday-times.co.uk

The full *Times* and *Sunday Times* newspapers, on the Net, before breakfast. Threatens to make print look redundant.

This is London
http://www.thisislondon.co.uk

Online version of London's afternoon daily, the *Evening Standard*, which doubles as a decent "what's on guide" to the British capital.

Ultimate Collection of News links
http://pppp.net/links/news/

Broad selection of magazines and newspapers.

USA Today
http://www.usatoday.com

News, sport, money, life, and weather from the US national daily.

The Village Voice
http://www.villagevoice.com

What's on in New York plus links to several other major US streetmags.

The Voice of America
http://www.voa.gov

Listen to audio clips of the day's news in various languages as you browse the staid megabroadcaster's other info.

PERSONAL

American Singles
http://www.as.org

Massive free international lonely hearts billboard.

Cupid's Network
http://www.cupidnet.com

Don't stay home alone playing on your computer. Join a few of these agencies, submit your interests – beer, cheap curry, Nukem, footy, engine numbers, and speed metal, say – and sit back and wait. Before long, you'll be Dukematching by candlelight.

Match.com
http://www.match.com

Browse for a perfect match. All entries come from the Net. Dip out here, then try: http://www.date.com

Pen Pal Directory
http://www.yahoo.com/Society_and_Culture/Relationships/Pen_Pals/

Exchange email with strangers.

RSVP
http://www.rsvp.com.au

Seek out a pedigreed Aussie.

Vampire Connection
http://www.cclabs.missouri.edu/~c667539/vwp/connect/

Give blood as an act of love.

POLITICS

Amnesty International
http://www.amnesty.org

"If you think virtual reality is interesting, try reality," says Amnesty International, global crusaders for human rights. Discover how you can help in its battles against militant regimes and injustice.

Australian Political Parties
http://www.liberal.org.au
http://www.npa.org.au
http://www.alp.org.au
http://www.democrats.org.au

Liberal, National, Labor, and Democrat parties' sites respectively, with news, history, policies and contacts (although few by email). Expect a flurry of fresh content when Howard pitches for another crack at the country's coffers.

British Political Parties
http://www.labour.org.uk
http://www.libdems.org.uk
http://www.conservative-party.org.uk

Now that the hustings are history, and the reality's set in, all's left is for Labour to deliver. Again, though it's unlikely you'll see much but press releases and policies on any of these pages before election time, they're still a good source for contacts to badger.

Noam Chomsky Archive
http://www.worldmedia.com/archive/

The works of Noam Chomsky, MIT Professor of Linguistics and outspoken critic of US foreign policy. He might change the way you read the world.

Conspiracies
http://www.mt.net/%7Ewatcher/
http://www.conspire.com

There's no doubt about it. Certain people are up to something and what's worse they're probably all in it together. If these exposés of the 60 biggest cover-ups of all time aren't proof

enough, then do your bit and create one more convincing:
http://www.turnleft.com/conspiracy.html

DeathNet
http://www.islandnet.com/~deathnet/open.html

A side-effect of DeathNet's euthanasia campaign was the
media's predictable focus on the Net as a medium for
encouraging suicide. Consequently a large slab of this "right
to die" library is dedicated to examples of press
dramatization.

Friends of the Earth
http://www.foe.co.uk

Find out about Friends of the Earth's latest campaign, your
nearest group, results of environment studies, or check out
how to join forces.

The Gallup Organization
http://www.gallup.com

About 20% of Gallup's online visitors fill out its
questionnaires and opinion polls. Not a bad response
compared to say, Barclays' callers requesting credit card
flyers. It also supplies results of past surveys, so you can
keep up to date with trends and ratings such as the fickle
swings of Slick Willy's popularity.

Greenpeace International
http://www.greenpeace.org

Apparently the happy ending starts here.

Hatewatch
http://www.hatewatch.org

Not everyone will agree the site's premise: "It's the ignorance
of hate groups and their ideologies that allow the spread of
these vile and poisonous ideas to continue." In fact, most
people argue the direct opposite. Whatever the case, there's a
bundle of nastiness linked from here, and you'll probably
agree that they do look pretty pathetic in the light of day.

Hempseed
http://www.hempseed.com

Score a free POP3 mail account that says you're pro dope for
rope.

InfoWar
http://www.infowar.com

Information on warfare issues from prank hacking to
industrial espionage and military propaganda.

Jane's IntelWeb
http://intelweb.janes.com

Brief updates on political disturbances, terrorism,
intelligence agencies, and subterfuge worldwide. For a full
directory of covert operations, see:
http://www.dreamscape.com/frankvad/covert.html

Neofeminism
http://www.neofeminism.com

Help beta test the platform preview of neofeminism.
According to its authors, this release updates and sorts out
interoperability problems between feminism, paleofeminism,
separatist feminism, postmodern feminism, Marxist
feminism, ecofeminism, and radical feminism. Don't forget to
report any bugs to the developers.

One World
http://www.oneworld.org

> Crisis news, submitted by a who's who of NGOs and charities, along with their plans. All sortable by country, date, and theme. Plus, daily archived RealAudio news from several short-wave broadcasters.

The Progressive Review
http://emporium.turnpike.net/P/ProRev/

> Washington dirt dug up from all sides of the fence.

Revolutionary Association of the Women of Afghanistan
http://www.rawa.org

> And you think you have problems with men.

Spunk Press
http://www.spunk.org

> All the anarchy you'll ever need organized neatly and with reassuring authority.

Trinity Atomic Test Site
http://www.envirolink.org/issues/nuketesting/

> See what went on, and what went off, fifty years ago, then file into the archives of high-energy weapon testing, and read who else has been sharpening the tools of world peace.

United Nations Development Program
http://www.undp.org

> Daily news of the UN's involvement in international affairs.

US Party politics
http://www.democratic-party.org
http://www.townhall.com

> There's unlikely to be anything new here from the Democrats until Bill dusts off his sax for Gore's campaign. However, the Conservative Town Hall has been in top gear, chirpily splattering dirt throughout the entire term. If only First Emperor Norton had got his way:
> http://www.zpub.com/sf/history/nort.html

RADIO

Looking for live Net radio? Download the Real Player first from: http://www.real.com, then check http://www.timecast.com for the latest broadcast listings.

Art Bell
http://www.artbell.com

Tune into the X-Files of radio via RealAudio.

BBC
http://www.bbc.co.uk

Becoming the broadcasting blockbuster online it is on the airwaves. That makes it somewhat daunting, but worth the exploration. Dig in and you'll find BBC TV, radio and World Service program mini-sites of varying quality, some with full length RealAudio archives. Take Radio 1, for example. If you miss Pete Tong, John Peel, or its swinging technology special, the Digital Update, you can catch them all online, anywhere in the world. Whatever you expect from the Beeb, be it education, news, sport or music, it's surfacing here.

Broadcast.com
http://www.broadcast.com

RealAudio, RealVideo, Netshow and VDOLIve broadcasts from over 250 radio and television stations, live sports and music, thousands of CDs on demand and more in the vaults.

BRS Radio Directory
http://www.radio-directory.com

Radio stations around the world with Web sites and, in many cases, live or archived audio feeds.

Crystal Radio
http://www.midnightscience.com

Build a simple radio that needs no battery.

Interface
http://www.pirate-radio.co.uk/interface/

Listen to live London pirate radio wherever you live.

NetRadio
http://www.netradio.net

Over 150 channels of streaming audio across a multitude of genres from drum'n'bass to country.

Police Scanner
http://www.policescanner.com

Live police, fire, aviation, and racetrack scanner feeds piped into RealAudio. Eavesdrop on busts in progress.

Phil's Old Radios
http://www.accessone.com/~philn/

If you've ever drifted to sleep bathed in the soft glow of a crackling Bakelite wireless, Phil's collection of vacuum-era portables may instantly flood you with childhood memories.

Radio Station WXYC
http://sunsite.unc.edu/wxyc/

Live broadcasts from college radio WXYC, the first real-time station on the Net.

Satco DX Satellite Chart
http://www.satcodx.com

Where to point your dish and what you can expect to receive.

Shortwave Radio Catalog
http://itre.ncsu.edu/radio/

If it's not on the Net, maybe it's crackling over the airwaves.
Find out what's on what frequency, and get the latest station
ID clips, maps, news, satellite info, propagation reports,
sunspot readings, spy station sitings, and much more.

Triple J
http://www.abc.net.au/triplej/

Listen to the world's coolest national
youth network live via RealAudio, or
flip through selections from its well-
rotated playlist.

Veronica FM Kits
http://www.legend.co.uk/~veronica/

Build your very own clandestine radio station for less than
the price of a PC, and join ranks with:
http://www.0171.com/theradio/pirateradio/pirateradio.html and
http://www.frn.net

Virgin Radio
http://www.virginradio.co.uk

Tune into London's Virgin FM live via RealAudio.

REAL ESTATE & HOMES

Ask the Master Plumber
http://www.clickit.com/bizwiz/homepage/plumber.htm

Save a small fortune by unblocking your own toilet.

Feng Shui
http://www.loop.com/~bramble/fengshui/

How to create the ambience of a Chinese restaurant.

Home Tips
http://www.hometips.com

Load your toolbox, roll up your sleeves, and prepare to go in.
More advice at: http://www.housenet.com and
http://www.naturalhandyman.com

Home Scout
http://www.homescout.com

Scan hundreds of US real estate databases at once.

International Real Estate Directory
http://www.ired.com

For the rare times in your life when you'll actively seek the attentions of a real estate hawker. Wherever you want to live, this site will have you sheltered in a flash.

Maui Buy the Inch
http://aloha-mall.com/buy-maui/

Stake out a square inch of Maui for only $15.99.

Pike Net
http://www.pikenet.com

Useful service that reviews and rates commercial real estate sites in over 250 market areas and 42 categories.

SmartCalc Financial Calculators
http://www.smartcalc.com

Figure out your monthly payments or what you can't afford.

UK Property Warehouse
http://www.uk-property.com

Well-organized, searchable warehouse of mostly UK properties for sale or rent. Also links to mortgage companies, removal firms, and everything else for moving home.

REFERENCE

Academic Info
http://www.academicinfo.net

Research directory aimed primarily at students and teachers.

Acronyms
http://www.ucc.ie/info/net/acronyms/acro.html

Before you follow IBM, TNT, and HMV in initializing your company's name, make sure it doesn't stand for something blue by searching through these 12,000 acronyms.

Altavista Translations
http://babelfish.altavista.digital.com

Translate text, including Web pages, between English and French, Spanish, Portuguese, Italian or German, in seconds. Run it back and forth a few times and you'll end up with something that wouldn't look out of place on a Japanese T-shirt. See also: http://www.globalink.com

alt.culture
http://www.altculture.com

Witty, digital A–Z of 1990s pop culture. Coupland meets *Encyclopaedia Britannica*. Fun to browse, maybe even enlightening, though don't blow your cool by admitting it.

Alternative Dictionary
http://www.notam.uio.no/~hcholm/altlang/

Insult your foreign pals in their mother tongue.

American ASL Dictionary
http://www.bconnex.net/~randys/

Learn sign language through simple animations.

AT&T's Toll-Free Directory
http://www.tollfree.att.net

Find those elusive 1-800 numbers and cut your phone bill. That is, if your online charges don't contra the savings.

BabyNamer
http://www.babynamer.com

Why not give your bub a cutesy name like Adolph? Apparently, it means "noble hero." That sounds nice. More suggestions to scar it for life at:
http://bnf.parentsoup.com/babyname/

Bartlett's Quotations
http://www.columbia.edu/acis/bartleby/bartlett/

Searchable database of smart remarks.

Britannica Online
http://www.eb.com

Buying this bulky set was never that practical, nor cheap. And it's not likely you'd ever read it all. So it makes more sense to leave it on a server where you can get at it as you need it, and leave it to EB to keep fresh. However, it's only free for a week. After that you or your masters will have to fork out.

Calculators Online
http://www.calculator.com

Awesome directory of some 6000 online tools to calculate everything from how much sump oil to put in soap, to the burden of bringing up brats.

Cliché Finder
http://www.westegg.com/cliche/

Submit a word or phrase to find how not to use it.

Encyberpedia
http://www.encyberpedia.com/eindex.htm

More of a directory of subject-orientated links than a genuine encyclopedia, but not a bad one all the same.

House of Evil Cheat
http://www.cheathouse.com

Thousands of college essays, termpapers and reports.

Jeffrey's Japanese/English Dictionary Gateway
http://www.wg.omron.co.jp/cgi-bin/j-e/

Translate English to Japanese and vice versa. View the output in plain English text or in Japanese characters either as images or via a Japanese character enhanced browser. It takes a while to get started, but there's plenty of help along the way.

LOGOS Dictionary
http://dictionary.logos.it/query/query.html

Searchable multilingual database which returns translations and example literary passages.

Megaconverter
http://www.megaconverter.com

Calculate everything from your height in angstroms, to the pellets of lead per ounce of buckshot needed to bring down an overcharging computer dealer.

One Look
http://www.onelook.com

Search more than 300 online dictionaries at once.

Online Dictionaries
http://www.bucknell.edu/~rbeard/diction.html

Linked to more than 500 dictionaries in 140 different languages.

Rap Dictionary
http://www.sci.kun.nl/thalia/rapdict/

Hip-hop to English. Parental guidance recommended.

Rhyming Dictionary
http://www.cs.cmu.edu/~dougb/rhyme.html

Find words that rhyme perfectly, just with the last syllable, or sound alike but are spelt differently, sorted by proximity in meaning to another word.

Roget's Thesaurus
http://www.thesaurus.com

The bible of big words finds life anew in hypertext. However, it's still useless.

Skeptics Dictionary
http://wheel.ucdavis.edu/~btcarrol/skeptic/dictcont.html

Punch holes through a bunch of popularly accepted superstitions and pseudo-sciences with this terse dinner-party deflator.

Study Web
http://www.studyweb.com

Ideal school research aid with thousands of leads split by topic.

Strunk's Elements of Style
http://www.columbia.edu/acis/bartleby/strunk/

English usage in a nutshell.

Symbols
http://www.symbols.com

Ever woken up with a strange sign tattooed on your buttocks? Here's where to find what it means without calling Agent Mulder.

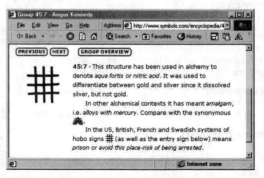

United States Postal Services
http://www.usps.gov

Look up a Zip code, track express mail, sort out your vehicle registration or just get down and philatelic.

What's in your name?
http://www.kabalarians.com/gkh/your.htm

According to the non-profit Kabalarians, who've been doing this stuff for over 60 years, names can be rendered down to a numerical stew and served back up as a character analysis. Look yourself up in here and see what a duff choice your folks made. Then blame them for everything that's gone wrong ever since. Of course, you could always revert to your Pacific island self:

http://www.hisurf.com/cgi-bin/DM/hawaiian_name.cgi?

What is?
http://whatis.com

Unravel cumbersome computer and Internet jargon without having even more thrown at you.

RELIGION

Anglicans Online!
http://www.anglican.org/online/

Gentle introduction to what Anglicans believe, with links to parishes, groups, and resources worldwide.

Avatar Search
http://www.AvatarSearch.com

Search the occult Internet for spiritual guidance and lottery tips.

Bhagavad Gita
http://www.iconsoftec.com/gita/

To view these PostScript Sanskrit pages of the Bhagavad Gita, the most sacred of Vedic literature, you'll need a program like GhostScript or a PostScript printer. However, if your Sanskrit is not up to scratch, you may find the English summary and translation easier going.

The Bible Gateway
http://www.calvin.edu/cgi-bin/bible/

Search the Bible as a database by textual references or passage. Or, turn scripture references into hyperlinks in your own documents by referring to the gateway in your HTML code.

Catholic Information Network
http://www.cin.org

Scripture, liturgy, early writings, Vatican documents, papal encyclicals, pronouncements, books, and other Catholic highjinks.

Chick
http://chick.com

Hard-core Christian pornography.

Christian Naturists
http://home.vistapnt.com/markm/

Frolic with other Christian funseekers, the way God intended.

Comparative Religion
http://www.academicinfo.net/religindex.html

Multifaith directory for religious academics.

Desecration Digest
http://www.christiangallery.com/digest.html

The ugly face of Christian fundamentalism.

The Global Hindu
http://www.hindunet.org

Hindu dharma – the philosophy, culture and customs.

The Holy See
http://www.vatican.va

Official Vatican showpiece. It's flashy, in six languages, and has to be said, boring beyond description. For more insight into the Pope's role, see: http://www.pacinst.com/antichri.htm

Homosexuals and the Church
http://www.qrd.com/QRD/religion/

Collection of links that reflect the church's attitude to sexuality.

Internet Satanic Syndicate
http://www.satanism.net

This lot has never enjoyed good press. If they're ever taken seriously it's only to be accused of some heinous crime against humanity, like backmasking racy slogans into heavy metal tracks, inciting suicide as a fashion statement, or killing the Czar and his ministers. According to these galoots, Satanism is a bona fide religion whose followers do not worship the devil, but follow their Darwinian urges to disinherit the meek of the earth.

Islamic Resources
http://latif.com

Links to Islamic FAQs, announcements, conferences, and social events, Qu'ran teachings, Arabic news, and the Cyber Muslim guide.

Jesus of the Week
http://www.phoenixnewtimes.com/extra/gilstrap/jesus.html

The original Mr Nice Guy in 52 coy poses per year. See if you can catch him wink at: http://www.fastlane.net/~sandman/jesus/

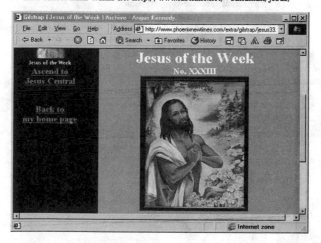

Magick

http://www.student.nada.kth.se/~nv91-asa/magick.html

Tunnels to alternative spiritualist groups, strange orders, superstitions, soothsayers, and mystical literature. All stuff you should know better than to believe in, though it still makes compulsive reading. Get to the Freemasons, Rosicrucians, Temple of the Psychic Youth, and Builders of the Atydium, as well as works on Voodooism, Druidism, divination, astrology, alchemy, and so much more – it casts an eerie light on the human condition.

Maven

http://www.maven.co.il

The Yahoo of Jewish/Israeli links.

Miracles Page

http://www.mcn.org/1/miracles/

Spooky signs that point towards a cosmic conspiracy.

Peyote Way Church of God

http://www.peyote.org

http://www.primenet.com/~idic/peyote.html

Unless you're Native American, or live in select southern US states, you stand to be locked up for finding God through the psychedelic cactus. Otherwise, feel free to fry your brain; just don't drive home from church.

Prophecy and Current Events

http://www.aplus-software.com/thglory/

You'll never guess who's coming to dinner. Don't bother cooking though, he's supposed to be a real whiz with food.

Table of Faiths

http://www.servtech.com/public/mcroghan/religion.htm

Links to info on various world religions, along with their principal saints, scriptures, and sects.

Universal Life Church

http://ulc.org/ulc/

You're already a member, just not aware of it yet. Ordain yourself a minister within seconds online and print out the certificate to frame for your bedroom wall.

The Witches' Voice
http://www.witchvox.com

Expresses a burning desire to correct misinformation about witchcraft, a legally recognized religion in the US since 1985.

SCIENCE AND SPACE

The Braintainment Center
http://www.brain.com

Start with a test that says you're not so bright, then prove it by buying loads of self improvement gear.

Business Card Menger's Sponge Project
http://world.std.com/~j9/sponge/

Build a Menger's sponge. You only need 66,048 business cards and some sort of reason.

Cool Robot of the Week
http://ranier.hq.nasa.gov/telerobotics_page/coolrobots.html

Clever ways to get machines to do our dirty work.

CICA Projects
http://www.cica.indiana.edu/projects/

These bods at the Center for Innovative Computer Applications are always up to something tricky. Whether it's stirring up Siamese Fighting Fish with animated challengers or weighting dices into four dimensions, they're not exactly sitting around watching the darts.

Documentation and Diagrams of the Atomic Bomb
http://neutrino.nuc.berkeley.edu/neutronics/todd/nuc.bomb.html

Gosh, here's how to make an atomic bomb. Let's hope this doesn't fall into the wrong hands.

Earth Viewer
http://www.fourmilab.ch/earthview/vplanet.html

View the Earth in space and time via this nifty simulator. Maps in real time to show the current positioning, lighting, and shadows.

Earthquake Information
http://www.civeng.carleton.ca/cgi-bin/quakes/

Stats and maps of the most recent quakes worldwide. For greater detail on the latest big one see:
http://www.gps.caltech.edu/~polet/recofd.html

Entomology Image Gallery
http://www.ent.iastate.edu/imagegallery/

If lice, ticks, mosquitoes, and potato beetles get you frisky, you'll sure leave this area feeling mighty aroused.

Exoscience
http://exosci.com

Scours the net for the latest astrophysics and astronomy news and particularly that relating to research into the origin, evolution, and distribution of life in the universe.

Interactive Frog Dissection
http://curry.edschool.virginia.edu/go/frog/

This step-by-step frog disembowelment was one of the Web's best-loved sites in its early days. Not because it's educational, interactive, and finely detailed. Nah, because it's so gruesome. All you have to do is pin a frog down, grab your scalpel, and follow the pictures. That's all very well, but what next – serve it up for lunch? Better a frog than a worm though: http://telcom.coos.k12.or.us/coquillstu/molls_place/worm.htm

History of Mathematics
http://www-groups.dcs.st-andrews.ac.uk/~history/

The life and times of various bright sparks with numbers.

Keirsey Temperment Sorter
http://www.keirsey.com/cgi-bin/keirsey/newkts.cgi/

Confirm what a beast you really are. Skeptics insist it's simply a psychological parlor game.

The Lab
http://www.abc.net.au/science/

Science features and news from the ABC, including fascinating weekly Q&As from Australian popscience superstar, Dr Karl Kruszelnicki.

Mars Home Page
http://mpfwww.jpl.nasa.gov

Get a bit more red dirt live from NASA's space safari before you stake out your first plot at: http://www.marsshop.com

MIT Media Labs
http://www.media.mit.edu

If you've read **Being Digital** or any of Nicholas Negroponte's **Wired** columns, you'll know he has some pretty tall ideas about our electronic future. Here's where he gets them.

NASA
http://www.nasa.gov

Top level of NASA's mighty Web presence. Its projects, databases, policies, missions, and discoveries are strewn across the Net, but you can find them all from here, if you persist. If you saw the first moon missions in the late 1960s, it's sure to bring back vivid memories of mankind's greatest step.

Netsurfer Science
http://www.netsurf.com/nss/

Subscribe to receive weekly bulletins on science and technology sites.

Net Telescopes
http://deepspace.physics.ucsb.edu http://www.telescope.org/rti/ http://inferno.physics.uiowa.edu

Probe deep space by sending requests to remote telescopes.

New Scientist
http://www.newscientist.com

Full features, back issues, daily bulletins, and scientific miscellany from the superlative science weekly.

Northern Lights – Aurora Borealis
http://www.uit.no/npt/homepage-npt.en.html

If you're ever lucky enough to see the aurora borealis during a solar storm, you'll never be able to look skyward with the same nonchalance again. It will challenge your notion of the visible universe and its relative stasis. This Norwegian planetarium does a commendable job in explaining a polar phenomenon that very few people understand. Except maybe these champs: http://www.geocities.com/CapitolHill/1606/akhaarp1.html

Nuclear Power Station

http://www.ida.liu.se/~her/npp/demo.html

Play Montgomery Burns and try to curb a meltdown.

PopSci

http://www.popsci.com

What's new in cars, computers, home technology, science, and electronics, from the editors of **Popular Science** magazine.

Rocketry Online

http://www.rocketryonline.com

Admit it, you've always wanted to build a rocket. Well, get to it.

Skeptics Society

http://www.skeptic.com

The Skeptics Society, a private organization of the intellectually curious and the perennially unconvinced, investigates the pseudosciences, paranormal, and claims of fringe groups. Subscribe to its magazine, order books and tapes, read newsletters, and find out what's new in the world of scientific inquiry.

Solar System Simulator

http://space.jpl.nasa.gov

Shift camp around the Solar System until you find the best view.

Space Calendar

http://newproducts.jpl.nasa.gov/calendar/calendar.html

Guide to upcoming anniversaries, rocket launches, meteor showers, eclipses, asteroid and planet viewings, occultations, and happenings in the intergalactic calendar.

Today's Space Weather

http://www.sel.bldrdoc.gov

If you're into short-wave radio or aviation, you'll know all about solar activity, its effects on communications and what you might do with a space weather report. If not, maybe you'll work it out from these pages. Then again, maybe you don't really need to know.

Volcano World

http://volcano.und.nodak.edu

Monitor the latest eruptions, see photos of every major volcano in the world and virtually tour a Hawaiian smoky without choking on sulfur fumes.

Web-Elements

http://www.shef.ac.uk/~chem/web-elements/

Click on an element in the periodic table and suss it out in depth.

Weird Science and Mad Scientists

http://www.eskimo.com/~billb/weird.html
http://www.student.nada.kth.se/~nv91-asa/mad.html

Free energy, Tesla, anti-gravity, aura, cold fusion, parapsychology, and other strange scientific projects and theories.

Why Files

http://whyfiles.news.wisc.edu

Entertaining explanations of the science behind current news topics.

SHOPPING

It's safe to say online shopping is finally here and, perhaps even, here to stay. Though it's not exactly a neatly organized experience, it certainly does offer advantages – particularly when you can't find something as cheaply, if at all, in your home town. In fact, finding a bargain has never been easier. You can visit several stores, in different parts of the world, all at once, simply by opening multiple browser windows. Or you could employ an agent like Bottom Dollar (see opposite), to find the best deal across several shops within seconds.

Of course, it helps if you know what you're buying, and with whom you're dealing, but these are the risks you always take with mail order. A good sign that a shop is serious is if it uses a secure server. This encrypts your details and makes it almost impossible for anyone to intercept them as they travel across the Net. But don't get too worried about someone stealing your credit card info surreptitiously – be more concerned about being overcharged, or regularly billed for a subscription you've tried to cancel. If you're tempted to flash your card in the red light zone, even as identification, expect to be played for a sucker. Outside this territory though, online fraud is exceptionally rare. All the same, do reconcile your statements, keep email records, and consult your bank if you strike problems. If your bank won't help, cancel your card immediately and shift your money. This applies doubly in the UK where the motto is often "sorry, it's not my job" rather than "the customer is always right." Eventually they might get the message.

The concept of shops bundled together into "cybermalls" is as good as dead. Today, most reputable businesses have their own root domain (eg roughguides.com). As with any Internet search, the best place to start is with the main directories and search engines. Yahoo, Excite, and Infoseek all have excellent shopping categories. Naturally, there are also several specialist shopping directories, a few of the best being: Shopomatic (http://www.shopomatic.com); All Internet Shopping Directory (http://www.all-internet.com); and Internet Shopper (http://www.internetshopper.com). Like every section, the following is only meant to get you off the ground. Within two clicks, you could be anywhere. See also our "**Books**" and "**Music**" sections for book and CD stores.

Auction Universe
http://www.auctionuniverse.com

Hock your castoffs across the Net. Buyers can instruct a bot to intelligently bid on their behalf and keep them posted on the progress. After the deal, there's the issue of payment and delivery to figure out. Being separated by an ocean might dampen proceedings.

Bottom Dollar
http://www.bottomdollar.com

Compare online prices of books, music, magazines, toys, movies, sporting goods, and computers across selected shops. Also try: Aureva (http://www.aureva.com), Virtual Outlet (http://www.virtualoutlet.com) and CompareNet (http://www.comparenet.com).

Catalog Mart
http://catalog.savvy.com

Why hunt through lists of catalogs, then join each separately when you can do it in bulk? Just choose all the product categories, send your details, and Catalog Mart will ensure your postie gets a few extra pounds to lug your way.

CatalogSite
http://www.catalogsite.com

Not every major US mail order house, but not far off it. Some offer online ordering but most simply another way to order their catalog.

CompUSA
http://www.compusa.com

Shop at the US computer megastore without being put off by the sales assistants.

Condom Country
http://www.condom.com

The mail order condoms, sex aids, books, and jokes are pretty harmless, but the mere mention of the penis size ready reckoner may prove disquieting to some. You'll find more of the same by wedging your favorite brand names between www and com

Conran Shop
http://www.conran.co.uk

Score a flash sofa online without having to suffer the indignity of sitting in it first.

Coolshopping
http://www.coolshopping.com

Be assured where it's "cool" to shop.

Floaty
http://www.floaty.com

The world's neatest tilt-and-something-nifty-happens pens, clocks, rings and watches.

Freeshop
http://www.freeshop.com

Hundreds of magazine trial subscriptions and assorted freebies.

Information Unlimited
http://www.amazing1.com

Awesome selection of serious weird science toys like Tesla coils, electro-hypnotizers, disorientation devices, class 4 laser kits and ultrasonic ray guns.

Interflora
http://www.interflora.com

Punch in your credit card number, apology, and delivery details, and land back in the good books before you get home.

Kellner's Fireworks
http://www.kellfire.com/fireworks.html

Mail order light explosives.

Khazana
http://khazana.com

Indian and Nepalese collectables purchased direct from the artisans and artists, with a "fair trade" policy of payment.

Lakeside Products
http://wholesalecentral.com/Lakeside/

Order the gags and novelties you could never afford when you really needed them. They're all here. Whoopee cushions, X-ray specs, itching powder, joke buzzers, and coffin piggy banks, ripped straight from the pages of your childhood comics. And, it's still the same company selling them.

Loot
http://www.loot.co.uk

British trash, real estate, and assorted classifieds.

Macys
http://www.macys.com

Order essentials like shirts and stockings online, or email a personal assistant to stock your entire wardrobe.

Marrakesh Express
http://uslink.net/ddavis/

Come my friend – I'll show you something special. If you've been pestered to the end of your tether by Moroccan carpet dealers, maybe this might breathe new life into those rugs you tried so hard to avoid.

Mind Gear
http://www.mind-gear.com

There's a theory that if you bombard yourself with light and sound of a certain frequency you'll be bludgeoned into a higher state of consciousness. Mind Gear sells various such devices, tapes, and potions to realign your noodle.

Mondotronics Robot Store
http://www.robotstore.com

Build machines that do exactly what they're told. Exterminate, exterminate!

New and Kewl
http://www.new-kewl.com

New and nifty gadgets on sale around the Net.

Newsclassified
http://www.newsclassifieds.com.au

Classifieds from Murdoch's Australian papers.

Onsale Online Auction Supersite
http://www.onsale.com

Bid on consumer electronics, sporting and computer goods.

Pet Nuke
http://www.petnuke.com

Beef up your home security with this prestigious nuclear ornament.

Pricecheck
http://www.pricecheck.co.uk

Cross check for the best UK rate on gas, electricity, mortgage, savings and new cars.

Sorcerer's Shop

http://www.sorcerers-shop.com

Attract love and fortune using bottled potions rather than charm and skill. If that doesn't work, you might have to resort to Voodoo: http://www.spellmaker.com

Spy Base

http://www.spybase.com

Get to know your neighbors better.

Tokyo Classified

http://www.tokyoclassified.com

Jobs, flats and bric-a-brac in the world's most expensive city.

Used Software Exchange

http://www.midwinter.com/usox/

Search for used software by type, price, currency, and platform. Works like a classified listing. You contact the vendor directly.

Yacht Broker
http://www.yachtbroker.com

Scan through the list of yachts on offer, find something in your price range, and then access a staggeringly detailed description complete with pictures of the craft. Once you've narrowed it down to two or three, you can email or phone to arrange a viewing. Theoretically, it can arrange delivery anywhere in the world.

SPORT

Abdominal Training
http://www.dstc.edu.au/TU/staff/timbomb/ab/

Get "abs like ravioli."

Australian Football League
http://www.afl.com.au

Aggregated news, live Netcasts and round highlights from the official home of aerial ping-pong.

Charged
http://www.charged.com

For all that falls under the banner of "extreme sports," from taking your pushbike offroad to the sort of sheer recklessness that would get you cut from a will.

CBS Sportsline
http://www.sportsline.com

US sports news, scores, gossip, and fixtures, including live play-by-play baseball action.

Cric Info
http://www.cricket.org

Cricket is some bizarre Zen thing. A test match can span five days in the blazing Faisalabad midsummer sun. Often without result. Yet buffs ponder every ball, awaiting the birth of some new statistic. But the ultimate indulgence is following such a match on the other side of the world, ball by ball, over the Internet, while periodically checking Cricinfo's stat tables during tea breaks. Ommm ...

ESPN Sportzone
http://espnet.sportszone.com

Live news, statistics, and commentary on major US sports.

Faith Sloan's Bodybuilding Site
http://www.frsa.com/bbpage.shtml

Galleries of the grimacing human form pushed to near-illogical extremes, as well as competition results, videos, fan mail addresses, workout advice, and links to vanity pages.

Fastball
http://www.fastball.com

Major league baseball scores, news, stats, games and discussion.

Flyfish.com
http://www.flyshop.com

Meeting point to trade tips and generally exaggerate about aquatic bloodsports. Don't let this one get away.

Goals – Global Online Adventure Learning Site
http://www.goals.com

Follow the progress of adventurous lunatics like Mick Bird, who's striving to become the first person to row around the world.

Golf.com
http://www.golf.com

Grab the latest news on chipping, driving, and putting tournaments worldwide. Then slip on your checkered strides, cruise into the travel section, and picture yourself in one of 25,000 listed courses belting a ball to your heart's content.

Internet Disc Shoppe
http://www.digimark.net/disc/

Why risk your fingernails in a rough sport like rugby or strain your back over a croquet stick when you can fling one of these blighters back and forth? They're totally foolproof and available where all good ice cream is sold.

Manchester United Football Club

http://www.sky.co.uk/manu/
http://www.iol.ie/~mmurphy/red_devils/mufc.htm

Get match reports, news and gossip from Old Trafford, and all the latest on Giggsy and the lads.

NBA.com

http://www.nba.com

Official home of the NBA with loads of pro basketball news, picks, player profiles, analyses, results, schedules, and highlight videos.

Rugby League

http://www.rleague.com

Read how 26 men bash themselves senseless, push each other's faces into the dirt as they're rising, and then meet for a drink afterwards. Stats, news and scores posted after every game.

Sailing Index

http://www.sailingindex.com

Neat directory of links to sailing resources like racing authorities, regatta bulletins, commercial suppliers, weather reports, cruising destinations, and clubs.

Scrum.com
http://www.scrum.com

Up-to-date rugby coverage from Five Nations to the Super 12.

SkiCentral
http://www.skicentral.com

Indexes more than 4000 ski related sites. Like snow reports, resort cams, snowboard gear, accommodation, and coming events in resorts across the world.

Sky Sports
http://www.sky.co.uk/sports/

Regular soccer, golf, boxing, tennis, cricket, rugby and superleague scores and news updates.

SoccerNet
http://www.soccernet.com

Daily Mail-driven shrine to all that's footy in Britain and a little bit beyond. But if it's European, Latin American, Australian or even Japanese you're after, you'll find a link to it here: http://www.justwright.com/rss/links.html

Sporting Life
http://www.sporting-life.com

Comprehensive coverage of all British sports including live cricket and football feeds.

SportsWeb
http://www.sportsweb.com

Sports news from Reuters, fresh off the wire.

Stats
http://www.stats.com

Pig in to an overflowing trough of baseball statistics.

Stockdog Server
http://www.stockdog.com/stockdog.htm

Keep up with who's who in the stockdog trials. Where the only two mammals with any mutual affection collaborate to corner a very stupid animal into an enclosure. This ambush is appraised by the dominant species while the subordinates inspect each others' equipment. Also includes some sturdy shots of startled sheep, if that's your scene.

When Saturday Comes
http://www.wsc.co.uk/wsc/

Britain's original football fanzine produces a self-described "half-decent Web page," with the daily news stories from the tabloids and a bit more besides.

World Surfing
http://www.goan.com/surflink.html

Regionally sorted links to the sort of dude stuff that real surfers live for. Like how to forecast waves, where El Niño's at, surfboard shops, Dick Dale riffs, surf reports and tons of surfcams. And for the only magazine tough guys are allowed to read in public, see: http://www.msp.com.au/tracks/

Wrestling.com
http://www.wrestling.com

Vent the frustration of helplessly watching your boofhead heroes being piledriven, suplexed, and moonsplashed, by spilling some hardway juice virtually. Though if you prefer seeing them simply smack each other in the head, drop by: http://www.boxing.com

Yahoo Sports
http://www.yahoo.com/Recreation/Sports/

Yahoo's Sports arm is undoubtedly the fattest bag of sports links you'll find. If you can't get to your healthy obsession within a couple of jumps from here, it probably doesn't exist.

SUPPORT

Adoption.com
http://www.adoption.com

International gateway for parents seeking to adopt or place children.

Alien Implant Removal and Deactivation
http://www.abduct.com/irm.htm

Discover, within a free three-minute phone call, how many times you've been abducted and which implants you're carrying. Then it's just a matter of surgically removing them and sorting out your mental health. Perhaps the latter is all that's needed.

Ask-a-Chick
http://www.ask-a-chick.com

Girl advice for confused boys.

Bastard Nation
http://www.bastards.org

Parent search advice, campaigns, and support with a tinge of humor.

Breakup Girl
http://www.breakupgirl.com

How to mend a broken heart and get on with your life. Or better still, reject them first:

http://www.xtra.co.nz/content/loveman/reject.html

Cyberspace Inmates
http://www.cyberspace-inmates.com

Strike up an email romance with a prison inmate, perhaps even one on death row.

Gulf War Veterans
http://www.gulfweb.org

Lest we forget.

National Center for Missing and Exploited Children
http://www.missingkids.org

Help locate missing children and track down abductors. The success rate to date has been about one in seven, which is more than 30,000 children. So be aware it exists and call if you can help.

Psychological Self-Help Resources
http://www.psych-web.com/resource/selfhelp.htm

Many psychological disorders can be self-cured. For some, it's the only solution. The answer usually comes through finding others who've overcome the same anxieties or neuroses and taking their advice. The Net is the perfect medium for this sort of interaction as it's easy to make contact and still maintain your privacy. This site lists hundreds of resources for such support.

Queer Resources Directory
http://www.qrd.org/qrd/

AIDS support, legal news, attitude trends, clubs, publications, broadcasts, images, political action, community groups, and assorted gay links. See also: http://www.datalounge.com

Silent Witness
http://www.getnet.com/silent/

Become a bounty hunter for the Phoenix police department. Just take the brief, get on the case, find your quarry, and call the toll-free number to claim your booty.

Weddings in the Real World
http://www.theknot.com

Get ready to jump the broom.

TELECOMMUNICATIONS

Free Fax Service
http://www.tpc.int

Transmit faxes anywhere in the world via the Internet for the price of your connection. In practice, coverage is limited and subject to delays. But give it a shot anyway.

J-Fax
http://www.jfax.com

Provides a unique phone/fax number in many cities that forwards your incoming faxes and voicemail as email attachments. Plus you can send faxes the same way. Costs less than Internet access.

RelayOne
http://relayone.msn.com

Have your email or attached document printed and delivered by first class post from the Royal Mail Electronic Services Centre in London.

What does your phone number spell?
http://www.phonespell.org

Enter your phone number and check all permutations of corresponding letters to see what it spells. The reverse lookup might be useful when choosing a number.

World Time & Dialing Codes
http://www.whitepages.com.au/time.shtml

International dialing info from anywhere to anywhere, including current times and area codes.

TIME

28 hour Day
http://www.kaplan.com/cellar/28hours.html

Living by a 28-hour day, 6-day week regime has a number of benefits, according to one Mr. Mike Biamonte. No more Mondays for one.

Date and Time Gateway
http://www.bsdi.com/date/
http://www.stud.unit.no/USERBIN/steffent/verdensur.pl

Click on a city to get the local time.

The Death Clock
http://www.deathclock.com

Watch the countdown to your final taxi.

EarthTime

http://www.starfishsoftware.com/products/et/activeet/activeet.html

Active X control that displays the times in your choice of
eight cities. But that's just the start. It can synchronize your
PC with an atomic clock across the Net, show the Sun's path
across the Earth and perform a mindboggling range of
measurement conversions. All that and it's free.

Freeminder

http://www.cvp.com/freemind/

Send yourself a timely email reminder.

Greenwich 2000

http://www.greenwich2000.com

Tick down the seconds to the new millennium, get ready for
celebrations, and link to the best of the Net's time resources.

International Earth Rotation Service

http://hpiers.obspm.fr

Ever get that feeling that your bed's spinning? The truth is
even scarier, as you'll find out here.

Java Clocks

http://www.developer.com/directories/pages/dir.java.util.clocks.html

Hundreds of clock applets to insert into Web pages or run as
lone applications.

Virtual VCR Clock

http://www.wvi.com/~odonnell/vcrclock.htm

You'll have to see it to understand.

TRANSPORT

Aircraft Shopper

http://www.aso.com

Troubled by traffic? Rise above it, with something from this
range of new, used, and charter aircraft. And if you can't fly,
then sign up for training or flight simulation.

All-In-One British Timetables
http://www.ukonline.co.uk/UKOnline/Travel/contents.html

Form access to timetables of leading UK carcass haulers like BA, Eurostar, British Rail, and National Express coaches plus links to just about everything else that moves across the Isles. Beats waiting on the phone.

Aviation Safety Records
http://www.faa.gov/asafety.htm

Way more goes wrong up in the air than you realize. Here's why you should be terrified to fly. If you're still not convinced then see and hear the results of overconfidence behind the joystick at: http://www.cam.org/~gilmour/

BAC Testing
http://www.copsonline.com/bac2.htm

Slurring your swearwords, wobbling all over the road, mounting gutters and knocking kids off bikes? Pull over and blow into this site.

DealerNet
http://www.dealernet.com

Locate, browse, compare specs, and read reviews of the latest new and used cars, boats, and speciality vehicles from trusty US dealers.

Deep Flight: In Pursuit of the Earth's Last Frontier
http://www.deepflight.com

Get your license from the world's first underwater aviation school so you can voyage to the bottom of the sea in an ultra-maneuverable space-age sub that looks like a jet fighter crossed with Thunderbird 4. Then if you'd like to scare the fish in your own custom-built U-boat, file an order at: http://ussubs.com

European Railways Server

http://mercurio.iet.unipi.it/home.html

Timetables, news, and groovy liveries created by ardent loco locos. Some are faithful reproductions depicting national color schemes, while others are fantasy sketches conjuring up futuristic engines.

Exchange and Mart

http://www.exchangeandmart.co.uk

Choose from over 50,000 used British bangers. As you can filter it down by locality, make, model, price, color, and more, it's actually superior to the print edition.

Layover

http://www.layover.com

Long wide loads of essential truckin' stuff, plus special features like the diary of a lonely trucker's wife and an Internet guide for prime movers and shakers.

License Plates of the World

http://danshiki.oit.gatech.edu/~iadt3mk/

Ring in sick, cancel your date, unplug the phone and don't even think about sleep until you've seen EVERY LICENSE PLATE IN THE WORLD.

NMRA Directory of World Wide Rail sites
http://www.rrhistorical.com/nmra/nmralink.html

Locophilial banquet of railroad maps, databases, mailing lists, transit details, and hundreds of shunts all over the Net.

No Risk: Used Car Buying
http://www.goodasnew.com

Do your homework before going toe to toe with Honest John.

Paramotor
http://cyberactive-1.com/paramotor/

According to this source, paramotors are the among the smallest, yet safest, aircraft. They require no license, weigh less than 65 pounds, can be lugged about in a backpack, assembled in under five minutes, and can soar to heights of 10,000 feet at up to 500 feet per minute. At less than $10,000, what are you waiting for?

Piaggio
http://www.piaggio.com

50 years have ticked away since Piaggio unleashed its first two-wheeled peepy-horned menace onto safe European roads. Yet even today many modern young nostalgics and potential kidney donors reckon the Vespa scooter remains the absolute quintessence of cool. You won't find disagreement here but you will learn more about its origins and what's yet to grace the piazza.

Professional Pilots Rumor Network
http://www.pprune.com

First hand tales of terror in the air.

Woman Motorist
http://www.womanmotorist.com

Features aimed at the demographic group that motor vehicle insurers prefer.

Yesterday's Tractors
http://www.ytmag.com

Tribute to the world's most criminally underrated convertibles.

TRAVEL

Travel is another huge area of the Net – and fast becoming one of its commercial successes as folks gain confidence to book flights and car rental online, and maybe travel with laptops to browse travel guides and what's on listings. Site selections below are only the tip of the iceberg. For impressive wads of links, check Excite and Yahoo! Travel.

A2Btravel.com
http://www.a2btravel.com

One-stop shop for travelling into, around, and out of the UK. Includes: flight booking; up-to-the-minute flight arrival and departure times; a massive hotel finder; car hire and price comparisons; ferry, bus and train timetables; traffic reports; and loads of travel tips and stories.

Adventurous Traveler Bookstore
http://www.gorp.com/atbook.htm

No matter how far you're heading off the track, this store has the guides, maps, and videos to help you on your way.

AESU
http://www.aesu.com

Reserve discounted US air departures.

Air Traveler's Handbook
http://www.cis.ohio-state.edu/hypertext/faq/usenet/
travel/air/handbook/top.html

Now that this FAQ-style travel cookbook has been converted to hypertext, it's quite easy to find your way around. It aims to wise you up to the tricks of the travel trade, help you beat the system, save you money, and get you home in one piece.

Amsterdam
http://clix.net/clix/amsterdam/

Certain people drool pavlovially at the mere mention of Amsterdam. Must be all the tulips or something. Whatever, the Dutch capital is most definitely wired.

Arab Net

http://www.arab.net

Bulging omniscient resource of rare detail comprising thousands of pages on North Africa and the Middle East, their peoples, geography, economy, history, culture, and, of course, camels. See also:

http://www.1001sites.com and http://www.i-cias.com

Art of Travel

http://www.artoftravel.com

25 chapters of advice on how to see the world on $25 a day.

Bargain Holidays (UK)

http://www.bargainholidays.com

Want to go somewhere, anywhere really, say tomorrow even, if it's cheap enough? See what you think of these fares.

British Foreign Office Travel Advice

http://www.fco.gov.uk

Use this service in conjunction with the US travel warnings when planning your next holiday in Afghanistan or Chad, but don't rely on it as a sole source: it's often hopelessly brief, or out of date, and tends to recommend that you contact the local consul.

Cheap Flights

http://www.cheapflights.co.uk

Scouts the travel market for the best deals on flights worldwide from UK airports, supported by ample links to airlines, agents, guideboks, weather, currency converters, etc.

CIA World Factbook

http://www.odci.gov/cia/publications/pubs.html

Encyclopedic summary of every country's essential stats and details. Like geographical boundaries, international disputes, climate, geography, economy, demographics, government, communications, and defense. Perfect for a school project though not quite enough for a military takeover.

Currency Converter

http://www.oanda.com

Convert between a choice of over 160 daily updated currencies or chart them at: http://pacific.commerce.ubc.ca/xr/xplot.html

Electronic Embassy

http://www.embassy.org

Directory of foreign embassies in DC plus Web links where available.

Erich's Packing Center

http://www.stetson.edu/~efriedma/packing.html

Erich lives for packing geometric shapes into boxes. Why not invite him over next time you're stuffing your rucksack?

Excite Travel

http://www.city.net

Regionally sorted digest of links to community, geopolitical, and tourist information from all around the globe. Choose a locality directly or zoom in from a larger region.

Expedia

http://www.expedia.com
http://www.expedia.co.uk

Microsoft intend to be the future face of travel online and Expedia is their tool. It's basically a travel agency, enabling online booking of flights (including last minute deals), cars, and (in a rather corporate manner) hotels, and, as such it's pretty damn good, fueling numerous other travel Web sites, as well as its own homepages. Booking aside, Expedia's best feature is its "Links" which include 10,000 travel sites, arranged by city or country destination.

Fielding's Danger Finder
http://www.fieldingtravel.com/df/
Adventure holidays that could last a lifetime.

Find a Grave
http://www.findagrave.com
Find out where celebrities are buried, and in some cases see their graves. It's hard to say whether reuniting the Three Stooges posthumously by juxtaposing their gravestones on a Web page falls within the bounds of good taste, but it certainly stops you in your tracks.

Hotel Net
http://www.u-net.com/hotelnet/
Find, appraise, and reserve European hotels. Not many choices but what's covered is well documented.

How far is it?
http://www.indo.com/distance/
Calculate the distance between any two cities.

InnSite
http://www.innsite.com
Search an enormous crawler-built database of bed and breakfast sites.

International Student Travel Confederation
http://www.istc.org
Where to get an international student identity card and what it's good for.

Internet Travel Services
http://www.itsnet.co.uk
UK travel cybermall and directory, most notable for its late-booking search. Often a source of bargain fares.

J-Links
http://www.islandtel.com/j-links.html

One of the better Japanese link banks – in English, anyway.
If you're up to reading Japanese, you can't do better than
Yahoo Japan at: http://www.yahoo.co.jp Catch is you'll also need a
Japanese browser. But that's merely a download from
Netscape or Microsoft away.

Journeywoman
http://www.journeywoman.com

Smart magazine-style guide for sassy sisters on the road
with regular features like gal-friendly city sites, holiday
romances, and where to shop 'til you drop.

Lonely Planet Guidebooks
http://www.lonelyplanet.com.au

Good for summaries of every country in the Lonely Planet
series along with basic info and health precautions. But of
most use for it's wealth of first-hand tales posted by
backpacking survivors. Find travel partners, advice, and
ideas for your next stint away from the keyboard.

Maps On Us
http://www.mapsonus.com

Punch in any US address and generate a local map, or key in
two for maps and directions on how to get from one to the
other. But even more impressive is that, since it's jacked into
the Yellow Pages, you can key in a business name and get
full details (and map), or go the other way, for example,
finding all the bars within ten square miles of a nuclear
reactor. See also: http://www.mapblast.com

MCW International Travelers Clinic
http://www.intmed.mcw.edu/ITC/Health.html

Not much more than token preparation for the bugs that
await your alimentary displeasure, but its links should help,
if not entirely dissuade. These include the American Society
of Tropical Medicine, the AMSTMH directory of Travel Clinics
& Physicians, and the International Society of Travel
Medicine. Like the consular warnings, it's all bad news, so be
prepared for the worst. See also http://www.tripprep.com

Moon Travel Guides
http://www.moon.com

Read excerpts, and in some cases the full text, of Moon's acclaimed travel books. Or catch Travel Matters, its thrice-yearly newsletter, published in full online.

Netfind Travel
http://netfind.aol.com/aol/Reviews/Regional/Travel/

Decent bundle of travel links. Sorted, rated, and reviewed courtesy of AOL.

No Shitting in the Toilet
http://www.noshit.com.au

Comic take on the peculiarities of low-budget travel.

Outside Online
http://outside.starwave.com

Current and back issues of **Outside** magazine, spanning all kinds of outdoor hands-grubbying from cycling the Alps to saving Botswanan fleabags from extinction.

Paris
http://www.paris.org

Virtual tour of popular Parisian museums, cafés, monuments, shops, railways, colleges, and such. All in the comfort of English – or, if you want to punish yourself, French.

Priceline.com
http://www.priceline.com

State how much you'd like to pay for a domestic or international ticket from anywhere in the US and see if anyone will take up your offer. You should get an answer within an hour.

QuickAddress
http://www.qas.com

Reconcile UK postcodes and streets.

Roadside America
http://www.roadsideamerica.com

Guide to the strange attractions that loom between squished animals on US highways.

Rough Guides
http://www.roughguides.com

Okay, we're biased but in its new incarnation this has to be the #1 travel Web site. It features the full text from over 20 of the Rough Guide travel guides, and a rolling program will see almost every destination the books cover online by the end of 1999. It's free, searchable, and linked to flight and car rental online ordering mechanisms. Coming soon are links out to every reviewed site and establishment that's online, from small jazz clubs to hotels.

Sidewalk
http://www.sidewalk.com

Microsoft Network's personalized entertainment guides to major US cities and Sydney. A potential rival to **Time Out** (see below) if Bill's people continue to provide the finance.

Streetmaps (UK)
http://www.streetmap.co.uk

Key in a UK postcode or street address and pull up a corresponding map. You might find it a tad sluggish compared to flipping through an A to Z. Mapquest (http://www.mapquest.com) also has London maps along with several other major cities worldwide.

Terraserver
http://www.terraserver.com

Want to see what your house looks like from a Russian spy satellite? Here's your best chance to find out.

Time Out
http://www.timeout.co.uk

Fish through **Time Out**, London's weekly listings guide's site, and you'll find no excuse to stay at home in not just London, but also Amsterdam, Berlin, Edinburgh, Madrid, New York, Paris, Prague, Rome, San Francisco, Sydney, Tokyo, and more to follow. With fortnightly updated tourist guides to each city, classifieds, postcard stores, city maps, sample features and, of course, the highlights of what's on.

Travelocity
http://www.travelocity.com

Fully-featured DIY air, car and hotel reservation and scheduling service that patches you into over 700 airlines, 34,000 hotels and 50 car rental companies via the SABRE network.

The Trip
http://www.thetrip.com

Reservations, flight tracking, low fare notification, airport maps, ground transport strategies, hotel reviews and more. Aimed specifically at the frequent business traveler.

Tourism Offices Worldwide
http://www.mbnet.mb.ca/lucas/travel/tourism-offices.html

Locate tourist offices around the world, and if there's a Web presence, link to it. It's pretty low-fi but another place to look.

Traffic and Road Conditions
http://www.accutraffic.com

Live traffic updates in various US cities.

Travel Window
http://www.seaforths.com

Flight and hotel reservation through Galileo, as used by thousands of travel agents worldwide.

Travelmag
http://www.travelmag.co.uk/travelmag/

Several intimate travel reflections monthly.

TravelWeb
http://www.travelweb.com

Flight and hotel booking service with a special late notice weekend hotel bargain finder.

UK Travel Guide
http://www.uktravel.com

Three-part insight into the British way of doing things, comprising an A to Z of traveling within and from the UK, an interactive UK map leading to regional pics and sites, and a beginner's guide to the "world's most cosmopolitan city." Plus more at: http://www.visitbritain.com

US Travel Warnings
http://travel.state.gov/travel_warnings.html

Essential information if you're planning to visit a potential
hot spot, but not necessarily the last word on safety. It only
takes an isolated incident with a foreign tourist to start
panic, but years to settle the fear. Don't ignore these
bulletins, but seek a second opinion before postponing your
adventure.

Virtual Tour of Jerusalem
http://www.md.huji.ac.il/vjt/

After you've taken this pleasant tour through the old city of
Jerusalem, scout around the rest of Israel by selecting each
region from a contact-sensitive map.

The Virtual Tourist
http://wings.buffalo.edu/world/

Click on the atlas interface to zoom into the region of your
choice. Once you're down to country level, choose between a
resource map, resource list, or general country
information. Could ultimately link you with any server in
the region.

World's Largest Subway Map
http://metro.jussieu.fr:10001/

Pick from a selection of major cities and choose a starting
and finishing destination to estimate the traveling time. It's
relatively entertaining but not really practical – after all, how
many rail networks run this smoothly?

The World Traveler Books & Maps
http://www.travelbookshop.com

Order from a wide range of travel literature, online.

Xerox PARC Map Viewer
http://mapweb.parc.xerox.com/map/

Build your own maps showing rivers, roads, rail lines,
borders, and other information, by specifying a location.
From none other than the inventors of the GUI (Graphical
User Interfaces), the mouse, and Ethernet.

Yahoo Travel

http://www.yahoo.com/Recreation/Travel/

> Yahoo's travel section is one of its best stacked areas, with links to thousands of travel and regional sites. Most have one-liners, rather than reviews, but they'll give you some idea of what to expect. It's broad, but uncritical.

WEATHER

The Daily Planet

http://www.atmos.uiuc.edu

> Meteorological maps, satellite images, and pointers to sources of climatic data, courtesy of the University of Illinois Department of Atmospheric Sciences.

Intellicast

http://www.intellicast.com

> International weather, radar tracking and half-hourly satellite feeds in a sleek shell.

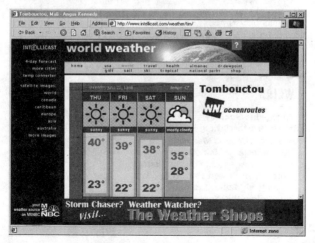

National Severe Storms Laboratory
http://www.nssl.uoknor.edu

These guys aren't put off by a bit of drizzle spoiling their ball game, they're out whipping up lightning rods on mountain peaks, trying to attract the big stuff. If tornadoes, blizzards, flash floods, thunderstorms, hurricanes, and cyclones are your idea of prime time viewing, you'd better read the bit on responsible storm chasing. It may just temper that Pavlovian frenzy for the car keys the next time a distant rumble snaps you from your post-prandial stupor.

World Climate
http://www.worldclimate.com

Off to Irkutzk next August? Here's where to find out what weather to expect.

World Meteorological Organization
http://www.wmo.ch

UN division that monitors global climate. Links to national bureaus worldwide.

World Weather
http://weather.yahoo.com
http://cnn.com/WEATHER/

Forecasts, charts, storm warnings, allergy reports, satellite photos and more for thousands of cities worldwide.

WEIRD

Aetherius Society
http://www.aetherius.org

When the Cosmic Masters from the Interplanetary Council need to give their message to Earth, Sir George King, their chosen Primary Terrestrial Mental Channel, must enter a Positive Yogic Samadhic Trance. Sort of like when Ramjet takes his protein pills.

Anders Main Page
http://www.student.nada.kth.se/~nv91-asa/

Immense and diverse digest that sways toward the occultish
side of spirituality, with a fair helping of transhumanism,
mad science, discordia, illumination, magic, and blatant
onanism.

The Ants are my friends
http://www.mcs.com/~bingo/lyrics/

Do you know someone who butts in all the time with "I
thought you said..." and then laughs? It's a pathological
disorder called Mondegreenism. The good news is you can
legally have them put down. The bad news is they're
everywhere: http://www.kissthisguy.com

Chocolate Toxicity in Dogs
http://www.netpet.com/articles/choc.tox.html

How to pop off a greedy mutt with household ingredients.

Church of the Subgenius
http://www.subgenius.com

Pipe-puffing Bob's three-fisted
surreal preaching. Beyond
description.

Clonaid
http://www.clonaid.com

Thanks to the Raelians, we now
know all life on earth was
created in extraterrestrial
laboratories. Here's where you
can buy genuine cloned human
livestock for the kitchen table.
Ready as soon as the lab's
finished.

Christian Guide to Small Arms
http://www.frii.com/~gosplow/cgsa.html

Then said he unto them, "But now, he that hath a purse, let
him take it, and likewise his scrip: and he that hath no
sword, let him sell his garment, and buy one." – Luke 22:36
Ouoh, it's not just your right, but your duty!

CNI Angel Gallery
http://www.cninews.com/CNI_Angels.html

Leading authorities point to evidence that angels may be alien frauds. Backed up at: http://www.mt.net/~watcher/

The Darwin Awards
http://www.officialdarwinawards.com

Each year, the Darwin Award is presented to the person who drops off the Census register in the most spectacular fashion. Here's where to read about the runners up and er ... winners.

Derm Cinema
http://www.skinema.com

Adds a whole new meaning to the term "skin flick."

Exploding Heads
http://www.mit.edu/people/mkgray/head-explode.html

Worried your head might explode? These tips identify early symptoms.

Faking UFOs
http://www.strw.leidenuniv.nl/~vdmeulen/deeper/Articles/UFOfake.html

Create your own crop circles to amuse New-Agers and the press.

FlyPower
http://www.flypower.com

We have the technology. We can build a bionic blowfly.

Fortean Times
http://www.forteantimes.com

Highlights and news from the print monthly that takes the investigation of strange phenomena consistently more seriously than itself.

Fractal Cow
http://www.fractalcow.com

This weirdzine won a "Weirdest Site of the Year" Webby in 1998 for its "Bert Is Evil" feature – currently suspended due to over-popularity.

Gallery of the Absurd
http://www.absurdgallery.com

Strange ways to sell strange stuff.

Geek Site of the Day
http://www.owlnet.rice.edu/~indigo/gsotd/

Further proof that geek is très hip. Each day, a new obsessive. Always entertaining.

George Goble's Page
http://ghg.ecn.purdue.edu

Engineer George demonstrates the power-user way to light a BBQ.

Great joy in great tribulation
http://www.dccsa.com/greatjoy/index.html

Biblical proof that Prince Chuck is the Antichrist and key dates leading to the end of the world. For more enlightenment, including how to debug the pyramids, see:
http://members.aol.com/larrypahl/lpahl.htm

Hutt River Province
http://www.wps.com.au/hutriver/

Leonard Casley got such a raw deal on his 1969 wheat quota
he officially seceded his 18,500-acre property from Western
Australia. The whole thing got so tied up in colonial red tape
that, to this day, no-one has marched in to reclaim the
territory. Consequently HRH Prince Leonard thinks it's quite
a lark to hand out passports, driver's licenses, and honors to
anyone who asks. Just fill out the forms.

Hyper-Weirdness
http://www.physics.wisc.edu/~shalizi/hyper-weird/

Links to some of the Web's most impassioned wells of
weirdness. You name it: UFOs, cults, political action groups,
extropians, fringe science, fantasy, and drugs. Water always
seems to find its own level.

Infamous Exploding Whale
http://www.xmission.com/~grue/whale/

Easy. Take one beached whale carcass, add half a ton of
dynamite, turn on the video, and run. In this case not all
went as planned.

Klingon Language Institute
http://www.kli.org/klihome.html

With multimedia language tutorials like this, it's a wonder
Klingon isn't more widely spoken. In fact, if Captain James T.
Kirk had a better grip on it perhaps the Enterprise would be
still in one piece. Oh, and don't miss **Hamlet** restored to the
Bard's native tongue.

Mind Control Forum
http://www.mk.net/~mcf/

Horrific tales of being remote controlled by Big Brother's
psychotronic devices. Surely, it can only be a matter of time
before it's built into Windows.

MouSing Theremin
http://www.swcp.com/~sells/mousing.htm

Make eerie sounds with your mouse.

Mozart's Musical Dice
http://sunsite.univie.ac.at/Mozart/dice/

Anyone can write music. Even you. Just by rolling a dice. Well that's what Mozart reckoned anyway. See for yourself, or be like U2 and toss a coin.

Mrs. Silk's Cross Dressing Magazine
http://www.mrs-silk.com

Mrs. Silk can furnish you with a variety of products to ensure that when you do step out of the closet, it's with style.

News of the Weird
http://nine.org/notw/

Chuck Shepard's syndicated column of bizarre news. Get it here, or subscribe to have it delivered direct to your mailbox, weekly.

Project Destination Moon
http://www.caus.org/destmoon.htm

Help fund the first civilian moon launch, which aims to get to the bottom of the funny business in the Sinus Medii region.

Reverse Speech
http://www.reversespeech.com

The theory is we speak the overt forward and the covert backward. You're not going to believe what Tony Blair, Bill Clinton and others are hiding. Or maybe you will.

Steps in Overcoming Urges
http://www.moonmac.com/Mormon_masturbation.html

Having trouble leaving it alone? Here's timely advice from our friends in Salt Lake City.

Strawberry Poptart Blow Torches
http://www.sci.tamucc.edu/~pmichaud/toast/

Insert Poptart, depress lever, aim, fire! How to turn an innocent kitchen appliance into a deadly incendiary device. But, so long as you adhere to strict laboratory procedures, no-one need get hurt, save the odd marshmallow bunny: http://www.pcola.gulf.net/~irving/bunnies/

Time Travel Devices
http://home.inreach.com/dov/tt.htm

Step back to a time that
common sense forgot.

Toilet-train Your Cat
http://www.rainfrog.com/mishacat/

How to point pusskins at the
porcelain. Literally.

Uncle Chuckie's
General Store
http://www.amargiland.com/
charles-cosimano/shop.html

Build a simple psionic
transmitter out of household
refuse to create widespread
terror and avenge traffic
fines.

The Under Ground Net
http://www.theeunderground.net

News as rolled out by Sollog's prophecies. Stay tuned for a
spate of nuclear terrorism live on CNN.

Vomitus Maximus Museum
http://www.vomitus.com

Take heed. Steve Connett's gallery of surreal sadism is not in
particularly good taste. Although it's one of the most popular
galleries on the Net, it's also the one most likely to invoke a
strong reaction. Don't say you weren't warned.

WearCam
http://www.wearcam.org

Steve has a Netcam fixed to his head. You see what he sees.
But that won't stop him having fun.

Weird World
http://monkey.hooked.net/m/chuck/

If you like what you see, you're in luck because Chuck's keen
to sell it off. But what exactly will you do with the likes of
David Koresh's business card or copies of Pee Wee Herman's

arrest report? And for the most disturbing real-life horror story you'll ever read, try the ill-fated Shuttle Challenger's final transcript.

Why Cats Paint

http://www.netlink.co.nz/~monpa/

New paintings by emerging feline artists, how to spot fakes, updates from the Museum of Non-primate Art, moggy masters caught on video, and merchandise including, and inspired by, the best-selling book of the same name. Of course, we knew it wouldn't be long before the big baboons bustled in on the action: http://www.gorilla.org/Art/

Usenet Newsgroups

Whatever you're into – hobbies, sports, politics, music, philosophy, business, and a thousand other pursuits – there's sure to be a Usenet newsgroup devoted to it. In fact, you might be surprised how many others share your interests. Usenet newsgroups provide a forum to meet like-minded people, exchange views, and pose those perplexing questions that have bugged you for years. And the groups are as much yours as anyone's, so once you have the feel of a group, jump in and contribute.

We provide the low-down on reading and posting to newsgroups on p.128. The following pages are brief directories of around 700 of the most interesting groups. That might seem a lot but it's only around three percent of the total. Not that anyone knows exactly, as many are only propagated within a local area and new groups are added daily.

We've excluded the newsgroups devoted to "adult interests" – sex, mainly, either talking about it or looking at it. If that's your bag, you don't need our help to browse the alt.sex, alt.binaries.pictures or the alt.personals hierarchy. If you do browse the murkier areas of sex Newsgroups – or the rackets discussed in the pirate software (.warez and .cracks), phone tampering (.2600), or other mischief-making groups – be aware that just because this stuff is readily available on the Net doesn't make it legal. So don't put anything on your hard drive, or email or post anything, you wouldn't like to defend in front of a jury. Oh, and beware pirate programs bearing surprise gifts . . .

NEWSGROUPS DIRECTORY

For ease of reference, we've broken down newsgroups into the following categories:

Arts, Architecture, and Graphics

ART

alt.artcom	Artistic community
rec.arts.fine	For art's sake
rec.arts.misc	Unclassified arts

ARCHITECTURE

alt.architecture	Building design/construction
alt.architecture.alternative	Non-traditional design

GRAPHICS AND LAYOUT

alt.3d	Three-dimensional imaging
alt.aldus.pagemaker	DTP with PageMaker
alt.ascii-art	Pictures in ASCII characters
alt.binaries.pictures.utilities	Image software
alt.cad	Computer-aided design
comp.cad.autocad	High-end graphic modeling
comp.fonts	Font speak
comp.graphics	Computer-created images
comp.graphics.animation	Creating moving images
comp.graphics.raytracing	Persistence of visionaries
comp.publish.prepress	Desktop publishing
comp.sys.mac.graphics	Macintosh graphic techniques

Authors and Books

REFERENCE

alt.usage.english	English grammar
comp.infosystems.interpedia	The Internet Encyclopedia
comp.internet.library	Electronic libraries

DISCUSSION

alt.books.purefiction	Pulp citations
alt.books.reviews	Join the critics

alt.books.technical	Technically speaking
alt.evil	Tales from the dark side
alt.fan.douglas-adams	Hitchhiking through the galaxy
alt.fan.holmes	Sherlock and Long John
alt.fan.james-bond	On His Majesty's Secret Service
alt.fan.philip-dick	Dick heads
alt.fan.pj-orourke	Rolling Stone Republican
alt.fan.tolkien	Lords of the Ring
alt.horror	Be afraid, be very afraid
alt.writing	Literary engineering
bit.listserv.rra-l	Romance Readers Anonymous
rec.arts.books	General book nook
rec.arts.poems	Poetry in motion
rec.arts.sf.reviews	Science fiction critique
rec.arts.sf.science	Science or science fiction?

Business and Finance

BUSINESS

alt.business	Get rich quick schemes
alt.business.import-export	International commerce
alt.business.misc	All aspects of commerce
alt.consumers.free-stuff	The Milky Bars are on us
alt.business.offshore	Tax planning
biz.comp.services	Commercial services postings
biz.general	Miscellaneous business schemes
biz.misc	Commercial postings
misc.consumers	Shopping advice
misc.consumers.house	House-hunting advice
misc.entrepreneurs	Pyramid building

FINANCE

misc.invest	Managing finances
misc.invest.forex	Foreign exchange students
misc.invest.real-estate	Position, position, position

misc.invest.stocks .... Stock market tips
misc.invest.technical .... Predicting trends
sci.econ .... Economic science
uk.finance .... UK financial issues

Buying and Selling

alt.cdworld.marketplace .... Trading compact discs
alt.co-ops .... Collaborative buying
alt.forsale .... Step right up
ba.market.misc .... Bay Area trading post
demon.adverts .... UK network's classifieds
la.forsale .... Los Angeles trading
misc.forsale .... Trading hierarchy
rec.arts.books.marketplace .... Online books trading
rec.arts.sf.marketplace .... Science fiction trading
rec.arts.comics.marketplace .... Buy and sell comics
rec.audio.marketplace .... Low price hi-fi
rec.autos.marketplace .... Trade your dream machine
rec.bicycles.marketplace .... Buying and selling bikes
rec.music.makers.marketplace .... Instrument trading
rec.music.marketplace .... Record and CD trading
rec.photo.marketplace .... Camera trading
rec.radio.swap .... Trading radios
uk.forsale .... UK trading post

Comedy and Jokes

alt.adjective.noun.verb.verb.verb .... Usenet wordplay
alt.binaries.pictures.tasteless .... Spoil your appetite
alt.comedy.british .... Best of British chuckles
alt.comedy.slapstick.3-stooges .... Pick three
alt.comedy.standup .... Comedy industry gossip
alt.devilbunnies .... They're cute, but want our planet
alt.fan.monty-python .... Cleese and chums
alt.flame .... Insults and abuse

Comics

Computer games

Computer technology

MISCELLANEOUS

COMPUTER HARDWARE

COMPUTER SECURITY

COMPUTER SOFTWARE

NETWORKING AND EMAIL

OPERATING SYSTEMS

Crafts, Gardening, and Hobbies

CRAFTS

GARDENING

HOBBIES

Dance and Theater

Drugs

Education

Employment

Fashion

Food and drink

Health and Medicine

alt.aromatherapy .... The essential oil
alt.backrubs .... Massage messages
alt.folklore.herbs .... Herbal superstitions and theories
alt.hygiene.male .... Keeping it clean
alt.med.allergy .... Fighting allergies
alt.skincare .... Looking good
alt.yoga .... Bending over backwards
bionet.virology .... Battling viruses
misc.fitness .... Staying svelte
misc.health.alternative .... Alternative healing
misc.health.diabetes .... Coping with diabetes
sci.bio .... Life sciences
sci.life-extension .... Drinking at the fountain of youth
sci.med .... Medicine, drugs, and regulations
sci.med.aids .... AIDS research
sci.med.dentistry .... Caring for teeth
sci.med.diseases.cancer .... Cancer advances
sci.med.immunology .... An ounce of prevention
sci.med.nursing .... Keeping patients
sci.med.nutrition .... Eating well
sci.med.pharmacy .... Beyond the labels

History, Archeology, and Anthropology

alt.archaeology .... Life in ruins
alt.folklore .... Miscellaneous legends
alt.folklore.ghost-stories .... Tales of spotted spooks
alt.folklore.science .... Tales of invention
alt.folklore.urban .... Urban legends and tall tales
alt.history.what-if .... What if Adam was gay?
alt.mythology .... Folk laureates
alt.revisionism .... Rewriting history
alt.war.civil.usa .... Yankees 1, Confederates 0
rec.org.sca .... Renaissance-era period play

sci.anthropology	Studying human evolution
sci.archeology	Can you dig it?
soc.history	Looking backwards

International culture

Almost every culture/ethnic group has a soc.culture and/or an alt.culture group. If yours doesn't, start one!

alt.chinese.text	Chinese character discussion
alt.culture	Cultural forum hierarchy
alt.culture.saudi	Arabian might
alt.culture.us.asian-indian	Native American culture
soc.culture	Cultural forum hierarchy
soc.culture.african.american	Afro-American affairs
soc.culture.yugoslavia	All ex-Yugoslav factions
uk.misc	All things British

Internet Stuff

BBS LISTINGS

alt.bbs	Bulletin board systems
alt.bbs.internet	BBSs hooked up to the Internet
alt.bbs.lists	Regional BBS listings

CYBERSPACE

alt.cybercafes	New café announcements
alt.cyberpunk	High-tech low-life
alt.cyberpunk.tech	Cyberpunk technology
alt.cyberspace	The final frontier
sci.virtual-worlds	Virtual reality

IRC

alt.irc	Internet Relay Chat material
alt.irc.questions	Solving IRC queries

NEWSGROUPS

alt.config .... How to start an alt Newsgroup
alt.culture.usenet .... Finishing school for Usenetsters
alt.current-events.net-abuse .... Usenet spamming
alt.test .... Posting practice
bit.admin .... Maintenance of bit.* Newsgroups
bit.general .... BitNet/Usenet discussion
bit.listserv.help-net .... Help on BitNet and the Internet
bit.listserv.new-list .... New list announcements
news.admin.misc .... Usenet administration
news.announce.newgroups .... Recently added groups
news.announce.newusers .... Usenet introduction
news.answers .... Usenet FAQ repository
news.groups .... New group proposals and voting
news.groups.questions .... Usenet help desk
news.lists .... Usenet statistics and lists
news.lists.ps-maps .... Usenet traffic maps
news.newusers.questions .... Newbie day care center

SERVICE PROVIDERS

alt.aol-sucks .... Grievances with AOL
alt.internet.access.wanted .... Locating service providers
alt.internet.services .... Net facilities and providers
alt.online-service .... AOL, CompuServe, et al.

WORLD WIDE WEB

alt.culture.www .... Web manners
alt.html .... Web authoring
comp.infosystems.www .... The Web information system
comp.infosystems.www.authoring.html .... Web authoring
comp.infosystems.www.misc .... Web techie discussion
comp.infosystems.www.providers .... Provider issues
comp.internet.net-happenings .... What's new on the Net
comp.lang.java .... Writing Java applets

Legal

Movies and TV

rec.arts.disney	Taking the Mickey
rec.arts.drwho	Help conquer the Daleks
rec.arts.movies	Movies and movie-making hierarchy
rec.arts.movies.reviews	Films reviewed
rec.arts.sf.movies	Science fiction movies
rec.arts.sf.tv.babylon5	Babylon 5 discussion
rec.arts.startrek.current	New Star Trek shows
rec.arts.startrek.fandom	Trek conventions and trinkets
rec.arts.tv	Television talk
rec.arts.tv.soaps	Parallel lives hierarchy
rec.arts.tv.uk	UK television talk
rec.video.production	Making home movies

Music

There are hundreds more specialist groups under the alt.music and rec.music hierarchies.

GENERAL

alt.cd-rom.reviews	Read before you buy
rec.music.info	Music resources on the Net
rec.music.misc	Music to any ears
rec.music.reviews	General music criticism
rec.music.video	Budding Beavis and Buttheads

POP

alt.elvis.sighting	Keep looking
alt.exotic-music	Strange moods
alt.fan.frank-zappa	The late Bohemian cultural minister
alt.fan.rolf-harris	King of the stylophone
alt.gothic	Dying fashion
alt.music.bootlegs	Illicit recordings
alt.music.brian-eno	Eno's worldly activities
alt.music.hardcore	Head banging
alt.music.kylie-minogue	Is she Elvis?

alt.music.lyrics .... Spreading the words
alt.music.peter-gabriel .... From Genesis to the Real World
alt.music.prince .... The artist formerly named after a dog
alt.music.progressive .... Almost modern music
alt.rock-n-roll .... Counterpart to alt.sex and alt.drugs
alt.rock-n-roll.metal .... Heavy, man
alt.rock-n-roll.oldies .... The golden years
rec.music.dylan .... Rolling Stone cover model
rec.music.gdead .... Jerry lives on

INDIE AND DANCE

alt.music.alternative .... Indie talk
alt.music.alternative.female .... Indie women
alt.music.canada .... Canadian indie scene
alt.music.independent .... Alternative pop
alt.music.dance .... Water? E? Okay, let's go
alt.music.hardcore .... Serious punks
alt.music.house .... Repetitive bleats
alt.music.jungle .... Rumble in the bassbin
alt.music.synthpop .... Keyboard capers
alt.music.techno .... Repetitive beats
alt.punk .... The attitude and the music
alt.rave .... Late-night loonies
rec.music.ambient .... Soundscapes
rec.music.industrial .... Metal machine music
uk.music.breakbeat .... Drumming base

WORLD MUSIC AND FOLK

alt.music.jewish .... Klezmer developments
alt.music.world .... Tango to Tuvan throatsinging
rec.music.afro-latin .... African, Latin, and more
rec.music.celtic .... Irish music mostly
rec.music.folk .... Folk/world music/singer-songwriters
rec.music.indian.classical .... Raga sagas
rec.music.reggae .... Rasta nation

COUNTRY

rec.music.country.western .... Both types, C & W

JAZZ

alt.music.acid-jazz .... Smooth movements
rec.music.bluenote .... Jazz and the blues

CLASSICAL

rec.music.classical .... Classical music
rec.music.early .... Early music

MUSIC MAKING

alt.guitar .... You axed for it
alt.music.makers.electronic .... Electric friends
rec.music.makers.guitar .... Six string along
rec.music.makers.synth .... Synthesize your mind

HI-FI AND RECORDING

rec.audio.high-end .... Audiophile equipment
rec.audio.opinion .... Hi-fi reviews
rec.audio.pro .... Professional sound recording

MUSIC UTILITIES

alt.binaries.multimedia .... Sound and vision files
alt.binaries.sounds.midi .... Music making files
alt.binaries.sounds.music .... Music files
alt.binaries.sounds.utilities .... Sound programs

Mysticism and Philosophy

alt.astrology .... Soothsaying by starlight
alt.chinese.fengshui .... Mystical interior design
alt.consciousness .... Philosophical discourse
alt.dreams .... Welcome to my nightmare
alt.dreams.castaneda .... Don Juan yarns

alt.hypnosis	You are getting sleepy
alt.magic.secrets	Letting the rabbit out of the hat
alt.magick	Supernatural arts
alt.meditation	Maintaining concentration
alt.paranet.paranormal	Psychic phenomena
alt.paranet.skeptic	Doubters
alt.paranet.ufo	It came from outer space
alt.paranormal	Bent-fork talk
alt.paranormal.channeling	Cosmic contacts
alt.philosophy.debate	The quest for truth
alt.prophecies.nostradamus	Deciphering the predictions
sci.skeptic	Questioning pseudo-science
talk.bizarre	Believe it or not
talk.philosophy.misc	Navel-gazing

Pets

alt.aquaria	Fishy things
alt.pets.ferrets	Polecats as toys
alt.pets.rabbits	Bunnies
rec.aquaria	Water wonderful life
rec.birds	Fine feathered friends
rec.pets	Animals in captivity
rec.pets.alligators	Tending the swamp
rec.pets.birds	Birds behind bars
rec.pets.cats	Kitty chat
rec.pets.dogs.misc	Canine capers

Politics and Media

CURRENT AFFAIRS/POLITICAL ACTION

alt.activism	Agitate, educate, and organize
alt.activism.death-penalty	For and against
alt.conspiracy.princess-diana	Whodunnit?
alt.current-events.bosnia	Bosnia-Herzegovinan strife

alt.current-events.russia	The rise and fall of the KGB
alt.gossip.royalty	Tabloid fodder
alt.india.progressive	Indian politics
alt.individualism	Hanging on to your ego
alt.obituaries	Death notices
alt.peace-corps	Volunteers abroad
alt.politics.british	The Blair bones
alt.politics.correct	Sanctimony
alt.politics.datahighway	Information Super-gridlock
alt.politics.greens	Ecological movements
alt.politics.libertarian	What it means to be free
alt.politics.radical-left	Take your Marx
alt.politics.reform	Changing the nation
alt.rush-limbaugh	Conservative US talk-radio activist
alt.society.civil-liberty	Knowing your rights
alt.society.conservatism	Playing it straight
aus.politics	Aussies trading insults
talk.politics.animals	Animal activism
talk.politics.china	Behind the bamboo curtain
talk.politics.medicine	Health care ethics
talk.politics.tibet	The Tibetan crisis
uk.politics	Life after Thatcher

POLITICAL THEORY

alt.conspiracy	Paranoia and corruption
alt.conspiracy.jfk	The Kennedy/Presley cover-up
alt.illuminati	Conspiracy theories and secrecy
alt.philosophy.objectivism	Ayn Rand's slant
alt.politics.correct	Elitist speech codes
alt.politics.economics	Economic reason
alt.politics.elections	Political motivation
alt.politics.org.misc	Look right, left, then right again
alt.politics.usa.constitution	Challenging it, mainly
alt.politics.usa.misc	US political free-for-all
talk.politics.misc	Get your piece of the action

SEXUAL POLITICS

alt.abortion.inequity .... Whose choice?
alt.culture.riot-grrrls .... Angry femmes
alt.dads-rights .... Custody battles
alt.fan.camille-paglia .... Flamboyant feminist
alt.feminazis .... Feminist flames
alt.feminism .... Sisters for sisters
alt.politics.homosexuality .... Gay power
soc.feminism .... Gender war zone
soc.men .... Men wanting more
soc.women .... Women wanting more

US PARTY POLITICS

alt.impeach.clinton .... Presidential peeves
alt.politics.democrats .... Democrat party discussion
alt.politics.usa.congress .... US congressional affairs
alt.politics.usa.republican .... Republican party reptiles
alt.president.clinton .... Spotlight on Clinton

MEDIA

alt.fan.noam-chomsky .... Media watchdogs
alt.journalism .... Hack chat
alt.journalism.freelance .... Unemployed lines
alt.news-media .... Don't believe the hype
alt.quotations .... The things people say
bit.listserv.words-l .... English language mailing list
biz.clarinet .... ClariNet newsfeed news
biz.clarinet.sample .... ClariNet news samples
uk.media .... UK media issues

Psychological support

For more support groups, see also "Health and Medicine"

GENERAL PSYCHOLOGY

alt.psychology.nlp	Neurolinguistic programming
alt.sci.sociology	Human watching
sci.psychology.misc	Troubleshooting behavior
sci.psychology.personality	Why you are you

SUPPORT AND EXPLORATION

alt.adoption	Matching parents and children
alt.child-support	Coping with split families
alt.contraceptives	Ecofriendly drugs
alt.cuddle	Drop in for a hug
alt.good.morning	Big sister of alt.cuddle
alt.homosexual	Talk to other gays
alt.infertility	Difficulty conceiving
alt.i-love-you	Valentine dazes
alt.lefthanders	Gaucherie
alt.life.sucks	Pessimism
alt.love	Mushy stuff
alt.med.cfs	Chronic fatigue syndrome
alt.med.fibromyalgia	Coping with fibromyalgia
alt.missing-kids	Locating missing children
alt.parenting.solutions	Dealing with kids
alt.recovery.aa	Sobering up
alt.romance	Love, exciting, and new
alt.sexual.abuse.recovery	Support for sexual trauma
alt.support	Dealing with crisis
alt.support.anxiety-panic	Coping with panic attacks
alt.support.arthritis	Easing joint pain
alt.support.asthma	Breathe easier
alt.support.attn-deficit	Attention deficit disorder
alt.support.big-folks	Big is better

alt.support.cancer	Cancer news and support
alt.support.depression	Serious cheering-up
alt.support.diet	Enlightenment through starvation
alt.support.eating-disord	Dealing with anorexia
alt.support.stop-smoking	Averting premature death
bit.listserv.autism	Autism mailing list
rec.org.mensa	Haiku club
soc.support.fat-acceptance	Be big and merry
soc.support.pregnancy	From conception to birth

Radio and Telecommunications

alt.radio.pirate	Lend your buccaneers
alt.radio.scanner	Eavesdropping
alt.radio.talk	Shock waves
rec.radio.amateur.misc	Hamming it up
rec.radio.broadcasting	Domestic radio
rec.radio.scanner	Airwave snooping
rec.radio.shortwave	Tuning in to the world
uk.radio.amateur	Best of British hams
uk.telecom	Fight call timing

Religion

alt.atheism	Dogma discussed
alt.bible.prophecy	Learn the exact date of the end
alt.buddha.short.fat.guy	Waking up to yourself
alt.christnet	Christian jamboree
alt.christnet.bible	Bible discussion and research
alt.christnet.christianlife	Living with Jesus
alt.christnet.dinosaur.barney	Barney for Jesus
alt.christnet.philosophy	He forgives, therefore he is
alt.christnet.second-coming.real-soon-now	Get ready
alt.christnet.sex	Christian attitudes to fornication
alt.freemasonry	The brotherhood
alt.hindu	Indian philosophy

alt.messianic .... Christ and other visionaries
alt.pagan .... Natural deities
alt.recovery.catholicism .... Getting over the guilt
alt.religion.christian .... Followers of Jesus
alt.religion.druid .... Full moonies
alt.religion.islam .... Being Muslim
alt.religion.mormon .... Joseph Smith's latter-day saints
alt.religion.scientology .... Hubbard out of the cupboard
alt.satanism .... Drop in for a spell
alt.zen .... Inner pieces
soc.religion.christian .... Followers of Christ
soc.religion.eastern .... Eastern religions
soc.religion.islam .... Followers of Mohammed
talk.origins .... Evolutionism versus creationism
talk.religion.misc .... Religious arguments

Science

GENERAL

alt.med.veterinary .... Animal doctoring
alt.sci.physics.new-theories .... Unproved postulations
alt.talk.weather .... Conversation openers
bionet.announce .... Biological news
bionet.biology.tropical .... Typically tropical lifeforms
bionet.microbiology .... Bug watching
bionet.software .... Biological software
sci.agriculture .... Dirty business
sci.chem .... Chemistry
sci.math .... Mathematically speaking
sci.misc .... Short-lived scientific discussions
sci.physics .... Physical laws
sci.physics.fusion .... Thermonuclear reactions
sci.stat.math .... Statistically speaking

ELECTRONICS

sci.electronics .... Totally wired
sci.electronics.repair .... Circuitry fixes

ENERGY AND ENVIRONMENT

alt.energy.renewable .... Alternative fuels
sci.bio.ecology .... The balance of nature
sci.energy .... Fuel for talk
sci.environment .... Ecological science
talk.environment .... Not paving the earth
uk.environment .... British ecological action

ENGINEERING

sci.engr .... Engineering sciences
sci.engr.biomed .... Biomedical engineering
sci.engr.chem .... Chemical engineering
sci.engr.mech .... Mechanical engineering

GEOLOGY

sci.geo.geology .... Earth science
sci.geo.meteorology .... Weather or not
sci.geo.satellite-nav .... Satellite navigation systems

Space and Aliens

alt.alien.research .... Identifying flying objects
alt.alien.visitors .... Here come the marchin' martians
sci.astro .... Staring into space
sci.space.news .... Announcements from the final frontier
sci.space.policy .... Ruling the cosmos
sci.space.shuttle .... Space research news

Sports

alt.fishing .... Advice and tall tales

alt.sports.baseball	Baseball hierarchy split by clubs
alt.sports.basketball	Basketball hierarchy split by clubs
alt.sports.darts	Pub sport
alt.sports.football	Gridiron hierarchy split by clubs
alt.sports.hockey	Hockey hierarchy split by clubs
alt.sports.soccer.european	European soccer
alt.sports.soccer.european.UK	British and Irish soccer
alt.surfing	Surfboard waxing
aus.sport.rugby-league	The world's roughest sport
misc.fitness.weights	Body building
rec.climbing	Scaling new heights
rec.equestrian	Horsing around
rec.martial-arts	Fighting forms
rec.running	Running commentary
rec.scuba	Underwater adventures
rec.skiing.snowboard	Snowboarding techniques
rec.skydiving	Jumping out of planes
rec.sport.basketball.pro	Professional basketball
rec.sport.boxing	Fighting words
rec.sport.cricket.info	Stats, scorecards, and cricket news
rec.sport.football.australian	Aerial ping pong
rec.sport.football.canadian	Canadian football
rec.sport.football.pro	Get grid ironed
rec.sport.golf	Driving the dimpled ball to drink
rec.sport.hockey	Hockey on ice
rec.sport.olympics	Sydney 2000, Mogadishu 2004?
rec.sport.paintball	Weekend warriors
rec.sport.pro-wrestling	Advanced cuddling
rec.sport.rowing	Gently down the stream
rec.sport.rugby.league	Fun game with an oval ball
rec.sport.rugby.union	Meet you down the maul
rec.sport.soccer	Some call it football
rec.sport.tennis	Racketeering
rec.sport.triathlon	Multi-event sports
uk.rec.sailing	Vomiting off Blighty

Transport

Travel

Software Roundup

The easiest way to stack up on Net software is to copy it from the free CDs given away with Internet or PC magazines. But if you want the latest versions as they're released, then go direct to the Net itself. This chapter lists a selection of the most popular and essential programs to get you started. They're all free – at least for a limited time – though some have superior commercial versions.

How to find the software files

We've given **Web locations** to download each program, so you can read about it first, decide if it's what you want, and make sure you get the newest version. If an address doesn't work, run the program's name through a search engine and look for a new address (See "Finding It", p.174). We're assuming you have a **Web browser that supports FTP**. If not, get one first.

It's a good habit to download everything into a **central directory (folder)**. Call it "download" or something appropriate. Once a program's downloaded, copy it to a temporary directory for installation. Once installed delete the contents of the temporary directory and either shift the original file into an archive or delete it. (See p.158 for How to set up your directory structure.)

All these files should **self-extract**, so installation should be as simple as following the prompts. If not, you'll need an archiving program such as **WinZip** or **Stuffit** (see p.157). Once extracted, read the accompanying text files for installation instructions. It's usually a matter of clicking on a file called install.exe or setup.exe in Windows, or on an install icon on the Mac.

Many programs come in **16-bit and 32-bit versions**. If you're running Windows 95, NT, OS/2, or a PowerMac, go for the faster 32-bit versions. These programs will not work with 16-bit operating systems like Windows 3.x or earlier Macs, nor 16-bit TCP/IP stacks like Trumpet Winsock and some old ISP and Online Service connection kits. Ask your provider if you're unsure.

AGENTS

COPERNIC .... PC
http://www.copernic.com
Query up to 30 search engines simultaneously.

NETATTACHÉ PRO .... PC
http://www.tympani.com
Download whole or part of Web sites for offline reading.

NEWSMONGER .... PC
http://www.techsmith.com
Emails you when something is mentioned in Usenet.

CHAT

CLEARPHONE .... Mac
http://www.clearphone.com
Talk and send video over the Net.

CU-SeeMe .... PC, Mac

http://www.cu-seeme.com

Video/audio Netconferencing. Works better at high bandwidths.

ICQ .... PC, Mac

http://www.mirabilis.com

Know when your friends are online, chat and send files.

INTERNET PHONE .... PC, Mac

http://www.vocaltec.com

The original Internet telephone.

MACIRC .... Mac

http://www.macirc.com

User-friendly IRC for the Mac.

MICROSOFT CHAT .... PC

http://www.microsoft.com/ie/chat/

Chat cutely through a cartoon character.

MIRC .... PC

http://www.mirc.co.uk

Most popular IRC client for PCs.

NET2PHONE .... PC, Mac

http://www.net2phone.com

Place calls through the Net to any conventional telephone.

NETMEETING .... PC

http://www.microsoft.com/netmeeting/

Real-time voice and video, applications-sharing, and multi-user whiteboard. Slots in nicely with the Internet Explorer bundle.

THE PALACE .... PC, Mac

http://www.thepalace.com

Chat and frolic in interactive animated rooms.

VDOPhone .... PC, Mac

http://www.clubvdo.net

Full-color video telephony even over a modem.

VISUAL IRC .... PC

http://virc.melnibone.org

Audio/visual/text IRC client with features to boot.

ONLIVE! TRAVELER .... PC

http://www.onlive.com/prod/trav/

Join, build, and talk in 3D Net colonies.

File Transfer and Handling

CUTEFTP .... PC

http://www.cuteftp.com

First-rate FTP client, resumes downloads.

FETCH .... Mac

http://www.dartmouth.edu/pages/softdev/fetch.html

Multiple connection, drag-and-drop file transfer with automatic decoding and resumes downloads.

GO!ZILLA .... PC

http://www.gozilla.com

Queue up multiple FTP sessions, resumes downloads.

NETFINDER .... Mac

http://www.ozemail.com.au/~pli/netfinder/

FTP with resume capabilities.

STUFFIT EXPANDER/DROPSTUFF .... PC, Mac

http://www.aladdinsys.com

Essential cross platform drag-and-drop decoding/archiving tool.

VIRUSCAN .... PC, Mac
http://www.mcafee.com
Top-notch virus scanner. Check regularly for signature updates.

WINZIP .... PC
http://www.winzip.com
Must-have PC file compression/decompression utility.

WS-FTP .... PC
http://www.ipswitch.com
Powerful feature replete FTP client that can integrate into Windows Explorer.

ZIPit .... Mac
http://www.awa.com/softlock/zipit/zipit.html
Zip and unzip for transfer between Mac and PC.

HTML Tools

When looking for HTML editing programs, don't forget that both Netscape Communicator and Internet Explorer include optional editors. They're not perfect but they work – a comment which typifies most of the specialized programs below. It's also worth seeing what other converters, add-ons and tools Microsoft has to offer at: http://www.microsoft.com/msdownload/

BBEDIT .... Mac
http://www.barebones.com
Hands-on HTML editor that excels in text manipulation.

BEYOND PRESS .... Mac
http://www.astrobyte.com
Convert Quark to HTML.

DREAMWEAVER .... PC, Mac
http://www.macromedia.com
Seriously powerful Web editor from the home of Shockwave.

DRUMBEAT .... PC
http://www.elementalsw.com
Drag and drop WYSIWYG editor that does just about everything.

GIF ANIMATOR .... PC
http://www.ulead.com
Animate and jazz up your Web graphics.

GOLIVE CYBERSTUDIO .... Mac
http://www.golive.com
Drag and drop WYSIWYG site builder that works from a DTP
perspective.

HOTDOG EXPRESS/PRO .... PC
http://www.sausage.com
Feature-packed, but somewhat slow, raw html editor.

PAGEMILL .... PC, Mac
http://www.adobe.com/prodindex/pagemill/main.html
The original WYSIWYG HTML editor.

ULEAD SMARTSAVER .... PC
http://www.ulead.com
Optimize your Web images.

VISUAL PAGE .... PC, Mac
http://cafe.symantec.com
Top-ranked WYSIWYG editor with bundled Java applets.

WEBMODELER .... PC
http://www.webmodeler.com
Site design and architecture planning tool.

Mail

Be sure to check the browser offerings from Microsoft (http://www.microsoft.com/ie/) and Netscape (http://home.netscape.com) first before shopping for an alternative. However, Netscape's mail isn't separable from its browser.

EUDORA/EUDORA LIGHT .... PC, Mac
http://www.eudora.com
Popular, powerful, and reliable, but would you pay when you can get the likes of Outlook Express for free?

OUTLOOK EXPRESS .... PC, Mac
http://www.microsoft.com/ie/mac/oe/
The best mail client around, bundled with IE4, or available on the Mac as a standalone.

PEGASUS MAIL .... PC, Mac
http://www.pegasus.usa.com
Feature-packed and free. A little unintuitive but worth considering.

Newsreaders

Again, unless you feel under-powered or your system can't handle it, you might as well stick to your browser's newsreader. Otherwise, these are among the most worthy alternatives.

AGENT/FREE AGENT .... PC
http://www.forteinc.com/forte/agent/agent.htm
Queues multiple articles and auto-decode binaries. Unrivaled.

GRAVITY .... PC
http://www.microplanet.com
Fast and powerful, with advanced search functions.

HOGWASHER .... Mac

http://www.asar.com

Online/offline reader with internal decoding and image viewing.

MT- NEWSWATCHER .... Mac

http://www.best.com/~smfr/mtnw/

Free binary-decoding newsreader, with speech recognition.

Plug-ins and ActiveX controls

Plug-ins and ActiveX controls are meant to extend your
browser's capacities. **Plug-ins** are more of a Netscape
thing, but will usually work with Internet Explorer as
well. You have to download and then install them.
ActiveX controls load automatically into Internet
Explorer, or Netscape when embellished with Scriptactive (http://www.ncompasslabs.com). Some, like the
increasingly essential **RealPlayer**, also have stand-alone
versions that can be useful if you don't have the system
resources to open a browser. This list is only a small
sample. For more, see:

Browsers.com (http://www.browsers.com),

BrowserWatch (http://www.browserwatch.com)

or open "About Plug-ins" from Netscape's Help menu.

ACROBAT .... PC, Mac

http://www.adobe.com/prodindex/acrobat/

View Portable Document Files within your browser.

BEATNIK .... PC, Mac

http://www.headspace.com/beatnik/

Listen to high quality interactive music in Web pages.

ENVOY .... PC, Mac

http://www.twcorp.com/plugin.htm

View Envoy documents in your browser.

KOAN .... PC, Mac

http://www.sseyo.com

Creates live music based on certain parameters.

LIGHTNING STRIKE .... PC, Mac

http://www.infinop.com

View highly compressed images.

LISTENUP .... Mac

http://snow.cit.cornell.edu/noon/ListenUp.html

Use Apple's PlainTalk to activate Web commands by speech.

MICROSOFT MEDIA PLAYER .... PC

http://www.microsoft.com/winmm/msmp.htm

Plays most popular multimedia formats, though not necessarily
the latest versions.

QWICKVIEW PLUS .... PC

http://www.inso.com

View over 200 file formats within your browser.

REALPLAYER .... PC, Mac

http://www.real.com

Essential real-time sound and video add-on or stand-alone.

SHOCKWAVE .... PC, Mac

http://www.macromedia.com/Tools/Shockwave/

View inline multimedia creations. Get it now.

TALKER .... Mac

http://www.mvpsolutions.com/PlugInSite/Talker.html

Reads Web pages aloud via Apple's text-to-speech conversion.

VISCAPE .... PC, Mac

http://www.superscape.com

Explore high-res 3D worlds.

VDOLIVEAC .... PC, Mac

http://www.clubvdo.net

Impressive live video viewer, but no threat to TV yet.

VIVO .... PC, Mac

http://www.vivo.com

Impressive streaming video player.

Servers

Setting up a server using your own PC or Mac is easy with the right software. Just read the Help files.

NETPRESENZ .... Mac

http://www.share.com/peterlewis/

FTP, Gopher, and Web server.

PERSONAL WEB SERVER .... PC, Mac

http://www.microsoft.com/ie/

Free Internet Explorer accessory.

QUID QUO PRO .... Mac

http://www.socialeng.com

Free Mac Web server.

SLMAIL/WINSMTP .... PC

http://www.seattlelab.com/prodsmtp.html/

SMTP/POP3 mail server with autoresponders and mailing lists.

WAR FTP .... PC

http://home.sol.no/jgaa/tftpd.htm

Full featured, yet free, FTP server demon.

WINGATE .... PC

http://www.wingate.net

Share a single dial-up link.

Sound and Vision

It's useful to keep an armory of audio, graphics, and video players that activate when you click on the file. Netscape and Internet Explorer can play most multimedia types, but dedicated programs can provide more power. See also under "Plug-ins and ActiveX controls."

ACDSEE .... PC
http://www.acdsystems.com
Extraordinarily fast graphics file viewer that integrates sublimely into Windows.

BME .... Mac
http://www.softlogik.com
Basic image editor.

COOLEDIT .... PC
http://www.syntrillium.com
Pro quality audio file processor.

GRAPHIC CONVERTER .... Mac
http://www.lemkesoft.de
View and convert over 100 image file types.

HYPERSNAP .... PC
http://www.hyperionics.com
Capture screen images, even in games.

IMAGEVIEWER .... Mac
http://www.imageviewer.com
Good for previewing and organizing images.

MIDIPLUG .... PC
http://www.yamaha.co.jp/english/xg/
MIDI jukebox and software synthesizer.

NET TOOB .... PC, Mac
http://www.nettoob.com
Play MPEG-1, MPEG, AVI and QuickTime movie files.

PAINT SHOP PRO .... PC
http://www.jasc.com
For heavy-duty graphics manipulation.

QUICKTIME .... PC, Mac
http://quicktime.apple.com
Play QuickTime (.mov) movie and 360 degree virtual reality files.

SOUND MACHINE .... Mac
http://www.kagi.com/rod/
Play, edit, and convert sound files.

For more specialist sound software see:
   http://www.maz-sound.com and
   http://www.hitsquad.com/smm/

TCP/IP, Timers, and Dialers

Be sure to regularly check **Apple**; http://info.apple.com for upgrades to Open Transport, MacTCP and its operating system. Rifle through **Microsoft**; http://www.microsoft.com for upgrades to Windows and Dial-up Networking.

CYBERGAUGE .... Mac
http://www.neon.com
Monitor your bandwidth

FREEPPP .... Mac
http://www.rockstar.com
Use in conjunction with MacTCP to enable PPP connectivity.

GEARBOX .... Mac
http://www.rockstar.com
Internet configuration management, dialer, and diagnostics.

OPEN TRANSPORT AND OT PPP .... Mac
http://www.apple.com/support/
Replaces MacTCP and MacPPP.

NEOTRACE .... PC
http://www.neoworks.com
Trace your connection graphically.

NETMEDIC .... PC
http://www.vitalsigns.com
Monitor your connection's wellbeing, and see what's holding
things up.

NETSCAN TOOLS .... PC
http://www.nwpsw.com
Ping, Finger, Traceroute, Whois and more. Get it.

TRUMPET WINSOCK .... PC
http://www.trumpet.com.au/wsk/winsock.htm
Reliable TCP/IP socket for Windows 3.xx. Includes Ping,
TCPMeter, and Traceroute.

WHATROUTE .... Mac
http://homepages.ihug.co.nz/~bryanc/
Includes Traceroute, Ping, DNS Query, Finger and Whois.

Telnet

Telnet is a powerful tool that enables you to **log into a
remote computer via the Net** to run programs or access
local data on UNIX servers (common in universities).
Although its technology is useful, there's less and less
call for it, as services move onto the Web and more tasks

become automated – and that's a blessing, as it requires learning a few UNIX commands.

To log on to a remote server, enter the server's address, and then follow the prompts. It may require a log-in and password, which you should presumably have. If you don't, try hitting return instead. If that doesn't work, you'll have to go back to where you got the address and get the log-in details.

PROTERM .... Mac
http://www.intrec.com
Efficient, feature-packed Telnet client.

ZOC .... PC
http://www.emtec.com
Highly configurable Telnet client with tons of features.

Web Browsers

Even with some thirty-odd browsers available for download, for most people the choice is really down to two: **Netscape Communicator** and **Internet Explorer**. Both are as superb as they are problematic and include a whole suite of add-ons that pretty much do everything from Internet telephony to tea making. Although it doesn't boast a large feature set, Opera is well worth checking out especially for older systems. Apart from taking less than a tenth of the disk space, it's also faster and handles multiple windows better than the other two. However, unlike them, it's not free. For an ominous list of failed alternatives, see: http://www.browserwatch.com and http://www.browsers.com

MICROSOFT INTERNET EXPLORER .... PC, Mac
http://www.microsoft.com/ie/

NETSCAPE NAVIGATOR/COMMUNICATOR .... PC, Mac
http://home.netscape.com

OPERA .... PC
http://www.operasoftware.com

Various other Tools

ADWIPER .... PC, Mac
http://www.adwiper.com
Choose not to download banner ads in IE4.

BACKWEB .... PC, Mac
http://www.backweb.com
Receive channels of "push" content.

BLUE SKIES .... PC, Mac
http://groundhog.sprl.umich.edu/blueskies.html
Hook into The Weather Underground.

HOURWORLD .... Mac
http://www.hourworld.com
World times, moon phases, almanacs and more.

NETCHRONOMETER .... Mac
http://www.kezer.net/netchrono.html
Synchronize your Mac clock across the Net.

NETMAGNET .... PC
http://www.peak.com
Superior Web cache, history handling and browser accelerator.

POINTCAST .... PC, Mac
http://www.pointcast.com
Have news, weather, sports and such "pushed" at you.

SURF EXPRESS .... PC, Mac

http://www.connectix.com/html/surfexpress.html

Speeds up your browsing process by reading ahead.

TARDIS .... PC

http://www.kaska.demon.co.uk

Synchronize your PC time online.

WEATHERTRACKER .... Mac

http://www.weathertracker.com

Install a global weather station on your desktop.

WETSOCK .... PC

http://www.locutuscodeware.com/

Delivers current US weather data to your Win95 system tray.

WINSTOCK .... PC

http://www.winstocksw.com

Stock tracking and portfolio management.

WINWEATHER .... PC

http://www.igsnet.com

Up-to-date international weather reports, forecasts, and images via the Net.

But that's not all

For more depth and the very latest, check in to one of the specialist software guides in our Web Guide's **"Search Tools and Directories"** section (see p.250).

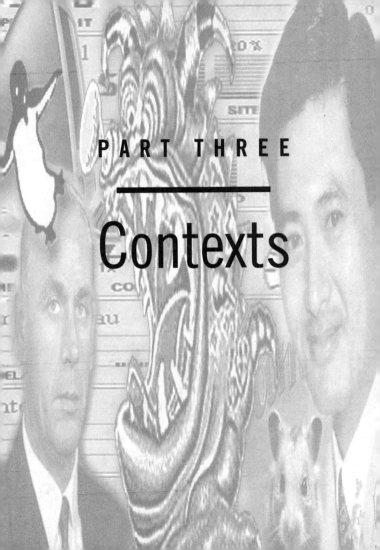

PART THREE

Contexts

A Brief History of the Internet

The Internet may be a recent media phenomenon but as a concept it's actually older than most of its users; it was born in the 1960s – a long time before anyone coined the buzzword "Information SuperHighway." Of course, there's no question that the Net deserves its current level of attention. It really is a quantum leap in global communications, though – right now– it's more of a prototype than finished product. While Bill Gates and Al Gore rhapsodize about such household services as video-on-demand, most Netizens would be happy with a system fast enough to view stills-on-demand. Nonetheless, it's getting there.

THE ONLINE BOMB SHELTER

The concept of the Net might not have been hatched in Microsoft's cabinet war rooms, but it did play a role in a previous contest for world domination. It was 1957, at the height of the Cold War. The Soviets had just launched the first Sputnik, thus beating the USA into space. The race was on. In response, the US Department of Defense formed the **Advanced Research Projects Agency (ARPA)** to bump up its technological prowess. Twelve years later, this spawned **ARPAnet** – a project to develop a military research network, or specifically, the world's first decentralized computer network.

In those days, no-one had PCs. The computer world was based on mainframe computers and dumb terminals. These usually involved a gigantic, fragile box in a climate-controlled room, which acted as a hub, with a mass of cables spoking out to keyboard/monitor ensembles. The concept of independent intelligent processors pooling resources through a network was brave new territory that would require the development of new hardware, software, and connectivity methods.

The driving force behind decentralization, ironically, was the bomb-proofing factor. Nuke a mainframe and the system goes down. But bombing a network would, at worst, only remove a few nodes. The remainder could route around it unharmed. Or so the theory went.

WIRING THE WORLD

Over the next decade, **research agencies** and **universities** flocked to join the network. US institutions such as UCLA, MIT, Stanford, and Harvard led the way, and in 1973, the network crossed the Atlantic to include University College London and Norway's Royal Radar Establishment.

The 1970s also saw the introduction of **electronic mail**, **FTP**, **Telnet**, and what would become the **Usenet newsgroups**. The early 1980s brought **TCP/IP**, the **Domain Name System**, **Network News Transfer Protocol**, and the European networks **EUnet** (European UNIX Network), **MiniTel** (the widely adopted French consumer network), and **JANET** (Joint Academic Network), as well as the Japanese **UNIX** Network. ARPA evolved to handle the research traffic, while a second network, MILnet, took over the US military intelligence.

An important development took place in 1986, when the US National Science Foundation established **NSFnet** by linking five university super-computers at a backbone speed of 56 Kbps. This opened the gateway for external universities to tap in to superior processing power and share resources. In the three years between 1984 and 1988, the number of host computers on the **Internet** (as it was now being called) grew from about 1000 to over 60,000. NSFnet, meanwhile, increased its capacity to T1 (1544 Kbps). Over the next few years, more and more countries joined the network, spanning the globe from Australia and New Zealand, to Iceland, Israel, Brazil, India, and Argentina.

It was at this time, too, that **Internet Relay Chat (IRC)** burst onto the scene, providing an alternative to CNN's incessant, but censored, Gulf War coverage. By this stage, the Net had grown far beyond its original charter. Although ARPA had succeeded in creating the basis for decentralized computing, whether it was actually a military success was debatable. It might have been bombproof, but it also opened new doors to espionage. It was never particularly secure, and it is suspected that Soviet agents routinely hacked in to forage for research data. In 1990, ARPAnet folded, and NSFnet took over administering the Net.

COMING IN FROM THE COLD

Global electronic communication was far too useful and versatile to stay confined to academics. Big business was starting to get interested. The Cold War looked like it was over and world economies were regaining confidence after the 1987 stock market savaging. Market trading moved from the pits and blackboards onto computer screens. The financial sector expected fingertip real-time data and that feeling was spreading. The world was ready for a people's network. And since the Net was already in place, funded by taxpayers, there was really no excuse not to open it to the public.

In 1991, the NSF lifted its restrictions on enterprise. During the Net's early years, its **"Acceptable Use Policy"** specifically prohibited using the network for profit. Changing that policy opened the floodgates to commerce with the general public close behind.

However, before anyone could connect to the Net, someone had to sell them a connection. The **Commercial Internet eXchange (CIX),** a network of major commercial access providers, formed to create a commercial backbone and divert traffic from the NSFnet. Before long, dozens of budding Access Providers began rigging up points of presence in their bedrooms. Meanwhile, NSFnet upgraded its backbone to T3 (44,736 Kbps).

By this time, the Net had established itself as a viable medium for transferring data, but it had one major problem. You could pretty much only find things if you knew where to look. And that process involved knowing a lot more about computers, and the UNIX computing language in particular, than most punters would relish. The next few years saw an explosion in navigation protocols, such as **WAIS**, **Gopher**, **Veronica**, and, most importantly, the now-dominant **World Wide Web**.

THE GOLD RUSH BEGINS

In 1989, Tim Berners-Lee of **CERN**, the Swiss particle physics institute, proposed the basis of the World Wide Web, initially as a means of sharing physics research. His goal was a seamless network in which data from any source could be accessed in a simple, consistent way with one program, on any type of computer. The Web did this, encompassing all existing infosystems such as FTP, Gopher, and Usenet, without alteration. It was an unqualified success.

As the number of Internet hosts exceeded one million, the **Internet Society** was formed to brainstorm protocols and attempt to co-ordinate and direct the Net's escalating expansion. **Mosaic** – the first graphical **Web browser** – was released, and declared to be the "killer application of the 90s." It made navigating the Internet as simple as pointing and clicking, and took away the need to know UNIX. The Web's traffic increased by 25-fold in the year up to June 1994, and domain names for **commercial organizations** (.com) began to outnumber those of educational institutions (.edu).

As the Web grew, so too did the global village. The media began to notice, slowly realizing that the Internet was something that went way beyond propeller heads and students. They couldn't miss it, actually, with almost every country in the world connected or in the process. Even the White House was online.

Of course, as word of a captive market got around, entrepreneurial brains went into overdrive. Canter & Seigel, an Arizona law firm, notoriously "**spammed**" Usenet with **advertisements** for the US green card lottery. Although the Net was tentatively open for business, crossposting advertisements to every newsgroup was decidedly bad form. Such was the ensuing wrath that C&S had no chance of filtering out genuine responses from the server-breaking level of hate mail they received. A precedent was thus established for **how not to do business on the Net**. Pizza Hut, by contrast, showed how to do it subtly by setting up a trial service on the Web. Although it generated wads of positive publicity, it too was doomed by impracticalities. Nevertheless, the ball began to roll.

THE HOMESTEADERS

As individuals arrived to stake out Web territory, businesses followed. Most had no idea what to do once they got their brand on the Net. Too many arrived with a bang, only to peter out in a perpetuity of "under construction signs." Soon business cards not only sported email addresses, but Web addresses as well. And rather than send a CV and stiff letter, job aspirants could now send a brief email accompanied with a "see my Web page" for further details.

The Internet moved out of the realm of luxury into an elite necessity, verging toward a commodity. Some early business sites gathered such a following that by 1995 they were able to charge high rates for advertising banners. A few, including Web **portals** such as **InfoSeek** and **Yahoo**, made it to the Stock Exchange boards, while others, like **GNN**, attracted buyers (in their case the Online Service giant, AOL).

But it wasn't all success stories. Copyright lawyers arrived in droves. Well-meaning devotees, cheeky opportunists, and info-terrorists alike felt the iron fists of Lego, McDonald's, MTV, the Louvre, Fox, Sony, the Church of Scientology and others clamp down on their "unofficial Web sites" or newsgroups. It wasn't always a case of corporate right but of might, as small players couldn't foot the expenses to test **new legal boundaries**. The honeymoon was officially over.

POINT OF NO RETURN

By the onset of 1995, the Net was well and truly within the public realm. It was impossible to escape. The media became bored with extolling its virtues, so it turned to **sensationalism.** The Net reached the status of an Oprah Winfrey issue. New tales of hacking, pornography, bombmaking, terrorist handbooks, and sexual harassment began to tarnish the Internet's iconic position as the great international equalizer. But that didn't stop businesses, schools, banks, government bodies, politicians, and consumers from swarming online, nor the major **Online Services** – such as CompuServe, America Online, and Prodigy, which had been developing in parallel since the late 1980s – from adding Internet access as a sideline to their existing private networks.

As 1995 progressed, Mosaic, the previous year's killer application, lost its footing to a superior browser, **Netscape**. Not such big news, you might imagine, but after a half-year of rigorous beta-testing, Netscape went public with the third largest ever NASDAQ IPO share value – around $2.4bn.

Meantime, **Microsoft**, which had formerly disregarded the Internet, released **Windows 95**, a PC operating platform incorporating access to the controversial **Microsoft Network**. Although **IBM** had done a similar thing six months earlier with **OS/2 Warp** and its **IBM Global Network**, Microsoft's was an altogether different scheme. It offered full Net access but its real product was its own separate network, which many people feared might supersede the Net, giving Microsoft an unholy reign over information distribution. But that never happened. Within months, Microsoft, smarting from bad press, and finding the Net a larger animal even than itself, aboutturned and declared a full commitment to furthering the Internet.

BROWSER WARS

As Microsoft advanced on the horizon, Netscape continued pushing the envelope, driving the Web into new territory with each beta release. New enhancements arrived at such a rate that competitors began to drop out as quickly as they appeared. This was the era of "This page looks best if viewed with Netscape." Of course, it wasn't just Netscape since much of the new activity stemmed from the innovative products of third party developers like **MacroMedia** (**ShockWave**), **Progressive Networks** (**Real Audio**), **Apple** (**QuickTime**), and **Sun** (**Java**). The Web began to spring to life with animations, music, 3D worlds, and all sorts of new tricks.

While Netscape's market dominance gave developers the confidence to accept it as the de facto standard, treating it as a kind of Internet operating system into which to "plug" their products, Microsoft, an old hand at taking possession of cleared territory, began to launch a whole series of free Net tools. These included **Internet Explorer**, a browser with enhancements of its own, including **ActiveX**, a Web-centric programming environment more powerful than the much lauded Java, but without the same platform independence, and clearly geared toward progressing Microsoft's software dominance. Not only was Internet Explorer suddenly the only other browser in the race, unlike Netscape, it was genuinely free. And many were not only rating it as the better product, but also crediting Microsoft with a broader vision of the Net's direction.

By mid-1997, every Online Service and almost every major ISP had signed deals with Microsoft to distribute its browser. At the time of writing, the browser battle continues, with Microsoft facing the US Department of Justice over its (logical but monopolistic) bundling of Internet Explorer as an integral part of Windows 98 – a move which could effectively render Netscape Communicator obsolete on the world's most populous operating platform.

FOUND ON THE INTERNET

Skipping back to late 1995, the backlash against Internet freedom had moved into full flight. The expression **"found on the Internet,"** became the news tag of the minute, depicting the Net as the source of everything evil from bomb recipes to child pornography. While editors and commentators, often with little direct experience of the Net, urged that "children" be protected, the Net's own media and opinion shakers pushed the **freedom of speech** barrow. It became apparent that this uncensored, uncontrollable new media could shake the very foundations of democracy.

At first politicians didn't take much notice. Few could even grasp the concept of what the Net was about, let alone figure out a way to regulate its activities. The first, and easiest, target was **pornography**, resulting in raids on hundreds of **private bulletin boards** worldwide and a few much publicized convictions for the possession of child porn. BBSs were an easy target, being mostly self-contained and run by someone who could take the rap. Net activists, however, feared that the primary objective was to send a ripple of fear through a Net community that believed it was bigger than the law, and to soften the public to the notion that the Internet, as it stood, posed a threat to national wellbeing.

In December 95, at the request of German authorities, **CompuServe** cut its newsfeed to exclude the bulk of newsgroups carrying sexual material. But the groups cut weren't just pornographers, some were dedicated to gay and abortion issues. This brought to light the difficulty in drawing the lines of obscenity, and the problems with publishing across foreign boundaries. Next came the **US Communications Decency Act**, a proposed legislation to forbid the online publication of "obscene" material. It was poorly conceived, however, and, following opposition from a very broad range of groups (including such mainstream bodies as the American Libraries Association), was overturned, and the decision later upheld in the Supreme Court. Several groups including the Family Research Council are presently working on a new version.

Outside the US, meanwhile, more authorities reacted. In **France**, chiefs of three major Access Providers were temporarily jailed for supplying obscene newsgroups, while in **Australia** police prosecuted several users for downloading child pornography. NSW courts introduced legislation banning obscene material with such loose wording that the Internet itself could be deemed illegal – if the law is ever tested. In **Britain**, in mid-1996, the police tried a "voluntary" approach, identifying newsgroups that carried pornography beyond the pale, and requesting that providers remove them from their feed. Most complied, but there was unease within the Internet industry that this was the wrong approach. That the same groups would migrate elsewhere and the root of the problem would remain.

But the debate was, or is, about far more than pornography, despite the huffing and puffing. For **Net fundamentalists**, the issue is about holding ground against any compromises in liberty, and retaining the global village as a political force – potentially capable of bringing down governments and large corporations. Indeed, they argue that these battles over publishing freedom have shown governments to be out of touch with both technology and the social undercurrent, and that in the long run the balance of power will shift toward the people, toward a new democracy.

WIRETAPPING

Another slow-news-day story of the mid-1990s depicted **hackers** gaining control of networks, stealing money, and creating havoc. It made great reading, but the reality was less alarming. Although the US Department of Defense reported hundreds of thousands of network break-ins, they claimed it was more annoying than damaging. While in the commercial world, little went astray except the odd credit card file. (Bear in mind that every time you hand your credit card to a shop assistant they would get the same information.) In fact, by and large, for an online population greater than the combined size of New York, Moscow, London, Calcutta and Tokyo, there were surprisingly few noteworthy crimes. Yet the perception remained that the Net was too unsafe for the exchange of sensitive information like payment details.

Libertarians raged at the US Government's refusal to lift export bans on crack-proof **encryption algorithms**. But cryptography, the science of message coding, has traditionally been classified as a weapon and thus export of encryption falls under the Arms Control acts.

Encryption requires a secret key to open the contents of a message and often another public key to code the message. These keys can be generated for regular use by individuals or, in the case of Web transactions, simply for one session upon agreement between the server and client. Several governments proposed to employ official escrow authorities to keep a register of all secret keys and surrender them upon warrant – an unpopular proposal, to put it mildly, among a Net community who regard invasion of privacy as an issue equal in importance to censorship, and government monitors as instruments of repression.

However, authorities were so used to being able to tap phones, intercept mail, and install listening devices to aid investigations, that they didn't relish giving up their freedom either. Government officials made a lot of noise about needing to monitor data to protect national security, though their true motives probably involve monitoring internal insurgence and catching tax cheats – stuff they're not really supposed to do, but we put up with anyway because if we're law-abiding it's mostly in our best interests.

The implications of such obstinacy go far beyond personal privacy. Business awaits browsers that can talk to commerce servers using totally snooper-proof encryption. Strong encryption technology has already been built into browsers, and approved for use with and between authorized financial bodies, to and from the USA. However, at present, it's illegal, or at least questionable, for a US citizen to export the most powerful technology encryption for private use.

THE ENTERTAINMENT ARRIVES

While politicians, big business, bankers, telcos, and online action groups like **CommerceNet** and the **Electronic Frontier Foundation**, fretted the future of privacy and its impact on digital commerce, the online world partied on regardless. If 1996 was the year of the Web, then 1997 was the year the **games** began. Netizens had been swapping chess moves, playing dress-up, and struggling with the odd network game over the Net for years, but it took id Software's **Quake** to lure the gaming masses online. Not to miss out, Online Services and ISPs took steps to prioritize game traffic, while hardcore corporate data moved further back on the shelves.

Music took off, too. **Bands and DJs** routinely simulcast, or exclusively played, concerts over the Net while celebrities like Michael Jackson, Joe Dolce, and Paul McCartney bared their souls in public chat rooms. Web pages came alive with the sound of music, from cheesy synthesized backgrounds to live radio feeds. Many online music stores like **CDNow** reported profits, while **Amazon** became a major force in bookselling.

And then there was the Net as a prime news medium. As **Pathfinder** touched down on Mars, back on Earth millions logged into NASA sites to scour the Martian landscape for traces of life. China marched into Hong Kong, Tiger Woods rewrote golfing history, Australia regained the Ashes, and Mike Tyson fell from grace, all live on the Net. In response to this breaking of news on Web sites and newsgroups, an increasing number of **print newspapers** began delivering online versions before their hard copies hit the stands. In 1997, if you weren't on the Net, you weren't in the media.

THE CASUALTIES

Not everyone had reason to party in 1997. **Cybercafés** – touted as the coolest thing in 1995 – tended to flop as quickly as they appeared, as did many small **Internet Service Providers**, if they weren't swallowed by larger fish. From over thirty **Web browsers** in early 1996, less than a year later, only two real players – Netscape and Microsoft – remained in the game. The also-ran software houses that initially thrived on the Net's avenue for distribution and promotion faded from view as the two browser giants ruthlessly crammed more features into their plug-and-play Web desktops. Microsoft, and scores of other software developers, declared that their future products would be able to update themselves online, either automatically or by clicking in the right place. So much for the software dealer.

Meanwhile, **Web TV** arrived delivering Web pages and email onto home TV screens. It offered a cheap, simple alternative to PCs, but to date has failed to find an immediate audience.

The whole **Web design industry** was due for a shake-out. Overnight Web cowboys – without the programming skills to code, the artistic merit to design, or the spelling standards to edit, yet who'd charged through the teeth for cornering the homepage design scam – were left exposed by the advent of ActiveX, Java, data processing, and print-standard art. New media had come of age. The top Web chimps reworked their résumés and pitched in with online design houses. Major ad agencies formed new media departments, and splashed Web addresses over everything from milk cartons to toothpaste tubes.

Bizarrely though, 1997's best known Web design team, **Higher Source**, will be remembered not for HTML handiwork, but for publishing their cult's agenda to top themselves in conjunction with the passing of the Hale Bopp comet. This was the Internet as a major news story in itself. Within hours of the mass suicide, several sites appeared spoofing both its corporate pages as well as its cult, **Heaven's Gate**. Days later, there were enough to spawn four new Yahoo subdirectories.

Back in the real world of **business and money**, major companies have played surprisingly by the book, observing netiquette – the Net's informal code of conduct. The marriage has been awkward but generally happy. Even the absurd court cases between blockbuster sites like **Microsoft Sidewalk v. TicketMaster** and **Amazon v. Barnes & Noble** (over the "biggest bookstore in the world" claim) did little to convince Netizens that they were witnessing anything more than carefully orchestrated publicity stunts. Indeed, many felt launching a

Web site without some kind of legal suit was a waste of free publicity. It just seemed like a bit of fun. And as big money flowed in, **bandwidths** increased, content improved, ma and pa scuttled aboard, and the online experience richened.

Alas, the same couldn't be said for the new school entrepreneurs. Low advertising costs saw **Usenet newsgroups and email in-trays** choked with crossposted get-rich schemes, network marketing plans, and porno adverts. Further, unprecedented **banks of email** broke servers at AOL, MSN, and scores of smaller providers. Netcom was forced to temporarily bar all mail originating from Hotmail, the most popular free Web email service, and consequent safe haven for fly-by-night operators due to the level of spam originating from its domain. At the same time, in July 1997, a mislaid backhoe ripped up a vital US backbone artery darkening large parts of the Net – something many had presumed impossible – and reducing the worldwide network to a crawl. The Net was nuclear-proof maybe, but certainly not invulnerable.

THE WORLD'S BIGGEST PLAYGROUND

By the end of 1997, the Net's population had skyrocketed to well over a hundred million. The media increasingly relied on it for research and, in the process, began to understand it. It could no longer be written off as geek-land when it was thrust this far into mainstream consciousness. Notable among the most recent arrivals were the so-called "grey surfers," predominantly retirees, who in some cases found it the difference between having few interests and few friends, and suddenly finding a reason to live. Indeed, the Net was looking not only useful, but essential, and those without it had good reason to feel left behind.

This new maturity arrived on the back of email, with the Web hot on its heels. As toner sales plummeted, surveys indicated that email had not only overtaken the fax, but possibly even the telephone, as the business communication tool of choice. However, at the same time, it could also lay claim to being the greatest time waster ever introduced into an office with staff spending large chunks of their days reading circulars, forwarding curios and flirting with their online pals.

Email's speed, and the ease in carbon copying an entire address book, brought new implications to the six degrees of separation. Something with universal appeal, like the infamous dancing baby animation, could be disseminated to millions within a matter of hours, potentially reaching everyone on the Net within days. And, as most journalists were by this stage hooked in, whatever circulated on the Net often found its way into other media formats. Not surprisingly, the fastest-moving chain emails were often hoaxes. One such prank, an address of sensible old-timer advice, supposedly delivered by Kurt Vonnegut to MIT graduates (but actually taken from Mary Schmick's Chicago Tribune column) saturated the Net within a week. Romeo & Juliet Director, Baz Lurhman, was so taken he put it to music resulting in the cult hit "Sunscreen", which even more incredibly was respoofed into a XXXX beer advert. All within six months.

On a more annoying note, almost everyone received virus hoaxes that warned not to open email with certain subject headings. Millions took them seriously, earnestly forwarding them to their entire address books. An email campaign kicked off by Howard Stern propelled "Hank, the ugly drunken dwarf" to the top of People's 100 Most Beautiful People poll as voted on the Net. Meanwhile the Chinese community rallied to push

Michelle Kwan into second place. But the biggest coup of all, was Matt Drudge's email leaking Bill Clinton's inappropriate affair with Monica Lewinsky, which sent the old world media into the biggest feeding frenzy since the OJ trial. Although it might not have brought down the most powerful man in the world, it showed how in 1998, almost anyone, anywhere could be heard.

THE SHOW MUST GO ON

In May 1998, the blossoming media romance with hackers as urban folk heroes turned sour when a consortium of good-fairy hackers, known as the L0pht, assured a US Senate Government Affairs Committee that they, or someone less benevolent, could render the Net entirely unusable within half an hour. It wasn't meant as a threat, but a call to arms against the apathy of those who'd designed, sold and administered the systems. The Pentagon had already been penetrated (by a talented Israeli hacker), and though most reported attacks amounted to little more than vandalism, with an increasing number of essential services tapped in, the probability of major disaster veered toward looking possible.

Undeterred, Net commerce continued to break into new territories. **Music**, in particular, looked right at home with the arrival of DIY CD compilation shops and several major artists such as Massive Attack, Willie Nelson and the Beach Boys airing their new releases on the Net, before unleashing them on CD. However, these exclusive previews weren't always intentional. For instance, Swervedriver's beleaguered "99th Dream" found its way onto Net bootleg almost a year before its official release.

By now, celebrity chat appearances hardly raised an eyebrow. Even major powerbrokers like Clinton and

Yeltsin had appeared before an online inquisition. To top it off, in April 1998, Koko, a 300-pound gorilla, fronted up to confess to some 20,000 chatsters that she'd rather be playing with Smokey, her pet kitten.

THE RED-LIGHT DISTRICT

Despite the bottomless reserves of free Web space, personal vanity pages and Web diaries took a downturn in 1998. The novelty was passing, a sign perhaps that the Web was growing up. This didn't, however, prevent live Web cameras, better known as **Webcams**, from enjoying a popularity resurgence. But this time around they weren't so much being pointed at lizards, fish, ski slopes or intersections, but at whoever connected them to the Net – a fad which resulted in numerous bizarre excursions in exhibitionism from some very ordinary folk. Leading the fray was the entirely unremarkable Jennifer Ringley, who became a Web household name simply for letting the world see her move about her college room, clothed and very occasionally, otherwise. She might have only been famous for being famous, but it was fame enough to land her a syndicated newspaper column about showing off and, of course, a tidy packet from the thousands of subscribers who paid real money to access Jennicam.

But this was the tame end of the Net's trade in voyeurism. And these were boom times for pornographers. Research suggested as high as 90% of network traffic was consumed by porn images. That's not to suggest that anywhere near 90% of users were involved, only that the images consume so much bandwidth. The story in Usenet was even more dire with more than 80% of the non-binary traffic hogged by spam and spam cancel messages. Meanwhile, the three top Web search aids, HotBot, Altavista and Yahoo, served click-through banners on suggestive keywords. However you felt about pornography from a moral standpoint, it had definitely become a nuisance.

THE BOTTLENECK

As 1998 progressed, **cable Internet access** became increasingly available, and even affordable in the USA. New subscribers could suddenly jump from download speeds of, at best, 56 Kbps to as high as 10 Mbps. Meanwhile several telcos, such as PacBell and GTE, began rolling out ADSL, another broadband technology capable of megabit access, this time over plain copper telephone wires. However, even at these speeds, users still had to deal with the same old bottleneck. Namely the Internet's backbone which had been struggling to cope with even the low speed dial-up traffic.

The power to **upgrade the backbone**, or more correctly backbones, lies in the hands of those who own the major cables and thus effectively control the Internet. Over the next few years, the global telecommunication big guns look set to starve the smaller players out of the market. And the emergence of Internet telephony has forced telcos to look further down the track at the broader scenario where whoever controls the Internet not only controls data, but voice traffic as well. They recognize that their core business could be eroded by satellite and cable companies. To survive, telcos need to compete on the same level, provide an alternative, or buy out their rivals. At the moment all three seem viable options.

There's little doubt their biggest competition will come from the skies. Apart from existing high-speed **satellite** downlink services from DirecPC, expect to see SkyStation's solar-powered stratospheric airships hovering over large cities and beaming down major megabits before the end of this century. And by 2002, Teledesic, from Gates,

Boeing, McCaw, and others, will launch several hundred low-orbiting satellites with the sole purpose of creating an alternative high-speed Internet backbone infrastructure accessible from anywhere on earth with a relatively small dish. So the Information SuperHighway may just be on its way. It's merely a matter of when, what it will cost and how you'll pay for it.

But the big question is, will it be for you? The answer is, most likely, yes. But you might not be able to justify spending on broadband unless you're earnestly intent on downloading video and high fidelity audio, and since you can already get that free with TV and radio, the decision is whether you're prepared to pay extra to do your own programming. In this scenario, you might expect the shops to pay for your bandwidth, in the same way they build car parks in the real world. You'd be hoping. But we will soon become blasé about the Net as a medium and focus on its content. As with magazines, it will be about what's in them, not the paper they're printed on.

Likewise, telcos have given in to **Internet telephony**. They see it's about the people at the end of the wires, not what they do with them. They just don't know how to work the bills. How this will pan out is anyone's guess, but the boundaries between email, chat, and voice will blur. Presumably this will mean cheaper long-distance phone calls and phone numbers that can move with you. This **new mobility** will induce many to leave their offices and work from home, and just as likely, while they're on holidays. Just don't be surprised if freedom from the office means never being able to escape work.

A BRIGHTER TOMORROW

Like it or not, the Net is the closest thing yet to an all-encompassing snapshot of the human race. Never before have our words and actions been so immediately accountable in front of such a far-reaching audience. If we're scammed, we can instantly warn others. If we believe there's a government cover-up, we can expose it through the Net. If we want to be heard, no matter what it is we have to say, we can tell it to the Net. And, in the same way, if we need to know more, or we need to find numbers, we can turn to it for help.

What's most apparent all up is that humanity looks in pretty okay shape. That's kind of ironic, because it didn't necessarily look that way before. But we've now been able to see that for every extreme there appears to be many more moderates; for every hate group, a thousand pacifists; and for every conspiracy theory, if not some sensible explanation, then at least a few attentive ears. We've been able to examine the weirdest and the worst the world has to offer and contrast it against a greater global theme. Now that our boundaries are so much easier to explore, the future of not only the Net, but the planet itself, surely looks brighter.

The problem with such rapid improvement is that our expectations grow to meet it. But the Net, even at age thirty, is only in its infancy. So be patient, enjoy it for what it is today, and complain, but not too much. One day you'll look back and get all nostalgic about the times you logged into the world through old copper telephone wires. It's amazing it works at all.

Net Language

The Internet hasn't always been a public thoroughfare: it used to be a clique inhabited by students and researchers nurtured on a diet of UNIX programming, scientific nomenclature, and in-jokes. Meanwhile, in a parallel world, thousands of low-speed modem jockeys logged into independent bulletin board networks to trade files, post messages, and chat in public forums. These groups were largely responsible for the birth of an exclusively online language consisting of acronyms, emoticons (smileys and such), and tagged text. The popularizing of the Internet brought these two cultures together, along with more recently, the less digitally versed general public.

Low online speed, poor typing skills, and the need for quick responses were among the pioneers' justifications for keeping things brief. But using Net lingo was also a way of showing you were in the know. These days, it's not so prevalent, though you're sure to encounter Netty terms in **IRC** and, to a lesser extent, in **Usenet and on Mailing Lists**. Since IRC is a snappy medium, with line space at a premium, acronyms and the like can actually be useful – as long as they're understood.

Shorthand: Net acronyms

It doesn't take long in IRC to realize that Net acronyms are peppered with the F-initial. It's your choice whether you add to this situation, but if you don't tell people to "f*** right off" in ordinary speech or letters, then FRO is hardly appropriate on the Net, and nor is adding F as emphasis. However, you may at least want to know what's being said. And, BTW (by the way), the odd bit of Net shorthand may be useful and/or vaguely amusing, even if unlikely to make you ROFL (roll on the floor laughing).

AFAIK	As far as I know
AOLer	America Online member
BOHICA	Bend over here it comes again
BBL	Be back later
BD or BFD	Big deal
BFN	Bye for now
BRB	Be right back
BTW	By the way
CUL8R or L8R	See you later
CYA	See ya
FB	Furrowed brow
FWIW	For what it's worth
GDM8	G'day mate
GRD	Grinning, running, and ducking
GR8	Great
HTH	Hope this helps
IMHO	In my humble opinion
IYSWIM	If you see what I mean
IAE	In any event
IOW	In other words
LOL	Laughing out loud
NRN	No reply necessary
NW or NFW	No way
OIC	Oh I see
OTOH	On the other hand
PBT	Pay back time
RTM or RTFM	Read the manual
SOL	Sooner or later
TTYL	Talk to you later
YL/YM	Young lady/young man
YMMV	Your mileage may vary
|LY| & +LY	Absolutely and positively

Smileys and emoticons

Back in the old days, it was common in Usenet to temper a potentially contentious remark with <grins> tacked on to the end in much the same way that a dog wags its tail to show it's harmless. But that wasn't enough for the Californian E-generation, whose trademark smiley icon became the 1980s peace sign. From the same honed minds that discovered 71077345 inverted spelled Greenpeace's bête noire, came the **ASCII smiley**. This time, instead of turning it upside-down, you had to look at it sideways to see a smiling face. An expression that words, supposedly, fail to convey. Well, at least in such limited space. Inevitably this grew into a whole family of **emoticons** (emotional icons).

The odd smiley may have its place in diffusing barbs, but whether you employ any of the other emoticons in use is up to your perception of the line between cute and dorky. All the same, don't lose sight of the fact that they're only mant to be fun :-). Anyway, that's up to you, so here goes:

:-)	Smiling	:-L~~	Drooling
:-D	Laughing	:-P	Sticking out tongue
:-o	Shock	(hmm)Ooo.. :-)	Thinking happy thoughts
:-(	Frowning		
:'-(	Crying	(hmm)Ooo.. :-(	Thinking sad thoughts
;-)	Winking		
X=	Fingers crossed	0:-)	Angel
: =)	Little Hitler	}:>	Devil
{}	Hugging	C)]	Beer
:*	Kissing	\V/	Vulcan salute
$-)	Greedy	\o/	Hallelujah
X-)	I see nothing	@}-`-,—	A rose
:-X	I'll say nothing	8:)3)=	Happy girl

A few other, mostly Japanese anime derived, work right way up:

@^_^@	blushing	^_^;	sweating
*^_^*	huge dazzling grin	T_T	major tears

If you still want more, try consulting a few unofficial dictionaries on the Web. Use "smiley dictionary" or "emoticon" as a search term at http://www.hotbot.com

Emphasis

Another common way to express actions or emotions is to add commentary within < **these signs** >.

For example:

<flushed> I've just escaped the clutches of frenzied train-spotters < removes conductor's cap, wipes brow >.

More commonly, and more usefully, Netizens also use **asterisks in email** to *emphasize* words, in place of bolds and italics. You simply *wrap* the appropriate word: Hey everyone look at *me*.

Misspellings and intracaps

Some clowns pointedly overuse **phonetic spellings, puns, or plain misspellings** (kewl, windoze, luzer, etc.) And wannabe crackers like to **intercapitalize**, L1Ke tHi5. You can safely assume they're either very young and trying to make an impression, total plonkers, or both.

Glossary

A

Access Provider Company that sells Internet connections. Known variously as Internet Access or Service Providers (IAPs or ISPs).

ActiveX Microsoft concept that allows a program to run inside a Web page. Expected to become a standard.

ADSL Asynchronous Digital Subscriber Line. High-speed copper wire connections at up to 6 Mbps downstream and 640 Kbps up.

Anonymous FTP server A remote computer, with a publicly accessible file archive, that accepts "anonymous" as the log-in name and an email address as the password.

Altavista Web and Usenet search engine at: http://www.altavista.digital.com

AOL America Online. Presently, the world's most populous Online Service.

Archie Program that searches Internet FTP archives by file name.

ASCII American Standard Code for Information Interchange. A text format readable by all computers. Also called "plain text."

Attachment File included with email.

B

Backbone Set of paths that carry longhaul Net traffic.

Bandwidth Size of the data pipeline. If you increase bandwidth, more data can flow at once.

Baud rate Number of times a modem's signal changes per second when transmitting data. Not to be confused with bps.

BBS Bulletin Board System. A computer system accessible by modem. Members can dial in and leave messages, send email, play games, and trade files with other users.

Binary file All non-plain text files are binaries, including programs, word processor documents, images, sound clips, and compressed files.

Binary newsgroup Usenet group that's specifically meant for posting the above files.

Binhex Method of encoding, commonly used by Macs.

Bookmarks Netscape file used to store addresses.

Boot up To start a computer.

Bounced mail Email returned to sender.

Bps Bits per second. The rate that data is transferred between two modems. A bit is the basic unit of data.

Browser Program, such as Netscape or Internet Explorer, that allows you to download and display Web documents.

C

Cache Temporary storage space. Browsers can store copies of the most recently visited Web pages in cache.

Client Program that accesses information across a network, such as a Web browser or newsreader.

Crack To break a program's security, integrity, or registration system, or fake a user ID.

Crash When a program or operating system fails to respond or causes other programs to malfunction.

Cyberspace Term coined by science fiction writer William Gibson, referring to the virtual world that exists within the marriage of computers, telecommunication networks, and digital media.

D

Digital signing Encrypted data appended to a message to identify the sender.

Direct connection Connection, such as SLIP or PPP, whereby your computer becomes a live part of the Internet. Also called full IP access.

DNS Domain Name System. The system that locates the numerical IP address corresponding to a host name.

Domain Part of the DNS name that specifies details about the host, such as its location and whether it is part of a commercial (.com), government (.gov), or educational (.edu) entity.

Download Retrieve a file from a host computer. Upload means to send one the other way.

Driver Small program that acts like a translator between a device and programs that use that device.

E

Email Electronic mail carried on the Net.

Email address The unique private Internet address to which your email is sent. Takes the form user@host

Eudora Popular email program for Mac and PC.

F

FAQ Frequently Asked Questions. Document that answers the most commonly asked questions on a particular subject. Every newsgroup has at least one.

File Anything stored on a computer, such as a program, image, or document.

Finger A program that can return stored data on UNIX users or other information such as weather updates. Often disabled for security reasons.

Firewall Network security system used to restrict external and internal traffic.

Flame Abusive attack on someone posting in Usenet.

Frag Network gaming term meaning to destroy or fragment. Came from DOOM.

FTP File Transfer Protocol. Standard method of moving files across the Internet.

G

GIF Graphic Image File format. A compressed graphics format commonly used on the Net.

Gopher Menu-based system for retrieving Internet archives, usually organized by subject.

GUI Graphic User Interface. Method of driving software through the use of windows, icons, menus, buttons, and other graphic devices.

H

Hacker Someone who gets off on breaking through computer security and limitations. A cracker is a criminal hacker.

Header Pre-data part of a packet, containing source and destination addresses, error checking, and other fields. Also the first part of an email or news posting which contains, among other things, the sender's details and time sent.

Homepage Either the first page loaded by your browser at start-up, or the main Web document for a particular group, organization, or person.

Host Computer that offers some sort of services to networked users.

HotBot Web search engine at: http://www.hotbot.com

HTML HyperText Markup Language. The language used to create Web documents.

HyperText links The "clickable" links or "hotspots" that connect pages on the Web to each other.

I

Image map A Web image that contains multiple links. Which link you take depends on where you click.

IMAP Internet Message Access Protocol. Standard email access protocol that's superior to POP3 in that you can selectively retrieve messages or parts thereof as well as manage folders on the server.

Infoseek Web and Usenet search service at: http://www.infoseek.com

Internet A co-operatively run global collection of computer networks with a common addressing scheme.

Internet Explorer The controversial Web browser produced by Microsoft.

Internet Favorites Internet Explorer directory that stores filed URLs.

Internet Shortcut Microsoft's terminology for a URL.

IP Internet Protocol. The most important protocol upon which the Internet is based. Defines how packets of data get from source to destination.

IP address Every computer connected to the Internet has an IP address (written in dotted numerical notation), which corresponds to its domain name. Domain Name Servers convert one to the other.

IRC Internet Relay Chat. Internet system where you can chat in text, or audio, to others in real time, like an online version of CB radio.

ISDN Integrated Services Digital Network. An international standard for digital communications over telephone lines, which allows for the transmission of data at 64 or 128 Kbps.

ISP Internet Service Provider. Company that sells access to the Internet.

J

Java Platform-independent programming language designed by Sun Microsystems. http://www.sun.com

JPEG Graphic file format preferred by Net users because its high compression reduces file size, and thus the time it takes to transfer.

K

Kill file Newsreader file into which you can enter keywords and email addresses to stop unwanted articles.

L

LAN Local Area Network. Computer network that spans a relatively small area such as an office.

Latency Length of time it takes data to reach its destination.

Leased line A dedicated telecommunications connection between two points.

Link In hypertext, as in a Web page, a link is a reference to another document. When you click on a link in a browser, that document will be retrieved and displayed, played or downloaded depending on its nature.

Linux A freely distributed implementation of the UNIX operating system.

Log on / Log in Connect to a computer network.

Lycos Web search service at: http://www.lycos.com

M

MIDI Musical Instrument Digital Interface. Standard adopted by the electronic music industry for controlling devices such as soundcards and synthesizers. MIDI files contain synthesizer instructions rather than recorded music.

MIME Multipurpose Internet Mail Extensions. Standard for the transfer of binary email attachments.

Mirror Replica FTP or Web site set up to share traffic.

Modem MOdulator/DEModulator. Device that allows a

computer to communicate with another over a standard telephone line, by converting the digital data into analog signals and vice versa.

Mosaic The first point-and-click Web browser, created by NCSA, now superseded.

MPEG A compressed video file format.

Multithreaded Able to process to multiple requests simultaneously.

N

Name server Host that translates domain names into IP addresses.

The Net The Internet.

Netscape Popular and influential Web browser – and the company that produces it.

Newbie Newcomer to the Net, discussion, or area.

Newsgroups Usenet message areas, or discussion groups, organized by subject hierarchies.

NNTP Network News Transfer Protocol. Standard for the exchange of Usenet articles across the Internet.

Node Any device connected to a network.

P

Packet A unit of data. In data transfer, information is broken into packets, which then travel independently through the Net. An Internet packet contains the source and destination addresses, an identifier, and the data segment.

Packet loss Failure to transfer units of data between network nodes. A high percentage makes transfer slow or impossible.

Patch Temporary or interim add-on to fix or upgrade software.

Phreaker Person who hacks telephone systems.

Ping A program that sends an echo-like trace to test if a host is available.

Platform Computer operating system, like Mac System 7.0, Windows 95, or UNIX.

Plug-in Program that fits into another.

POP3 Post Office Protocol. An email protocol that allows you to pick up your mail from anywhere on the Net, even if you're connected through someone else's account.

POPs Points of Presence. An Access Provider's range of local dial-in points.

Post To send a public message to a Usenet newsgroup.

PPP Point to Point Protocol. This allows your computer to join the Internet via a modem. Each time you log in, you're allocated either a temporary or static IP address.

Protocol An agreed way for two network devices to talk to each other.

Proxy server Sits between a client, such as a Web browser, and a real server. They're most often used to improve performance by delivering stored pages like browser cache and to filter out undesirable material.

Push Technique where data appears to be sent by the host rather than requested by the client. Email is a type of push.

R

RealAudio Standard for streaming compressed audio over the Internet. Supported by recent versions of

Netscape Navigator and Internet Explorer. The player and encoding tools are downloadable from: http://www.real.com

Robot Program that automates Net tasks like collating search engine databases or automatically responding in IRC. Also called a Bot.

S

Search engine Database of Web page extracts that can be queried to find reference to something on the Net.

Server Computer that makes services available on a network.

Signature file Personal footer that can be automatically attached to email and Usenet postings.

SLIP Serial Line Internet Protocol. Protocol that allows a computer to join the Internet via a modem and requires that you have a pre-allocated fixed IP address configured in your TCP/IP setup. Has almost completely been replaced by PPP.

SMTP Simple Mail Transfer Protocol. Internet protocol for transporting mail.

Spam Inappropriately post the same message to multiple newsgroups or email addresses.

Streaming Delivered in real time instead of waiting for the whole file to arrive, eg Real Audio.

Stuffit A common Macintosh file compression format and program.

Surf To skip from page to page around the Web by following links.

T

TCP/IP Transmission Control Protocol/Internet Protocol. The protocols that drive the Internet.

Telnet Internet protocol that allows you to log on to a remote computer and act as a dumb terminal.

Troll Prank newsgroup posting intended to invoke an irate response.

Trumpet Winsock Windows program that provides a dial-up SLIP or PPP connection to the Net.

U

UNIX Operating system used by most service providers and universities. So long as you stick to graphic programs, you'll never notice it.

URL Uniform Resource Locator. The addressing system for the World Wide Web.

Usenet User's Network. A collection of networks and computer systems that exchange messages, organized by subject into newsgroups.

UUencode Method of encoding binary files into text so that they can be attached to mail or posted to Usenet. They must be UUdecoded to convert them back. Better mail and news programs do this automatically.

V

Vaporware Rumored or announced, but non-existent, software or hardware. Often used as a competitive marketing ploy.

W

Warez Software, usually pirated.

The Web The World Wide Web or WWW. Graphic and text documents published on the Internet that are interconnected through clickable "hypertext" links. A Web page is a single document. A Web site is a collection of related documents.

Web authoring Designing and publishing Web pages using HTML.

World Wide Web See Web, above.

WYSIWYG What You See Is What You Get. What you type is the way it comes out.

Y

Yahoo The Web's most popular directory at: http://www.yahoo.com

Z

Zip PC file compression format that creates files with the extension .zip using PKZip or WinZip software. Commonly used to reduce file size for transfer or storage on floppy disks.

Zmodem A file transfer protocol that, among other things, offers the advantage of being able to pick up where you left off after transmission failure.

Still confused . . .

Then try the PCWebopaedia (http://www.pcwebopedia.com)
  What is? (http://www.whatis.com)
  and the CyberDorktionary
  (http://www.latech.edu/~jlk/jwz/dorktionary/)

Further Reading

The best way to find out more about the Net is to get online and crank up a search engine, but sometimes it's more convenient – and maybe more enjoyable – to read about it in a book or magazine. Among Internet mags, good reads include the US-based *Internet World* and cyberstyle bible *Wired*, the British-based *Internet*, *Connect*, and *.net*, and the Australian *Internet.au*. PC magazines have now moved in on the same territory and often cover the technical issues in better depth.

Books about the Net are harder to recommend as they date so quickly – it's hardly worth opening one that's more than a year old. This guide should be more than enough to get you started. However, the techie manuals can be handy when you need to check specifics, and don't feel like trawling the Net for them. Following are a few volumes that might prove useful, plus a selection of Net-related tales and discussions.

Techie manuals

Billy Barron and Jill Ellsworth *The Internet Unleashed*, (SAMS, US). Quality doorstopper covering most aspects of the Internet in reasonable depth.

Adam Engst *The Internet Starter Kit* (Hayden, US). Step-by-step guidance, plus software. For Mac/Windows.

Web-site design

Chris Baron and Bob Weil *Drag 'n' Drop CGI Enhance Your Web Site Without Programming* (Addison-Wesley, US). Add interactivity to your site without having to learn code.

Vincent Flanders and Michael Willis *Web Pages That Suck* (Sybex, US). Learn what not to do in site design. Hard copy of: http://www.webpagesthatsuck.com

Ian S. Graham *HTML 4.0 Sourcebook* (John Wiley & Sons, US). Web builder's reference chest.

Louis Rosenfeld and Peter Morville *Information Architecture for the World Wide Web* (O'Reilly & Assoc., US). Design sites that work rather than just look pretty.

Special interests

Lisa Hughes and Tim Benton *The Internet* (Hodder, UK). Illustrated hobby guide to the Net for kids.

Jeff James *The Internet and Multiplayer Gaming Bible* (St Martin's Press, US). Where to find the action and what to pack.

Thomas Mandel and Gerard Van der Leun *Rules of the Net* (Hyperion, US). As if. But a book that, despite its oxymoronic title, is packed with sound advice.

Scott Mueller *Upgrading and Repairing PCs* (QUE, US). Overcome your fear of chips and bits.

Robbin Zeff, Brad Aronson *Advertising on the Internet* (John Wiley & Sons, US). Campaigning in the new media.

Web directories

Lorna Gentry, Kelli Brooks, and Jill Bond *New Rider's Official Internet and World Wide Web Yellow Pages* (New Riders, US). Although there's nothing particularly official about this fat Web directory, it does list 10,000 of the most worthwhile sites.

Harley Harn *Internet & Web Yellow Pages* (McGraw-Hill). Big phonebook style Web directory with a mass of sites sorted by subject and briefly reviewed.

Net culture

Ric Alexander (ed.) *Cyber-Killers* (Orion, UK). Arresting anthology of network terrorism, robot crime, and virtual murder from authors such as William Gibson, Terry Pratchett, and J G Ballard.

Joey Anuff, Ana Marie Cox, and Terry Colon *Suck: Worst Case Scenarios in Media, Culture, Advertising and the Internet* (HardWired, US). Highlights from Suck (http://www.suck.com).

Constance Hale *WiredStyle* (HardWired, US). An elegant primer of English usage for techie editors. How should you line-break Web addresses? It's all here.

Michael Hyman *PC Roadkill* (IDG, US). Humorous exposé of computer industry warfare.

Jonathan Littman *The Fugitive Game* (Little Brown, US). Catching super-hacker Kevin Mitnick.

Nicholas Negroponte *Being Digital* (Knopf, US/Hodder, UK). The MIT luminary and *Wired* luminary stabs at the future.

Charles Platt *Anarchy Online: Net Sex Net Crime* (Harper Prism, US). A rational take on the issues surrounding online crime, porn, and the freedom of speech lobby.

Neil Randall *The Soul of the Internet* (Thomson, US). The Net, its history, and those who made it happen.

Michael Wolff *Burn Rate* (Simon & Schuster, US). Hilarious and illuminating account of the birth of new media capitalism by the founder of the NetGuide series.

Still want more?

If your local bookstore falls a bit short in the computer section try one of the online bookstores in our Web directory (see p.64), or, if you'd rather read them for free online, see what's on offer at:

http://hoganbooks.com/freebook/webbooks.html

PART FOUR

ISP Directory

Internet Service Providers

The directories following list major Internet Service Providers (ISPs or IAPs) in Britain, North America, Australia, New Zealand, Asia, and beyond. They are by no means complete and inclusion shouldn't be taken as an endorsement. We've concentrated on the larger, established providers with multiple dial-in access points, as these are what most users require. There are, in addition, hundreds of local Access Providers, catering for individual cities and states.

Your first priority is to find a provider with **local call access**, preferably without paying a higher tariff for the convenience. If you can't find one from our lists, ask around locally, or sign up temporarily, get online, and consult one of these **Net directories**:

http://www.the-list.com (global)
http://www.netalert.com (global)
http://www.cynosure.com.au/isp/ (Australia)
http://www.internet-magazine.com/isp/ (UK)
http://www.isps.com (USA)

Unfortunately, these lists aren't anywhere near comprehensive either. Nor do they offer advice. For something more subjective, check out local **computer/Internet publications**; in the UK, for example,

Internet magazine (http://www.internet-magazine.com) runs monthly performance charts. If you're still having problems, once online, try posting to the newsgroup: alt.internet.services

What to ask your provider

Choosing an Access Provider is an important decision. You want a reliable, fast connection; good customer support; and a company who are going to stay in the game, so you never need to change account or (worse) email address. The best advice is to **ask around, read magazine reviews, and find out what others recommend.** If someone swears by a provider, and they seem to know what they're talking about, give it a go. That's about the best research you can do.

So if you know someone who's hooked up, ask them: Is it fast and reliable? Does it ever get so slow they feel like giving up? Do they ever have difficulty collecting or sending mail? Do they often strike a busy tone when dialing in? Are the support staff helpful? Have they ever been overcharged?

If you're not in that boat, and have to do your own research, look for answers to the following questions – maybe by calling a few of the Freecall numbers listed in the sections following and asking for their information packs and access software. It might seem laborious but it's not as painful as being stuck with poor access.

Okay, here goes with the IAP/ISP grilling . . .

How long have you been in business, who owns the company, and how many subscribers do you have?

First up, you need to know with whom you're dealing. Big operators may offer certain advantages like national and even global dial-up points, security, guaranteed access, stability, and close proximity to the high-speed backbone. However, they can be slow to upgrade because of high overheads and may have dim support staff. Small younger providers can be more flexible, have newer equipment, more in-tune staff, cheaper rates, and faster access, but conversely may lack the capital to make future critical upgrades. There aren't any rules; it's a new industry and all a bit of a long-term gamble.

Can I access for the price of a local call?

If you have to pay long-distance rates, it will cost you more. Many providers maintain a toll-free national number, however it might incur a surcharge. Get a local number if possible and ask if it has multiple points of presence (POPs).

What is your maximum user to modem ratio?

The lower this ratio, the less chance you'll strike a busy tone when you call. As a yardstick, anything over 10:1 should start sounding warning bells that they're under-equipped.

Do you connect directly to the backbone and at what speed?

The closer you are to the backbone and the more bandwidth you have at your disposal, the faster you'll surf the Web. A quality provider should be proud to send you a topology map of its peer connections. This will tell you from whom it buys its connection, with whom it exchanges data, and the size of its internal network. It's easier to get it as a map so you can compare it with others at your leisure. It may help you figure out whether its network is fast and reliable. Good signs are its own transcontinental and international links, a direct link into the backbone, multiple routing options, and high-speed connections. A lot of people balk at this question but next to a reliable mail server, it's actually what matters most.

Do you use POP3 for email?

POP3 is pretty close to a must. It enables you to pick up your mail from a cybercafé, at work, or wherever you can get online. If they don't use it, ask how you would pick up mail remotely. For example, you can pick up AOL mail by logging in over the Net with its software. But that can be a pain. If they support IMAP, that's even better as it gives you added control over your mailbox. As yet though, it's rare.

What are your support hours?

It's not essential to have 24-hour support, but it's a bonus to know someone will be there when you can't get a line on the weekend or at 11pm.

What is your start-up cost?

Avoid paying a start-up fee if possible – though if it includes a decent start-up kit with a copy of the latest version of Netscape or Internet Explorer, it could be worth the savings in download time and bother.

What software do you supply – is it 32 bit, and will it work with Netscape or Microsoft Internet Explorer?

Likewise avoid paying for start-up software. Some providers recommend commercial packages, others provide their own. Whatever you're getting, if it doesn't work with Netscape or Internet Explorer, forget it – and if you're running Windows 95, you don't want 16 bit software.

What are your ongoing monthly charges?

Most providers charge a monthly fee, with some that's your only cost. This is common in the UK where local calls are charged by time. Elsewhere it often forms a base rate with certain time constraints. In these cases there's often an array of annoying plans based around how much time you plan on being online.

What are your usage charges?

In most countries where local calls are free or untimed, you'll be charged for the amount of time you're connected. In many cases your monthly charge will include a number of free hours per month or day. Find out if unused hours can be used as future credits.

Are there any premium charges?

Premium charges are one of the main drawbacks with the Online Service giants such as CompuServe, which provide quality commercial databases as well as Internet access. But having to pay extra to use certain services is not necessarily a bad thing, as you don't want to have to subsidize something you don't use.

Will I be charged extra if I go over a download limit?

This mainly applies to cable and satellite operators who charge a base rate per month, up to a limited number of Mb. Once you go over the limit, you're billed extra per Mb. Avoid this kind of plan if possible.

Is it cheaper to access at certain times?

In an effort to restrict traffic during peak times, providers may offer periods with reduced or no online charges. Think about when you're most likely to use your connection. Try during the cheap period. If you can't connect, it's slow, or you'd rarely use it at that hour, then it's no bargain.

Can you support my modem type and speed?

Modems like talking to their own kind. When modems aren't happy with each other, they connect at a slower rate. It's not much use if your 56K modem can only connect at 28.8 Kbps. Ask what connection speeds they support. If it's lower than your modem's top speed, look elsewhere.

Do you, or will you soon, offer high-speed access such as ISDN, ADSL or CDSL?

If the answer's yes, find out the cost all up, including the hardware, wiring, rental, and call charges. If it's affordable, ask for installation contacts. In some parts of the US, for example, ISDN installation is only about $20.00, and thereafter costs the same as a telephone. CDSL and ADSL are the ones to watch out for; they're much faster.

Do you carry all the newsgroups in Usenet? If not, how many do you carry and which ones do you cut?

Usenet has more than 25,000 groups and it's still growing. That's 95% more than you'll ever want to look at in your lifetime. Most providers carry only a portion, but it's still usually over 60%. The first ones to be axed are often foreign language, country specific, provider specific, and the adult (alt.sex and alt.binaries) series. If you particularly want certain groups, your provider can usually add them, but it may have a policy against certain material.

What will my email address be, and how much do you charge to register a domain name?

You usually have the option to choose the first part of your email address. You might like to use your first name or nickname. This will then be attached to the provider's host name. Check if your name's available and what the host name would be. You don't want a name that could reflect badly on your business plans. For instance, if you register with the UK Service Provider Demon, your email address will end with demon.co.uk – perhaps not the ideal choice for a priest (although one vicar who used the first edition of this book reckons it's a conversation point).

If you want your own domain name, a provider should be able to register your choice for you. For instance, if John Hooper trains ducks to use computers, he could register duckschool.com and give himself the email address **john@duckschool.com**. Then it would be easy to remember his address, just by thinking about who he is and what he does.

How much does it cost for personal Web page storage?

Most Access Providers include a few megabytes of storage free so you can publish your own Web page. In general, if you go over that megabyte limit there'll be an excess charge.

INTERNATIONAL ISPs

Most Access Providers only operate in one country (or the US and Canada). For truly **international access**, which may be a priority if you plan to use the Net on your travels (see our "On The Road" chapter – p.217), consider one of the following.

Provider	Web address	Points of Presence
AOL	http://www.aol.com	Worldwide
CompuServe / SpryNet	http://www.compuserve.com	Worldwide
IBM Global Net	http://www.ibm.net	Worldwide
Microsoft Network	http://www.msn.com	Worldwide
Netcom	http://www.netcom.com	North America, UK

For phone numbers – and more details – of the above, see our "Online Services" (p.43).

BRITAIN

Provider	Telephone number	Web Address
BT Internet	0800 800 001	http://www.btinternet.com
Cable & Wireless	0500 200 980	http://www.cwcom.co.uk
Cable Internet	0500 541 542	http://www.cableinet.co.uk
CIX	0845 355 5050	http://www.cix.net.uk
Demon Internet	0181 371 1234	http://www.demon.net
Direct Connection	0800 072 0000	http://www.dircon.net

Easynet	0541 594 321	http://www.easynet.co.uk
IBM Global	0990 426 426	http://www.ibm.net
Netcom	01344 395 600	http://www.netcomuk.co.uk
Netkonect	0171 345 7777	http://www.netkonect.net
NTL Internet	0800 607 608	http://www.ntli.com
Prestel Online	0990 223 300	http://www.prestel.co.uk
SAQ	0800 801 514	http://www.saqnet.co.uk
UUNet (Pipex Dial)	0500 474 739	http://www.uk.uu.net
Virgin Net	0500 558 844	http://www.virgin.net

EUROPE

Provider Web address	Telephone number Points of Presence
Algonet http://www.algonet.se	08 5875 8740 Sweden
BitMailer http://www.bitmailer.com	01 402 1551 Spain
Centrum http://www.centrum.is	511 7000 Iceland
Deutsches Provider Network http://www.dpn.de	0203 309 3101 Germany
Easynet http://www.easynet.fr	01 44 54 53 33 France, UK
Eunet Traveller http://traveller.eu.net	30 countries in Europe, North Africa, USA

FranceNet	01 43 92 14 49	
http://www.francenet.fr	France	
GlasNet	095 229 0631	
http://www.glasnet.ru	Russia	
Hellas Online	01 62 96 300	
http://www.hol.gr	Greece	
Internet Finland	09 4780 8470	
http://www.icon.fi	Finland	
Ireland Online	01 855 1739	
http://www.iol.ie	Ireland	
Itnet	010 650 3781	
http://www.it.net	Italy	
LvNet	777 7777	
http://www.lvnet.lv	Latvia	
NetMedia	04 856 0600	
http://www.netmedia.co.il	Israel	
Pingnet	01 439 1313	
http://www.pingnet.ch	Switzerland, Liechtenstein	
Scandinavia Online	22 58 38 00	
http://www.sol.no	Norway	
T Online	0800 330 1000	
http://www.t-online.de	Germany	
Telepac	1 800 200 079	
http://www.telepac.pt	Portugal	
XS4all	020 620 0294	
http://www.xs4all.nl	Netherlands	

NORTH AMERICA

Provider Web address	Telephone number Points of Presence
AT&T WorldNet http://www.att.net	800 967 5363 USA
Brigadoon http://www.brigadoon.com	800 386 1414 USA
Concentric Networks http://www.concetric.net	800 745 2747 USA, Canada
EarthLink Network http://www.earthlink.com	800 395 8425 USA, Canada
GTE Internet http://www.gte.net	800 927 3000 USA
IBM Internet Connection http://www.ibm.net	800 821 4612 USA, Canada
iStar http://www.istar.ca	888 GO ISTAR Canada
Locus http://www.locusonline.com	888 590 2677 USA, Canada, Japan, UK
MCI Internet http://www.mci.com	800 550 0927 USA
MindSpring http://www.mindspring.com	800 719 4660 USA
Netcom http://www.netcom.com	800 638 2661 USA, Canada
PSINet http://www.psi.com	800 395 1056 USA, Canada

| Prodigy | 800 848 8990 |
| http://www.prodigy.com | USA |

| Sprint | 800 747 9428 |
| http://www.sprint.com/sip/ | USA |

| SpryNet | 800 777 9638 |
| http://www.sprynet.com | USA, Canada |

| Sympatico | 800 773 2121 |
| http://www.sympatico.ca | Canada |

AUSTRALIA

Provider	Telephone number	Web address
Connect.com.au	1300 360 223	http://www.Connect.com.au
GigaNet	1800 686 884	http://www.giga.net.au
IBM Global Network	132 426	http://www.ibm.net
Magnet	1800 809 164	http://www.magnet.com.au
One.Net	1300 303 312	http://www.one.net.au
Ozemail	132 884	http://www.ozemail.com.au
Telstra Big Pond	1800 804 282	http://www.bigpond.com.au

NEW ZEALAND

Provider	Telephone number	Web address
Clear Net	0800 888 800	http://www.clear.net.nz
Telecom XTRA	0800 28 99 87	http://www.xtra.co.nz
Voyager	0800 869 243	http://www.voyager.co.nz

ASIA

Provider Web address	Telephone number Points of Presence
Brain Net http://www.brain.net.pk	42 541 4444 Pakistan
Global Online http://www.gol.com	03 5341 8000 Japan, USA, Canada
Internet Thailand http://www.inet.co.th	642 7065 6 Thailand
Jaring http://www.jaring.my	03 966 5000 Malaysia
Mackay http://www.mky.com	02 2696 3999 Taiwan
Mongolia Online http://www.magicnet.mn	1 312 063 Mongolia
Pacific Surf http://www.pacific.net.sg	1 800 872 1455 Singapore
Pinter http://www.pacific.net.id	3190 0162 Indonesia
VSNL http://www.vsnl.net.in	22 264 1544 India

REST OF THE WORLD

Provider Web address	Telephone number Points of Presence
Africa Online (Prodigy) http://www.africaonline.com	781 395 5500 (US) (233 21) 226802 (Ghana) (254 2) 243775 (Kenya) (255 51) 116088 (Tanzania) (263 4) 702 202 (Zimbabwe) (225) 21 90 00 (Ivory Coast)
Impsat http://www.impsat.com.ar	01 318 8333 Argentina, Latin America
Cybernet http://web.cybernet.com.br	21 553 5577 Brazil
DataNet http://www.data.net.mx	118 4577 Mexico
Egypt Online http://www.egyptonline.com	202 395 4111 Egypt
Global Internet Access http://www.global.co.za	0800 11 39 38 South Africa
Itinet http://www.itinet.net	305 577 9750 (Miami FL) Argentina, Chile, El Salvador, Guatemala, Honduras, Nicaragua, Panama, Puerto rico, Dominican Republic, Venezuela, Paraguay, Spain and Florida.

INDEX

C

D

E

50 things to do
with this book

You're on the Net, so where now? Has it all been worth the effort? Here, in no particular order, are 50 ideas of things to do with your online time. Just key in the Web address or go to the page in this book for instructions.

1. Look yourself up on the Web
http://www.hotbot.com

2. Reignite an old flame
See p.171

3. Become a magazine publisher
See p.200

4. Check a movie star's résumé
http://www.imdb.com

5. Assume another identity
See pp.118 & 185

6. Advise the US President
http://www.whitehouse.gov

7. Flirt with a stranger
See p.180

8. Deactivate an alien implant
See p.372

9. Work from the Bahamas
See p.217

10. Sort out your weeds
http://www.gardening.com

11. Do battle in QuakeWorld
See p.197

12. Tune in to foreign radio
See p.345

13. Natter by Netphone
See p.190

14. Rekindle your childhood interests
See pp.128 & 160

15. Make your first million
See p.295

16. Get fanatical about football
See p.368

17. Move to Mars
http://www.marsshop.com

18. Confirm you're mad
http://www.mentalhealth.com

19. Plan an adventure
See p.380

20. Jam with other musicians
http://www.resrocket.com

21. Build an atomic bomb
See p.357

22. Witness a whiteout in Tromso
http://www.cs.uit.no/~ken/images/big/weather.jpg

23. Buy a frilly bra
http://www.brasdirect.co.uk

39. Show off your baby snaps
See pp.112 & 200

40. Consult a mad scientist
http://madsci.wustl.edu/

41. Ordain yourself
See p.356

42. Indulge in hypochondria
http://www.pharminfo.com

43. Learn to be cool
http://www.geocities.com/SunsetStrip/4160/big.html

44. Chat with a pop star
http://www.sonicnet.com

45. Argue with the experts
See pp.123 & 128

46. Attend a live gig
http://www.liveconcerts.com

47. Master your own music compilation CD
See p.322

48. Join the Foreign Legion
http://www.specialoperations.com

49. Find that rare book
http://www.bibliofind.com

50. Email someone your favorite song
See p.113

Got a favorite site or activity on the Net?
Then let us know by email at: angus@easynet.co.uk